A's Bad as It Gets

ALSO BY JOHN G. ROBERTSON

*The Babe Chases 60: That Fabulous 1927 Season,
Home Run by Home Run* (1999; paperback 2014)

*Baseball's Greatest Controversies: Rhubarbs, Hoaxes,
Blown Calls, Ruthian Myths, Managers' Miscues and
Front-Office Flops* (1995; paperback 2014)

A's Bad as It Gets
Connie Mack's Pathetic Athletics of 1916

JOHN G. ROBERTSON *and*
ANDY SAUNDERS

McFarland & Company, Inc., Publishers
Jefferson, North Carolina

LIBRARY OF CONGRESS CATALOGUING-IN-PUBLICATION DATA

Robertson, John G., 1964–
   A's bad as it gets : Connie Mack's pathetic Athletics of 1916 / John G. Robertson and Andy Saunders.
       p.   cm.
   Includes bibliographical references and index.

   ISBN 978-0-7864-7818-7 (softcover : acid free paper) ∞
   ISBN 978-1-4766-1347-5 (ebook)

   1. Philadelphia Athletics (Baseball team)—History.
2. Philadelphia Athletics (Baseball team)   3. Mack, Connie, 1862–1956.   I. Saunders, Andy, 1983–   II. Title.
   GV875.P44R64 2014
   796.357'64097481109041—dc23   2014001720

BRITISH LIBRARY CATALOGUING DATA ARE AVAILABLE

© 2014 John G. Robertson *and* Andy Saunders. All rights reserved

No part of this book may be reproduced or transmitted in any form or by any means, electronic or mechanical, including photocopying or recording, or by any information storage and retrieval system, without permission in writing from the publisher.

On the cover: Philadelphia Athletics first baseman Stuffy McInnis (National Baseball Hall of Fame Library, Cooperstown, N.Y.)

Manufactured in the United States of America

McFarland & Company, Inc., Publishers
   Box 611, Jefferson, North Carolina 28640
       www.mcfarlandpub.com

Although they are all no longer with us, this book is dedicated to those hardy and thick-skinned individuals from the 1916 Philadelphia Athletics who endured, from beginning to end, perhaps the worst season any MLB team suffered through during the 20th century: Jack Nabors, Tom Sheehan, Joe Bush, Amos Strunk, Stuffy McInnis, Wally Schang, Whitey Witt, Charlie Pick, Nap Lajoie, and, of course, Connie Mack. Special mention also goes to William G. Weart, the cheerful scribe from the Philadelphia *Evening Telegraph* who steadfastly chronicled the dismal exploits of those 1916 A's on a national level for the readers of *The Sporting News*. Bless your departed souls. You deserve happiness in the hereafter.

Table of Contents

Acknowledgments	ix
Preface	1
The Last Hurrah: The 1913 Victory Banquet	5
Connie Mack: The Architect of the A's (Part 1)	7
Connie Mack: The Architect of the A's (Part 2)	13
Connie Mack's First Dynasty: 1910 to 1914	20
Prelude to Disaster: Spring Training 1916	33
April: Despair and Hope	46
May: Hope and the High-Water Mark	55
June: Reality Tramples Optimism	70
July: The Depths of Ineptitude	84
August: The "Little Tonic Team of Baseball" Rises from Its Nadir	104
August 26: The Masterpiece Among the Rubbish	120
August 28 to Season's End: Playing Out the String	126
Heroes and Pleasant Surprises, Villains, Disappointments and Busts	149
The Aftermath and Beyond	154
Whatever Happened To...?	165
Were the 1916 A's Really the Worst MLB Team of the 20th Century?	170
The 1916 Philadelphia Athletics Season	175
Chapter Notes	179
Bibliography	180
Index	181

Acknowledgments

For a work such as this to come to fruition, help is required from many sources and individuals. In many ways, doing detailed baseball research has never been easier thanks to the wonders of modern technology that were in the realm of science fiction when we started penning scholarly articles for sports publications in the early 1980s. Be that as it may, we would like to thank those people and groups who provided special assistance—even if they had no idea they were helping us.

First and foremost: The wealth of box scores of the 1916 season (and other seasons) available through Retrosheet.org was invaluable. This project would have been virtually impossible without that easily accessible motherlode of data. We were only too glad to add to that fantastic website's vast array of information with a couple of contributions of our own based on tidbits of information we came across purely by accident while looking through century-old editions of *The Sporting News*. The human effort required to compile such a vast cache of MLB data is truly staggering.

The materials available from the irreplaceable Society for American Baseball Research (SABR) were, as usual, tremendously helpful. As SABR members in good standing we have unlimited access to the online microfilms of *The Sporting News* via a link to a website called PaperofRecord.com. Being able to have any issue of "The Bible of Baseball" all the way back to 1886 at the click of a mouse was extremely convenient for this project. Moreover, the old newspapers were a total joy to peruse. They truly chronicled an era when baseball was the undisputed king of sports in America. Furthermore, the ongoing SABR biography projects provided wonderful background information on many of the 1916 A's, their opponents, and other ballplayers mentioned in the book.

Statistics, schedules, obituaries, and other information from the websites TheDeadballEra.com, Baseball-Reference.com, and Baseball-Almanac.com were always handy to consult, and were consulted with great frequency. Indispensible might be an appropriate adjective to describe those sources.

It was also a pleasant and wholly unexpected surprise to find a complete set of *Baseball Magazine* articles from 1914 through 1916 nicely re-created by some anonymous, baseball-loving soul on the website la84foundation.org. Thank you for your time and efforts, whoever you are.

Thanks also go John W. Horne, Jr. of the National Baseball Hall of Fame in Cooperstown, New York. The images that appear in this book come from the Hall's photo archives. His swift assistance in this project was a great help.

On the interpersonal side, there were the librarians at the main branch of the public library in Cambridge, Ontario, and at the Pioneer Park branch of the Kitchener (Ontario) Public Library who expended efforts well beyond the ordinary to try to assist us in obtaining obscure reference materials. They were not always successful, but we appreciated their enthusiasm, professionalism, and diligence nevertheless.

—John G. Robertson and Andy Saunders, February 2014

Preface

The 1916 A's—In Rhyming Couplets

The Philadelphia Athletics of nineteen fifteen
Were as terrible a ball club as had ever been seen.

But then they exceeded Connie Mack's fear:
They were even worse the very next year.

The Red Sox, White Sox, and teams of renown
Battered Mack's pitching when they came to town.

Amateurs, college boys, and so many more
Came searching for fame at old Connie's door.

But no-hopers, has-beens, and rookies galore
Couldn't help the A's in their quest to score.

Slugger Shag Thompson was supposed to be hacking,
But when he got no hits he was soon sent packing.

With a pair of hurlers at two and thirty-six,
Connie's pitching woes were too numerous to fix.

Wally Schang was a good man to have behind the plate,
But he got hurt on Opening Day—how's that for fate?

Schang moved to the outfield and had a two-homer game.
It set an MLB record—too bad nobody came.

Young Billy Meyer substituted for Schang
Until appendicitis sidelined him ... dang!

A youthful novice shortstop named Whitey Witt
Was bad with the glove—but at least he could hit.

At third base was stationed inept Charlie Pick
His array of errors made everyone sick.

Outfielder Jimmy Walsh was pleasant and nice,
But umpire Brick Owens ejected him twice.

Stuffy McInnis still starred in the game—
Except when a charley horse pulled him up lame.

*An eleven-game losing streak should have been plenty
But later that year the A's upped it to twenty!
Napoleon Lajoie was a star we all knew.
When he called it quits he was near forty-two.
A raw rookie catcher couldn't handle the shame.
He simply quit baseball after one lousy game.
Prospects came and went; they were virtually nameless
But manager Mack—he was totally blameless.
Connie tried his darnedest with moves that were foxy.
He even used a fellow whose first name was Moxie!
Just thirty-six wins were all they could glean.
Their losses? They totaled one-seventeen.
That's even worse than the '62 Mets.
Baseball fans know that's as bad as it gets.
The other AL clubs set a blistering pace:
The A's were forty games off seventh place!
Outfielder Rube Oldring couldn't be trusted.
He walked out on the team totally disgusted.
But Bullet Joe Bush—you can't call him a quitter:
On August 26 he tossed a no-hitter!
Mack's misfits staggered home both beaten and sore.
Hard to believe they were champs just two years before!*

Ah yes, the infamously inept 1916 Philadelphia Athletics...

What can you say about a major league baseball team that finished a 154-game season with an astonishingly poor record of 36 wins, 117 losses, and one tie for a miserable .235 winning percentage? A team that finished 54.5 games out of first place in the eight-team American League—and 40 games out of seventh place? A team that allowed 329 more runs than it scored? A team that lost 20 games in a row after enduring an earlier streak of 11 straight defeats? A team that lost 19 consecutive road games? A team with two starting pitchers who posted a combined record of 2–36? A team that went 2–28 in July? A team whose top young batting prospect was released after starting the season 0 for 17? A team that featured a pitcher who finished the season on a skein of 19 consecutive losses? A team that lost one of its few star players when he nearly killed himself running headlong into a concrete wall? A team whose pitching staff walked a combined 29 batters in two consecutive games? A team whose pitching staff had three 20-game losers? A team whose best rookie lost a triple when he missed first base on the same day he was honored by his hometown admirers? A team that had one of its hometown newspapers rooting for it to set a new league record for consecutive losses? A team whose pitcher was so sure his teammates wouldn't score another run for him on a sweltering day that he deliberately threw a game-ending wild pitch to escape from the hot sun? A team that had a brooding young prospect quit pro baseball after a rough game? A team, in one of its rare good outings, that had a batter become the first player in MLB history to hit home runs from both sides of the plate in a nearly empty ballpark? A team that had a runner on third base thrown out at home plate when a following batter singled? A team that had a petulant veteran outfielder retire in disgust partway through the season—only to cheerfully join a pennant contender a few weeks later? A team whose longest winning streak was a mere two games? A team that made 312 errors—an average of more than two per game—including 11 in a doubleheader? A team whose Opening Day shortstop would become a convicted double-murderer and whose rookie replacement would make 78 errors? A team with a pitching staff so bad that it led the American League in complete games because its bullpen was virtually useless?

Years later, the esteemed Connie Mack tried his best to describe such a rotten team—the very team he had molded and managed through those dismal days of 1916. "Yes, we were bad—very bad—that year,"[1] he succinctly told biographer Fred Lieb in 1944, stating the patently obvious.

What made the 1916 Philadelphia A's so stunningly awful was that a mere two seasons earlier ballplayers clad in the same familiar Athletics uniforms had been widely hailed as one of the most formidable MLB teams ever assembled. However, baseball economics, a costly bidding war from an upstart professional league, and Connie Mack's desire to rebuild the team completely turned the 1910, 1911 and 1913 World Series champion Athletics into a bottom-feeding bunch. The once proud and dynastic A's of just a few years before were sadly reduced to the laughingstocks and whipping boys of the American League in 1916. According to renowned baseball guru Bill James, the 1914 A's fabled "$100,000 infield" was the greatest ever assembled. By 1916, the pitiless writers at *Baseball Magazine* were calling the error-prone A's the "$10 infield" and commonly referring to Mack's team as the "Pathetics."

In 1916 the Athletics were little more than the other AL teams' football, according to William G. Weart, the overly sympathetic Philadelphia correspondent of *The Sporting News*. Weart, the main baseball writer for the *Philadelphia Evening Telegraph*, was an unabashed homer and a Mack admirer who tried to put his best spin on the A's dreary goings-on every week in his *TSN* column throughout the long and hopeless summer. However, even Weart gave up trying to come up with positive things to say about the A's by early August when they had lost 20 straight games and their winning percentage had dropped humiliatingly below .200. Actually he gave up on the Athletics only for a little while. Before very long, though, Weart's Pollyanna-like outlook on the team re-emerged and he proffered heady predictions of great things for his heroic Mackmen in the 1917 season without very much concrete evidence to support such boundless optimism. "In short, they were pretty bad," succinctly wrote George Robinson and Charles Salzburg, the authors of the quaintly titled *On a Clear Day They Could See Seventh Place*. The twosome apportioned 26 pages of their 1991 book on bad MLB teams to the futile 1916 Philadelphians.

You can say the 1916 Philadelphia Athletics were quite possibly the worst MLB team to step onto a diamond in the 20th century—worse than the 1904 Washington Senators, worse than the comedic expansion New York Mets of 1962, worse than the 1935 Boston Braves, worse than any collection of ballplayers the pitiful St. Louis Browns ever threw together purporting to be a big-league baseball team. Worse even than the staggeringly bad 2003 Detroit Tigers, if one cares to venture into the 21st century in search of awful MLB clubs for the purposes of comparison. They were also worse than two other Athletics teams from that same era that certainly merit consideration among MLB's all-time stinkers— Connie Mack's woebegone gangs from both 1915 and 1919. Let's be blunt: A team has to be uniquely rotten to eclipse those two teams. Unfortunately no team photo of the 1916 A's is known to exist, despite the best efforts of the Philadelphia Athletics Historical Society to obtain one. Perhaps the revolving-door nature of the team's roster made such a photo instantly obsolete and thus pointless.

The 1916 Philadelphia Athletics were epically bad, monumentally bad, famously bad, and catastrophically bad. *Baseball Magazine*, a leading sports periodical of the day, concurred in its August 1916 edition, mocking them as "a misfit crowd in every possible fashion." The A's were indeed bad in every possible way imaginable—and in some ways that still defy belief. This is how the debacle happened.

The Last Hurrah: The 1913 Victory Banquet

The victory celebrations were uncharacteristically subdued that October evening in 1913 for Connie Mack's World Series champion Philadelphia Athletics. Certainly their recent diamond triumph, a convincing five-game Fall Classic win over the hated National League champion New York Giants, ought to have been cause once again for revelry and delight. The World Series victory was the Athletics' third in four years and undoubtedly confirmed to the sporting public that the Mackmen, as the sports writers sometimes affectionately referred to the A's, were clearly in a class of their own and Philadelphia was indeed the baseball capital of America.

But this time the happiness and satisfaction of ultimate victory was tempered by tragedy: Harry Davis, Jr., the 13-year-old son of Athletics coach and part-time player Harry Davis, had suddenly died on Monday, October 13—two days after the Mackmen had clinched the 1913 World Series and just a day after the team had returned to Philadelphia. *The Sporting News*, baseball's august and revered trade publication, reported on October 16 that the cause of death had been "a combination of indigestion and heart disease." Decades later, Davis's SABR biographer, Mike Grahek, wrote that the teenager had died of an undiagnosed liver ailment "reportedly exacerbated by the excitement of the Athletics' victory." Harry Sr. was almost as much of a fixture with the A's as Connie Mack, having been with the club all but one year since the team began play as a charter member of the American League in 1901. He had led the AL in home runs for four consecutive years from 1904 to 1907 and was, by all accounts, Mack's de facto second in command with the Athletics.

Young Harry was well known to all the Athletics players, having been a regular attendee at Shibe Park. Elder Harry had frequently allowed his son to partake in on-field activities with the ballplayers, and the teenager had enthusiastically done so during the recent Fall Classic. Pitcher Eddie Plank, who had boarded with the Davis family during the 1913 season, was so heartbroken by the boy's death that he canceled a special victory celebration that had been scheduled in his hometown of Gettysburg, PA.

Such was the gloom surrounding the team that there was even talk of canceling the gaudy civic celebrations planned for Philadelphia, too, but mayor Rudolph Blankenburg would not hear of it. After all, he was campaigning for re-election in the autumn of 1913—and any type of association with a local championship team, even something as tenuous as hosting a banquet for them, provided too much of a golden chance for good publicity. Instead, the festivities were simply postponed until a week after young Harry Davis's funeral. The A's famed "$100,000 infield" served as pallbearers.

When the appointed time came, the Philadelphia Police Band accompanied the triumphant A's as they paraded the three miles from Shibe Park to a lavish banquet at the Bellevue-Stratford Hotel. Large numbers of enthusiastic admirers gathered along the sidewalks and cheered their invincible baseball heroes along the whole of the procession. Like the previous gatherings that had followed the Athletics' World Series triumphs in 1910 and 1911, at the banquet there were the usual banter, jokes, blustery after-dinner speeches and testimonials. But the unbridled joy of victory was plainly absent this time because of the specter of young Harry Davis's sad demise. No matter, though: With a team as dominant, talented, and cohesive as the 1913 Athletics, more World Series championships and much happier victory banquets would surely follow Connie Mack's famous White Elephants in the next few years.

Connie Mack: The Architect of the A's (Part 1)

> For the first half of the 20th century, [Connie Mack] was probably the best-loved and most respected man in any field in America. —Norman L. Macht, *The Ballplayers*

> Connie Mack. There was a wonderful person.... He really respected his fellow man. If you made a mistake, Connie never bawled you out on the bench, or in front of anybody else. He'd get you alone a few days later, and then he'd say something like, "Don't you think it would have been better if you'd made the play this way?" And you knew damn well it would have been better. No question about it. He knew what he was talking about. [He] never raised his voice.... In my opinion Connie Mack did more for baseball than any other human being—by the example he set, his attitude, the way he handled himself and his players.... He was a true gentleman in every sense of the word. —Rube Bressler, in *The Glory of Their Times*

One simply cannot think about the Philadelphia Athletics without thinking of Connie Mack. The two are as inseparable as ham and eggs, Laurel and Hardy, and Proctor and Gamble. When one reads a newspaper account of an A's game from 1901 to 1950, there is almost always a reference to baseball's "Tall Tactician" whether it was necessary for the story or not. For many fans of the grand old game, Mack was, quite simply, the personification of Philadelphia baseball.

The man who became such a fixture in Philadelphia and Pennsylvania was actually born out of state in East Brookfield, MA, on December 22, 1862. Cornelius McGillicuddy was the third of seven children born to Michael and Mary (McKillop) McGillicuddy. Both Michael and Mary had emigrated from Ireland to the United States as children in the mid 1840s. Michael was a wheelwright, and East Brookfield was a mill town. It was a good fit for him. Michael was not present when his famous son was born; he was serving a hitch with the 51st Massachusetts Regiment at the time. Apart from the appalling lists of casualties that the Civil War brought to every community in New England, times were good in East Brookfield during the period when Connie took his first breath.

Shoes were the big commodity in 1862, and the town's factories were busily operating day and night to meet the demands of their biggest customer—the War Department of the federal government. The Union Army seemingly had an insatiable need for footwear, and East Brookfield's industries were only too happy to provide it for them.

Michael returned from the war an alcoholic, broken in spirit from the horrors he had seen on the battlefields. He was frequently unable to work. Mary McGillicuddy became the driving force of the family. She instilled the values of hard work and frugality that stayed with Connie and his siblings all their lives. Beginning at the age of nine, Connie worked 12-hour shifts at a local cotton mill during the summer when school was out. Connie permanently quit school at age 14 and got a job at a shoe factory, shaping soles and cutting heels, to help provide for his younger brothers and sisters. School never held much attraction to young Cornelius anyway. He was gangly and awkward and had trouble fitting his tall frame behind a typical 19th-century school desk. By the time he was 15 he was already six feet tall. Connie showed leadership qualities even in those days. He rose to the position of assistant foreman at the shoe factory by age 21 and was earning a princely salary of $15 per week.

But being a foreman in an East Brookfield shoe factory was not Connie's destiny in life. He was an amateur baseball player of some repute at a time when baseball was just about the only wholesome recreation available for active young men. The country had fallen in love with the new sport—its rules had been codified by Alexander Cartwright in 1846. New England was especially a hotbed for the new national pastime. Connie loved to play anywhere on the field, but he found that catching was his forte. In the 1880s, catchers did not wear gloves. They typically stood in a slight crouch well behind home plate, and, more often than not, caught pitches on one hop. Now standing anywhere from 6'1" to 6'4" (various biographers disagree on his true height), Connie used his position as backstop as a command post to act as field general. His unmistakable, shrill, piping voice positioned his teammates around the diamond. Within a short time, Connie was the starting catcher on East Brookfield's amateur team where, not surprisingly, he acquired the pejorative nickname "Beanpole" as he tipped the scales at only about 150 pounds—a weight that would seldom change much throughout his long adult life. Displaying his natural leadership skills, he eventually ascended to the team's captaincy.

More meaningful baseball beckoned. Connie, who now answered to "Mack," played for minor pro teams in both Meriden and Hartford in the Connecticut State League. So likable and popular was Connie in Meriden that the fans presented him with a gold watch. By 1886 he had signed with Washington of the National League. (Supportive fans there would be equally enamored with Connie; they would present him with a silver tray as a token of their affection.)

It was the beginning of a solid 11-year major league career in which Mack played the vast majority of games as a catcher, although he ended up playing every position in the majors except third base and pitcher. Being a major leaguer in the 1880s was hardly a glamorous existence. In a 1955 interview, Mack recalled his first train trip to spring training seven decades earlier. "We traveled four to a berth and when it came to meal tips, the manager would put down a silver dollar for the whole team."[1]

Mack never was much of a hitter, compiling a lifetime average of just .244. Pro baseball was a bit of a culture shock for the virtuous man from East Brookfield who, at the insistence of his mother, did not smoke, drink, or use profanity. Those traits made him different from almost all his contemporaries. Ty Cobb once said, "When I began playing the game, baseball was about as gentlemanly as a kick in the crotch."[2] Consider that Mack started in pro baseball two decades *before* the Georgia Peach. Mack knew that even major leaguers were held in low esteem by most respectable folks in the 1880s. "Baseball was mighty exciting to me [back then]," he noted, "but there is no blinking at the fact that at the time the game was thought, by solid sensible people, to be only one degree above grand larceny, arson, and mayhem."[3] During the 19th century, the managers of respectable hotels would often refuse to rent rooms to riffraff. Professional baseball clubs often fell within the boundaries of that unflattering description.

In 1887 Mack married Margaret Hogan, the sister of one of his Meriden teammates, pitcher Willie Hogan. Together they had three children.

Though virtuous off the field, Mack wasn't above a bit of chicanery and rule-twisting while plying his trade behind the plate. He chattered constantly in an attempt to distract the batter. Every once in a while Mack was known to tip an opponent's bat if he thought he could get away with it. Mack's most renowned bit of deceit was the sham foul-tip ruse. In the 1880s, if a catcher caught a foul tip on the fly, the batter was out regardless of the count. Mack mastered mimicking the sound of a ball just touching a bat, often fooling the sole umpire into thinking that he had caught a foul tip when he really had not. It is generally believed that Mack's skill at this deception brought about the modern rule, instituted in 1891: an out can only occur on a foul tip as the third strike of a strikeout.

One of those 11 major league seasons was spent with the Buffalo Bisons of the ill-fated 1890 Players' League. The PL was a gallant attempt by the players to form their own circuit and thereby free themselves from the odious reserve clause that was a standard part of every professional ballplayer's contract. The clause, in effect, bound each player to his team in perpetuity and therefore kept all players' salaries artificially and pitifully low. They either re-signed with their old clubs for each season or were shut out of pro baseball entirely. Mack invested his life savings of $500 in shares of the Buffalo team and lost every cent when the Bisons and the entire league went bust.

When the PL folded after one costly season, Mack returned to the NL as a member of the Pittsburgh Pirates in 1891. (There was some dispute as to whether Mack belonged to Boston's American Association club or Pittsburgh. Baseball's Board of Control ruled in favor of the Pirates.) He stayed in Pittsburgh until he finished out his playing career in 1896. In 1892, Mack's wife Margaret passed away, leaving him a 29-year-old widower with three children all under the age of five.

Late in the 1894 season, with the disappointing Pirates sitting in seventh place in the 12-team NL, the team was in desperate need of a change. Club owner William W. Kerr had lost confidence in manager Al Buckenberger. Kerr believed the popular, quick-witted, and analytical Mack had the potential to be good managerial material and was the man who ought to take over the reins of the mediocre Pittsburgh club. After giving the offer some thought, Mack obliged. After all, he was nearing 32, he couldn't run so well anymore, and he was starting to feel the aches and bruises commonly associated with aging catchers more acutely. Moreover, a broken leg he suffered in 1893 had greatly effected his productivity. Managing just might be the ideal way for Mack to extend his career in the grand old game.

The Pirates had 23 games left on their schedule when Mack managed the first of his 7,755 career regular-season games on September 3, 1894. The Pirates drubbed Washington, 22–1, for win number one of 3,731—a staggering figure not likely to be approached by anyone any time soon. (Mack is nearly 1,000 wins ahead of his closest rival, John McGraw, who compiled 2,763 wins. He is more than 1,000 victories ahead of third-place Tony LaRussa, who won 2,728 games.) "My we made a lot of runs that day,"[4] Mack pleasantly recalled to reporters 50 years later when his golden anniversary of baseball managing was observed. The following day the Pirates lost 14–13 to the Giants in New York City, for Mack's first of 3,948 career losses—another number of stratospheric proportions. (Next highest on the list is Bucky Harris with 2,218 losses—a mere 56.2 percent of Mack's total.) The Pirates went 12–10–1 in those final 23 games of 1894. Mack was officially Pittsburgh's player-manager, but he would drastically reduce his own playing time over the next two seasons.

The 1895 and 1896 NL campaigns would prove to be largely unsuccessful for the Pirates—but Pittsburgh fans were used to losing baseball seasons. Mack's 1895 Pirates started well, had the city's hopes raised, and were in front in the pennant chase as late as August 9. By the end of the tumultuous season, though, they had astonishingly slumped to seventh place with a 71–61 record. Things were nearly as bad in 1896. After an encouraging spring training, the Pirates couldn't find their stride. They never threatened the front-runners and staggered home in sixth place with a mediocre 66–63–2 mark. Owner Kerr, after promising not to meddle in the daily operations of the Pirates, proved to be an ongoing irritant to Mack, often sending him telegrams during road trips that bluntly second-guessed his managerial decisions. Mack's contract was not renewed for 1897. His days in the NL were over.

Enter Ban Johnson, a one-time sports journalist from Cincinnati whom Mack knew only slightly. Johnson was keenly aware that Mack's services would not be renewed in Pittsburgh. By 1896, Johnson was running the Western League, a minor league outfit headquartered in Chicago. Johnson wired Mack an invitation to meet him in his office regarding a job vacancy with the WL's Milwaukee club. Johnson, who admired Mack's gentlemanly image and thought it would be good for his circuit, wanted the deposed Pirates manager to take over the WL's operations in Milwaukee. Mack would be his own boss—an appealing notion to a strong-minded and purposeful soul like Cornelius McGillicuddy. Mack knew his playing days were over. By 1896 he was a widower with three children who needed steady employment. Mack was also impressed by the go-getter aura exuded by Johnson, who told Mack he had big plans for his Western League. Mack accepted Johnson's offer. He uprooted his family from Pittsburgh and moved to Wisconsin for the 1897 season.

Johnson was not exaggerating when he told Mack he would run the whole Milwaukee operation. His four seasons in the city known for suds provided some valuable education in the business end of the national pastime. "I did most everything there but sell tickets," Mack told biographer Fred Lieb half a century later. "We didn't have the luxury of a road secretary or a business manager. Managing the ball club on the field was only part of my job; I signed the players, made the trades, arranged our railroad transportation, found hotels for the players, and paid all the bills."[5] In other words, Connie Mack the ex-ballplayer learned in Milwaukee how to be Connie Mack the baseball magnate. The lessons of baseball finances he learned in Milwaukee never left him. When the mood struck him, Mack would play in an occasional game, too. Mack's teams would finish third, third again, fourth, and second in his four seasons in Wisconsin. Before the 1900 season, Johnson changed the Western League's name to the loftier sounding American League.

At the year-end meeting of the AL on October 14, 1900, Johnson boldly declared the AL would exist as a major league for the 1901 season. He moved clubs into Baltimore, Cleveland and Washington, three of the four cities the National League had abandoned after the 1899 season when it contracted from an ungainly 12-team loop to an eight-team outfit. All three were pleased to get big-league baseball back in town and eagerly joined the new league. Johnson also saw Philadelphia as promising ground for a new AL franchise, even though a National League team had been doing good business there since 1883. Johnson figured Mack would be the ideal man to run the AL club in the City of Brotherly Love, even though he had absolutely no roots there.

Mack was instructed to get in contact immediately with Ben Shibe, a prominent local sporting goods manufacturer, to establish the new version of the Philadelphia Athletics. (Johnson insisted the Philadelphia AL club re-establish the distinguished nickname that harkened back to the earliest days of amateur baseball in the Pennsylvania city. It had been used as recently as the late 1880s by Philadelphia's American Association Club when the AA held major league status.) Shibe owned A. J. Reach & Co. He was told his company would exclusively provide baseballs for the league if he got aboard the AL's bandwagon. Shibe eagerly took the bait and was given 50 percent ownership of the Philadelphia club. Mack got a 25 percent share. A temporary playing ground called Columbia Park, largely made up of wooden bleachers, was quickly erected at the intersection of Twenty-Ninth Street and Columbia Avenue. It could accommodate only about 9,500 paying customers, but it would have to suffice until a grander baseball palace could be built if everything went according to plan.

Connie Mack, age 38, having traveled the baseball road from East Brookfield to Meriden, Hartford, Washington, D.C., Buffalo, Pittsburgh, and Milwaukee, had become the manager and part-owner of the nascent Philadelphia Athletics of the new American League—a position he would prominently hold for the next half-century. In the process he would become just as baseball historian Norman L. Macht described him: one of the most beloved and iconic sports figures of the 20th century.

Connie Mack: The Architect of the A's (Part 2)

Behind the saintly, grandfatherly appearance of the 6'1" 150-lb, ramrod-straight, blue-eyed Mr. Mack, there was a complex personality, a blend of patience and impetuosity, kindness and stubbornness, tightfistedness and generosity. He never raised his voice and seldom confronted a player in front of his teammates, but he could put a man in his place with a cutting sarcastic comment. He disdained swearing but sometimes cut loose with a salty barrage. To strangers of any age who approached him in a hotel lobby or dining room, he was invariably courtly and pleasant. Despite a tendency to mispronounce some names and forget others, he had an unfailing memory for the faces of old friends from his hometown, East Brookfields, Massachusetts, and gave them a genuinely warm welcome when they came to Boston to see the Athletics play.—Norman L. Macht, *The Ballplayers*

[Mack] became the game's patriarchal image, as singular in his way as McGraw, Mathewson, Cobb, Ruth, Dean, DiMaggio, and Jackie Robinson were in theirs. For fans who grew up following the game in the 1920s, 1930s, 1940s, and early 1950s, he was there, an indomitable monument, and always an old man, benign of face and reputation, a cornerstone of the national game, grandfather to every pitched ball and base hit, with billing above his team, for they were "Connie Mack's A's."— Donald Honig, *Baseball America*

Had Connie Mack's playing and managing career ended in Pittsburgh at the end of the 1896 season, he would likely be little known today except to the most studious devotees of 19th-century baseball. He was a steady yet unspectacular major league catcher who had managed to stick around in the majors for 11 seasons by employing his skills to the fullest and applying guile and baseball smarts. His two-plus seasons at the helm of the Pittsburgh Pirates were not especially impressive. (Mack's managerial record in Pittsburgh was 149–134.) He certainly would not have been considered for induction into the National Baseball Hall of Fame based upon any of those ordinary credentials. The best thing ever to happen to Connie Mack was his landing in Philadelphia at the head of one of the better teams in Ban Johnson's newly formed American League.

(A year later, John McGraw, the player-manager of the AL's Baltimore Orioles, publicly predicted that the Athletics would be "the white elephants" of the new major league. Amused by McGraw's wild attempt at fortune-telling, the A's quickly adopted the white elephant as their team emblem—and have retained it for more than a century.)

As a minor circuit, the Western League/American League had operated with something close to friendly relations with the established National League until Ban Johnson gambled on major league status in 1901. The AL clubs would now brazenly raid all eight NL clubs, luring their star players away with better pay. The prime target for the Philadelphia Athletics was naturally the Phillies' popular second baseman Napoleon (Larry) Lajoie, who had been impressing local fans with his hot bat since 1896. With a bit of chicanery, which involved Lajoie being paid his salary via a third party, the gregarious Lajoie jumped his existing contract and signed with the Athletics.

The much-awaited home opener in Philadelphia was twice postponed by rain, but 10,547 fans squeezed into the tiny ballpark on Friday, April 26, 1901, to see the first AL game in the city's history. Mayor Samuel Ashbridge, a politician who recognized a good opportunity to endear himself with the locals, was on hand to throw out the ceremonial first pitch. All signs pointed to a gala beginning—but Mack's team committed seven errors that afternoon and lost 5–1 to Washington on a noticeably waterlogged field. Lajoie got three of the Athletics' eight hits, though, and was well on his way to an outstanding offensive campaign. The Athletics ultimately had to settle for fourth place in their initial AL season, but they competed well at the gate with the NL's Phillies, who finished second in their pennant chase.

Lajoie, 26, simply set the AL afire in 1901, winning the league's Triple Crown, leading it in every meaningful offensive category, including a .426 batting average. Lajoie was so feared at the plate in 1901 that on May 23, in a game versus the Chicago White Sox, he was intentionally walked with the bases loaded to prevent him from having a chance at hitting a game-tying grand slam. It was the first time in 20 seasons, and only the second time in an MLB game, that a batter had been intentionally passed with the bases full. (Only four other players have been so "honored" in all the years since: Del Bisonette, Bill Nicholson, Barry Bonds and Josh Hamilton.)

Big problems, however, arose for Lajoie and the Athletics in 1902. The Phillies, understandably miffed at Lajoie's contract-jumping and how much he had done to make the Athletics the better professional baseball attraction in Philadelphia, obtained a legal injunction, upheld by the state's Supreme Court, that prevented Lajoie from playing anywhere in Pennsylvania—unless, of course, he was back in a Phillies uniform. AL president Ban Johnson was beyond outraged by the ruling. In a statement from Chicago published in the April 22,

1902, issue of *The Sporting News,* Johnson likened it to reviving slavery. Not surprisingly, in the very same newspaper, St. Louis Cardinals president William Hart presented a polar opposite viewpoint: He applauded the verdict of the court, declared it a complete victory for the NL, and boldly predicted "a speedy disintegration of the American League." It was wishful thinking on Hart's part, as the AL had just transferred its Milwaukee club to St. Louis for the 1902 season; Hart undoubtedly resented the competition of another major league team in his city. Be that as it may, such was the lingering bitterness and animosity between the two major leagues of professional baseball as the 1902 season got under way.

Despite Johnson's angry public vow to fight the court's decision to the last, four games into the new season Mack reluctantly dealt his biggest star and the AL's most prominent drawing card to the Cleveland Broncos. In Ohio, Lajoie became the centerpiece attraction for the franchise for many years, although the thrill of playing on a pennant-winning club always eluded him. Lajoie became so beloved a fixture in Cleveland baseball that the team was often referred to as "the Naps" during his 13 seasons there. He played the rest of the 1902 season carefully avoiding the state of Pennsylvania and its legal entanglements. Once the two major leagues made peace with each other in 1903, Lajoie was free again to play legally in the Quaker State. Lajoie would return to Philadelphia to finish out his career with the woeful 1915 and 1916 Athletics. His final MLB game coincided with a rare high point for the 1916 A's.

Despite the unavoidable loss of Lajoie, the Athletics roared to the AL pennant in 1902, winning the flag by five games over the second-place St. Louis Browns. The Athletics packed Columbia Park all season, drawing more than 420,000 fans—a great total by the standards of that era. Eddie Plank, Rube Waddell, and Bert Husting were the mainstays of the Athletics' pitching staff. Husting was a curious flash in the pan. He got married that August and never played another MLB game after 1902. Heavily influenced by his wife's desire for a stable home life, Husting opted for the security of a career in law in Wisconsin over professional baseball. Husting was just 24 when he walked away from the game forever. Plank, known for his constant fidgeting and dawdling on the mound, would be a reliable starter on Mack's squad for more than a decade. Although Plank never had a single eye-popping statistical year, perhaps with the exception of 1912, when he went 26–6, he was perennially among the AL's top five hurlers. He would become MLB's most successful left-hander until Warren Spahn and Steve Carlton came along decades later.

Then there was the unforgettable Rube Waddell. The burly left-hander was brilliant on the mound with his overpowering fastball. Even though he joined the team in June, he struck out 210 batters in $276\frac{1}{3}$ innings in 1902. That would be a great statistic today. It was even more spectacular in an era when batters generally eschewed home-run swings and were content to connect for singles. Waddell would pitch superbly for the Athletics for six seasons, and lead the AL in strikeouts every year. He was, however, Mack's notorious problem child. Waddell was, in many ways, a little boy in a man's body. He was immature, terribly unreliable, horrible at managing his money, and easily distracted by fire alarms, puppies, toys, or other shiny objects within his eyesight. A frequent imbiber (*The Sporting News*, baseball's de facto newspaper of record, once referred to him as a "souse-paw"), Waddell wasn't quite sure how many women he had married. On one occasion in Florida during spring training, Mack discovered Waddell wrestling alligators at a local wildlife park. Another time he was seen leading a parade on a day he was supposed to be pitching. Mack's widowed mother lived in his house and helped her son, a widower since 1892, raise his children. He often privately complained to his mother about the troubles Waddell's vagaries were causing both him and the team. Mrs. McGillicuddy would nod and listen politely to her frustrated son's plentiful grievances with the problematic Rube, but then would gently remind him that Waddell consistently won ballgames for him. The matron of the house spoke the bottom-line truth. Mack grudgingly put up with Rube's crazy shenanigans for another half-decade until the pitcher's teammates finally had had enough of his antics and demanded he be traded. After Connie's death, Mack's daughter, Ruth Mack Clark, told a reporter, "Dad always had a gleam in his eye when he told stories about Rube Waddell. Dad really loved the Rube."[1]

The 1902 AL pennant (with no subsequent World Series; that tradition did not begin until 1903) was the first of six Connie Mack would win through 1914. The Boston Pilgrims (soon to become the Red Sox) took AL honors in both 1903 and 1904. The Athletics came home a distant second in 1903, 14.5 games back of Boston, and fifth in 1904, even though they finished 11 games over .500. Waddell struck out 302 AL batters in 1903 and 349 in 1904—the latter was an MLB record that stood for more than 60 years until Sandy Koufax of the Los Angeles Dodgers bettered it with 382 strikeouts in 1965. More than a century later, Waddell's strikeout mark has never been equaled by any other AL left-hander.

The Pilgrims struck a major victory for the fledgling AL in 1903 by beating the favored Pittsburgh Pirates in eight games in a best-of-nine World Series—the first meaningful post-season meeting between the two rival leagues. Old animosities ran hard, though. There was no World Series in 1904. John McGraw, the manager of the NL champion New York Giants, had left the AL in July 1902, on very bad terms after Ban Johnson had suspended him. McGraw disassociated himself with the AL and joined the Giants as their new manager. McGraw, purely out of spite—and with the blessing of team owner John T. Brush (who himself was no fan of the AL because the junior circuit's New York club was drawing large numbers of fans)—simply refused to pit his NL champion Giants against the Red Sox in a World Series because nothing required him to do so. Of course it was a public-relations disaster in a sports-minded country that craved as much baseball as possible. Soon afterwards a formal agreement between the two major leagues made an annual World Series mandatory for each circuit's champion.

Mack's 1905 Athletics returned to the top of the standings, edging the Chicago White Sox by just two games to cop the AL flag. The tightness of the pennant race drew more than 550,000 fans to Columbia Park that year, testing its capacity to the breaking point. The Athletics' pitching was superb that season. Eddie Plank was becoming Mack's reliable anchor, almost compiling better stats (24–12) than the eccentric but dominant Rube Waddell (27–10)—but Plank had nowhere near Waddell's phenomenal total of 287 strikeouts. Young Andy Coakley was also becoming a formidable force on the mound, winning 18 games, as did Albert (Chief) Bender.

McGraw's Giants again won the NL pennant as they had in 1904—and this time there would be a World Series. Two major stories surround the Series. The first was the "straw hat incident": On September 8, while Mack's club was waiting to change trains on a railroad platform in Providence, RI, Waddell supposedly suffered a crippling shoulder injury while engaging in boisterous horseplay with Andy Coakley over the wearing of a straw hat after Labor Day. Waddell was unable to participate in the World Series. Rumors persist to this day that Waddell may have been corrupted by gamblers to feign an arm injury and sit out the Series. Mack dismissed the idea entirely, noting that glory—not money—inspired the Rube. Was Waddell really badly injured? Perhaps. The next season Waddell had a disappointing 15-17 record, the only year he had a sub-.500 record for the Athletics.

The second story—a much more positive one—was the utterly masterful pitching performance of New York's fabulous 25-year-old, college-bred right-hander, Christy Mathewson. Matty threw three complete game shutouts in just six days against the overmatched A's—a mind-boggling achievement to today's fan who is accustomed to five-man rotations and strict pitch counts. After the Series concluded, *The Sporting News* rightly hailed Mathewson in its October 19 issue as "the premier of all pitchers." Few fans or baseball writers would disagree. Philadelphia suffered a fourth shutout, this one at the hands of Joe McGinnity. In the A's lone win, all their runs were unearned. Thus the Giants' pitching staff posted an unbeatable 0.00 ERA for the Series. The A's excellent team ERA of 1.67 seems enormous by comparison. Philadelphia collectively batted an anemic .155 in the Series. "Mathewson was the greatest pitcher who ever lived," said Mack years later. "He had knowledge, judgment, perfect control and form. It was wonderful to watch him pitch when he wasn't pitching against you."[2] The

Athletics smartly opted to play their two World Series home games at the more spacious Baker Bowl, the Phillies' home ballpark on Lehigh Avenue, and drew in excess of 17,000 fans to each game. The A's wouldn't play another World Series game until 1910.

During his first decade as the manager of the White Elephants, Mack's familiar conservative attire and deportment was a constant. He never wore a uniform during a game, eschewing it for a simple business suit, usually with a high-collar shirt, and always with a necktie. Mack's chapeaus changed with the times, though, from straw hats to fedoras. He looked more like a banker, a stock broker, or a furniture salesman than a baseball manager. But his business-like approach to managing and deportment earned him respect from everyone in the game. No ballplayer on his team ever dared call him Connie. It was always a more reverential "Mr. Mack." Likewise, he addressed his players by their given names rather than by their familiar nicknames. Chief Bender, Mack's all-time favorite pitcher, was always called "Albert." Mack insisted on good behavior from his players, especially on the diamond. "There is room for gentlemen in any business,"[3] Mack would tell them. Surprisingly, on road trips Mack never insisted on curfews or bed checks for his Athletics, believing the players were both adult and professional enough to get their proper rest, although he seemed to have an uncanny knack for knowing when an Athletics player had stayed out all night. Because he didn't wear a uniform, Mack usually assigned a player to take the A's lineup to the umpire at the pregame meeting. Mack constantly positioned and repositioned his players when they were in the field. A gentle wave of his scorecard usually did the trick. Mack's presence in the dugout became iconic. Said legendary broadcaster Ernie Harwell, "A tall thin man waving his scorecard from the dugout: that's baseball."[4]

The 1906 Athletics failed to repeat as champions. The Chicago White Sox club that went down in baseball history as the "Hitless Wonders" took top honors in the AL and then scored a sensational, utterly stunning six-game triumph over the heavily favored Chicago Cubs in the only all-Chicago World Series to date. Mack's Athletics finished 12 games behind in fourth place. The next three years the AL pennant belonged to Ty Cobb's Detroit Tigers, although Mack would maintain to his dying day that a hotly disputed interference call—involving a police officer stationed on the field—in a key late-season game with Detroit cost his team the 1907 pennant. The A's finished a close second in both 1907 and 1909 and a disappointing sixth in 1908. The Tigers managed to lose all three World Series despite the presence of Cobb, Sam Crawford, and Hall of Fame manager Hughie Jennings. Cobb, not quite 23 years old when the 1909 season ended, would never again play in a World Series.

Despite no pennants being flown in Philadelphia from 1906 to 1909, the city's AL franchise was moving upward in status. In 1908 ground was broken for a new, modernized ballpark for its AL club. Tiny Columbia Park had clearly outlived its usefulness as baseball ascended into a greater era of prosperity. Grander and more spacious digs were required for MLB clubs to host their ballgames. Newly christened Shibe Park, situated at the corner of North 21st Street and West Lehigh Avenue, was MLB's first fully steel-and-concrete stadium—an indication of how popular, significant and profitable MLB had become over the course of the decade since peace between the two rival leagues was declared.

On Monday, April 12, 1909, the Opening Day proceedings at Shibe Park created a near riot. More than 30,000 excited fans showed up and were granted admission while at least another 15,000 who wanted to see the game were turned away when there was no more room. Overwhelmed and panicky club officials closed the gates hours before game time, turning the disappointed outsiders into a howling mob of thousands, according to one local newspaper's account, whose sheer weight forced open one of the padlocked gates. Hundreds of people poured into the ballpark without paying admission. An estimated 7,000 spectators saw that first game standing seven-deep in Shibe Park's outfield, held back by ropes stretched between the left field seats and the right field bleachers—a common site at big games in those days. An estimated 6,000 more fans caught the action free of charge from perches on various rooftops around the block.

"It seemed as if all of Philadelphia was there," declared the April 13 edition of Philadelphia's *Public Ledger*, engaging in only a slight bit of hyperbole. Mayor John E. Reyburn rightly called the new baseball facility a "pride to the city" and cheerfully threw out the ceremonial first ball of the 1909 season. The Athletics did their part by handily thumping the Boston Red Sox, 8–1, that afternoon despite all the chaos surrounding the inaugural. "We certainly were mighty proud of our park," recalled Mack decades later. "Baseball was still in the wooden grandstand stage, and our plant was the first built entirely of steel and concrete. We wondered whether we could ever fill those long rows of seats."[5]

Shibe Park would host MLB for 62 years, exclusively the home of the Phillies when the A's left town after the 1954 season. It would witness some of the highest quality baseball ever played in the American League—and some of the absolute worst.

Connie Mack's First Dynasty: 1910 to 1914

Although Mack had won two AL pennants in the first decade of the twentieth century, his 1910 Athletics were truly the first club in Mack's championship dynasty. Finishing with 102 wins against just 48 losses, the A's left every other AL club in the dust. The second-place New York Highlanders were barely on the radar screen, 14.5 games behind the White Elephants.

The 1910 Athletics did everything well. Infield regulars were veteran first baseman Harry Davis, cocky, college-bred second baseman Eddie Collins, reliable shortstop Jack Barry, and third baseman John Franklin (Home Run) Baker, who got his nickname by hitting two timely 1911 World Series clouts. Three-quarters of the soon-to-be-famous "$100,000 Infield" were in place. Jack Coombs, Cy Morgan, Albert (Chief) Bender, and Eddie Plank ably took care of most of the team's pitching. Bender's stellar hurling would forever be held in high esteem by Mack. Years later Mack declared, "If I had all the men I've ever handled in their primes and there was one game I wanted to win above all others, Albert [Bender] would be my man."[1] Mack was not alone in his praise for Bender, who was advertised as a full-blooded Chippewa, but actually had a father who was German-American. Ty Cobb called him the brainiest pitcher he ever faced. Mack put Bender's smarts to good use, occasionally employing him as the third-base coach because he was so adroit at stealing the opposing team's signs.

Keenly aware of his native heritage, Bender once humorously taunted a critical and overwhelmingly Caucasian crowd by yelling, "You ignorant, ill-bred foreigners! If you don't like the way I am doing things out there, why don't you just pack up and go back to your own countries!"[2]

The Athletics faced off against the last of the great Chicago Cubs teams in the 1910 World Series. The first two World Series games ever played at new Shibe Park were won by the home team, 4–1 and 9–3, on October 17 and 18. The action shifted to Chicago's West Side Grounds where the Athletics took a 3–0 stranglehold on the World Series with a 12–5 rout. A four-game sweep seemed to be in the offing, but a late-inning collapse in the fourth game resulted in a ten-inning 4–3 Cubs' win. Undaunted, the Athletics used a five-run eighth inning in Game 5 to win, 7–2. When Jack Barry fielded Johnny Kling's grounder in the ninth inning and stepped on second base to force out Jimmy Archer, Connie Mack had his long-awaited first World Series championship. He, his club, and the whole of Philadelphia rejoiced at the good news.

"There can be no question that the better team won," declared *The Sporting News* in its October 20, 1910, issue, "and no man would dare say the victory of the Athletics over the Cubs was a fluke. Mack's machine outplayed and outclassed [Chicago manager Frank] Chance's great combination. What is more, Mack outgeneraled Chance. The latter permitted his men to go into the Series ill-prepared for the struggle."

Philadelphia was unabashedly thrilled. The *Philadelphia Times*, an evening newspaper, published a special World Series edition after the final out was made. Some 300,000 copies were quickly sold. Some 50,000 excited fans gathered near Broad Street Station to fete their returning, conquering heroes in a huge victory parade. It was a grand time to be an A's fan—and to be Connie Mack. After 20 lonely years of being a widower, Mack himself celebrated his World Series triumph by marrying Katherine Hallahan, who would bear him five more children between 1911 and 1920.

More glory was in store for Mack and his charges in 1911. The Athletics took their second consecutive AL flag, the first time that feat had been achieved by a Connie Mack–managed team. The A's started slowly, winning just one of their first seven contests. In comparison, Detroit won 23 of their opening 25. It took until August 4 before the White Elephants overtook the Tigers for good and turned the 1911 AL pennant race into a runaway. Detroit finished far in the distance, 13.5 games back of the Athletics, despite Ty Cobb batting an unworldly .420.

The A's strengthened their lineup for 1911 with the addition of John Phalen (Stuffy) McInnis, a 20-year-old first baseman from Gloucester, MA. After two years in a reserve role, McInnis replaced 37-year-old veteran Harry Davis, who had been a fixture on the Athletics' roster since 1901. (Excluding the 1912 season, when he unhappily managed the struggling Cleveland Naps for one season, Davis would have a place on Mack's roster as a player-coach through 1917 and continue solely as an A's coach until 1927.) McInnis didn't have great power, but he batted .321 in 1911 and eventually became one of baseball's most difficult batters to strike out. He is said to have acquired his unusual nickname as an amateur when spectators cheered on his stellar defensive work with "That's the stuff, kid! That's the stuff!" A wizard with the glove, the baby-faced McInnis rounded out the last piece of the A's fabulous "$100,000 Infield." Though sadly forgotten or ignored by many current baseball fans, the 1914 version of the foursome is rated by stats guru Bill James as the greatest MLB infield of all time.

The 1911 World Series would be a rematch of the 1905 Series—the A's versus the New York Giants. By virtue of the Giants winning a coin toss, it opened at the Polo Grounds on October 14. Christy Mathewson bested Chief Bender in a 2–1 pitchers' duel. With the two cities situated so close to one another, the Series alternated between New York City and Philadelphia for each game. The Athletics found Shibe Park's familiar surroundings comfortable and won Game 2, 3–1. The A's managed only four hits, but one was a two-run homer by Frank Baker. Eddie Plank got the win for the home team. Back at the Polo Grounds the following day, Game 3 looked to be a certain Giants win, but Baker was again the hero; his solo homer off Mathewson in the top of the ninth inning forced extra innings. John Franklin Baker was forever known as Home Run Baker from that point onward. (He had led the AL with 11 home runs that season, a measly total by modern standards but certainly eye-catching in 1911.) During the game Baker had been intentionally spiked at third base by the Giants' Fred Snodgrass. The visiting Athletics won 3–2 in 11 innings and Baker was lauded as a battle-scarred hero. Jack Coombs went the distance for the victorious A's.

Six days of rain delayed the next World Series contest until October 24, irking fans, players, reporters, and baseball's moguls alike. When play finally resumed, the Giants plated two runs in the top of the first inning of Game 4. Philadelphia score three times in the fourth inning and once in the fifth to win, 4–2. Bender threw a seven-hitter for the victory. Rube Oldring, a largely unheralded outfielder, blasted a three-run homer in the third inning of Game 5, but the Giants staged a late rally, scoring twice in the ninth inning and once in the tenth to force a sixth game back in Philadelphia on October 26. The Giants' winning run came on Fred Merkle's sacrifice fly which scored Larry Doyle—sort of. Doyle's slide beat the throw to the plate by a considerable margin, but Doyle actually slid wide of the plate. Magisterial umpire Bill Klem properly lingered near the plate for a few moments, waiting for an Athletics appeal play that was never made. Mack later told reporters he knew Doyle had indeed missed home plate but thought it unsporting to make an appeal when Doyle arrived so far ahead of the throw. When the series ended, Mack further stated, "If any of my players had raised the point about Doyle's run, I would have felt so sore that I believe I would have taken him by the scruff of the neck and thrown him over the grandstand."[3] The November 2, 1911, edition of *The Sporting News* fawningly declared Mack's refusal to appeal Doyle's game-winning run to be "one of the finest acts of sportsmanship known to the game." Even during the frequent dismal periods of A's baseball until Mack's retirement decades later, *TSN* would almost always refer to Mack in reverential terms.

Game 6 was close only until the fourth inning, when the Athletics scored four times off Red Ames. A seven-run seventh inning completely salted things away for the defending champions. The A's cruised home with a 13–2 rout for their second straight World Series title. The Athletics thus became the first team under the best-of-seven World Series format to lose the first game and still capture the laurels. Old reliable Harry Davis contributed five RBI in the six games, as did Home Run Baker. The customary victory parade down the thoroughfares of Philadelphia and testimonial banquet followed. Connie Mack's Athletics were firmly entrenched at the top of the baseball world.

The Sporting News declared in that same November 2 issue that the A's were deserving champions. "The climax of the World Series, when the Athletics won by 13 to 2, undoubtedly put the lid on a whole lot of discussion as to which was the better team," concluded *TSN*. "The first five games were so hard fought that some were not disposed to grant that the Athletics were superior to the New Yorkers. But the sixth game left no doubt as to which manager has the better bunch of ball players."

The next season, 1912, proved to be the lone off-season in the 1910–1914 dynasty years of the A's. An excellent Boston Red Sox team won 105 games to take the AL flag that year. Philadelphia's 90 wins was good enough only for third place, one shy of second-place Washington's 91 triumphs. Thirty-one of those Senators wins came via the reliable right arm of Walter Perry Johnson, a likable, soft-spoken fellow from Kansas who was quickly becoming the most dominant fireballer in MLB. Eddie Plank's pitching could hardly be blamed for the A's not winning a third consecutive AL pennant. He went 26–6. Boston went on to beat the New York Giants in the memorable—even epic—1912 World Series that required eight games to complete because of a tie game controversially called due to darkness.

Philadelphia returned to the top of the standings in 1913, taking the AL flag fairly comfortably by 6.5 games over Washington. Plank and Bender continued to be the most reliable members of the A's pitching staff, although Carroll (Boardwalk) Brown, Bullet Joe Bush, and Byron Houck contributed 17, 15, and 14 wins respectively. Again the Giants won the NL pennant. Again they would try to win the World Series for the first time since 1905.

The Series began on October 7 at the Polo Grounds, where Home Run Baker performed his post-season magic once again. His two-run homer provided the difference in the Athletics' 6–4 win. As in 1911, the teams traveled from one city to the next for each game. Game 2 was very reminiscent of 1905 as Christy Mathewson, in his last World Series hurrah, shut out the A's, 3–0, at Shibe Park on October 8, although it took him ten innings to do it. Eddie Plank was the hard-luck loser. The A's jumped all over Jeff Tesreau early in Game 3 and romped, 8–2. Twenty-year-old Bullet Joe Bush went the distance for the victors, allowing just five New York hits, becoming the youngest pitcher to win a World Series game. "Giants Slain by Mere Boy" declared a headline in the October 10 *Boston Globe*. At Shibe Park in Game 4, Chief Bender was staked to a 6–0 lead but nearly let the advantage slip away. Five late Giants runs made things somewhat uncomfortable for Connie Mack, but his charges managed to hang on for a nail-biting 6–5 win. The following day, at the Polo Grounds, Christy Mathewson pitched the last World Series game in his illustrious career. He went the distance, but so did Eddie Plank. The A's won, 3–1, and captured their third World Series in four seasons. Remarkably, Mack did not use a substitute in the entire series except for giving catcher Wally Schang the day off for Game 2.

Many baseball writers justifiably declared these Athletics to be the greatest ball club ever assembled, although *The Sporting News* curiously declared the Athletics' victory to be "hollow" because, in their correspondents' eyes, the Giants did not put up much of a struggle, "crumpled weakly," and "could not find a flaw in the Mackmen." Said *The Sporting News* in its October 16 edition, "The Series, which ended Saturday in an overwhelming triumph for Philadelphia's Athletics, was so one-sided that it lacked the interest incited by some of the previous similar contests and fell far short of other years in brilliance and good baseball." It was the third consecutive World Series defeat absorbed by the Giants, equaling the dubious feat of the 1907–1909 Detroit Tigers, the only pennant winners Ty Cobb ever played for in his long and illustrious career.

In 1914, all things seemed rosy for the Athletics—at least on the surface. Although the season began on a sad note with news of Rube Waddell's death from pneumonia at age 37 (somewhat fittingly on April Fools' Day), Mack's team comfortably won the AL pennant with a 99–53 record, 8.5 games ahead of the runner-up Boston Red Sox. Superb pitching was the A's strength; it was truly phenomenal. Chief Bender went 17–3. Bob Shawkey was 15–8. Eddie Plank was 15–7. Joe Bush went 17–13. Herb Pennock recorded an 11–4 mark. Rube Bressler was 10–4. Weldon Wyckoff was 11–7. The A's recorded 24 shutouts. There was, however, a permanent distraction throughout the 1914 season—an upstart professional circuit called the Federal League.

In 1912, a baseball promoter named John T. Powers created an independent new circuit called the Columbian League. However, one of its main investors got cold feet and the entire enterprise folded before a single game was ever played. Powers tried once more in 1913. He created a six-team league with teams located in Chicago, Cleveland, Pittsburgh, Indianapolis, St. Louis, and Covington, KY. This time Powers christened his organization the Federal League, and served as the circuit's first president.

The FL was, in baseball terms, an "outlaw league" because it did not abide by the National Agreement on player contracts that was in place throughout organized baseball. Depending on one's point of view, the FL's outlaw status allowed it to either "recruit" or "raid" players from the established MLB clubs. Not surprisingly, the underpaid stars of the day were only too happy to listen to offers of double the salaries they were presently receiving from the clubs in the two established major leagues. Few AL and NL regulars were not offered FL contracts. Several up-and-coming minor leaguers were wooed by generous sums, too. During the FL's first season, Powers initially served as the league's president, but he was shortly replaced by the ambitious James A. Gilmore. Armed with deep-pocketed backers and an abundance of courage, Gilmore declared the FL a major league for the 1914 season and expanded the circuit to eight teams—the same size as both the NL and AL. Four of the teams operated in territory already occupied by NL or AL clubs (or both): Chicago, Pittsburgh, St. Louis and Brooklyn. Some of the well-to-do financiers of the Federal League included oil baron Harry F. Sinclair, ice magnate Phil Ball, and George S. Ward of the prominent Ward Baking Company.

The cash bonanza was constantly on the minds of Mack's A's, who generally weren't among the best paid players in the big leagues despite their continuing dominance on the diamond. Mack could always cry poverty. Attendance at Shibe Park was never as great as one might expect. AL umpire Billy Evans was always quick to remark that the champion A's deserved far better support at the gate than they customarily got. Those Athletics who weren't lured away in 1914 by FL money certainly considered jumping in 1915 if the FL was still in business and the price was right. Walter Johnson, baseball's brightest pitcher, initially signed a three-year FL contract with the Chicago Whales, but reneged when his Washington Senators put forth an acceptable counter-offer. This was typical of the negotiations that star players used during the FL bidding war: pay me significantly more or I'll jump to the Feds. Boston's Tris Speaker, a terrific hitter and the best defensive center fielder of his generation—perhaps ever—saw his Red Sox salary nearly triple after his threat of leaving. In an era of tight-fisted owners, Charles Comiskey of the White Sox and Connie Mack/Ben Shibe seem to have been the AL's most parsimonious and least likely to give in to their star players' escalating demands. Shibe Park, despite its clear improvement over insufficient Columbia Park, still had a huge number of 25-cent bleacher seats. Mack's only sources of income were gate receipts, the cut his team received from every road game it played, and, of course, the profit he could make by selling his players' contracts to rival clubs whenever the temptation of quick cash became too great. Following 1914, the temptation was almost always too great.

For most of the 1914 season, the scuttlebutt among Mack's players was how much cash they could make by joining FL clubs in 1915. Danny Murphy, a beloved member of all five Athletics' pennant-winning teams to that time, especially irked Mack because he was now working as a player-scout for the Brooklyn Feds, and openly courted the players on Mack's 1914 team. Mack was no fool and wanted to preserve one of baseball's great assemblages of talent. Eddie Collins was given a significant raise, as was Home Run Baker. Deep down, Mack hoped the FL would fold so he could retain all his stars for 1915 and beyond.

Despite the obvious distraction the FL provided in 1914, the Philadelphia Athletics continued where they left off in 1913 and won the AL pennant again without too much difficulty. With the pennant virtually assured, Mack took Chief Bender out of the A's rotation and sent him on a scouting trip to watch the surprising Boston Braves play a series. The Braves, a longtime cellar-dwelling club, had lost 16 of their first 19 games of 1914, and were languishing in last place in the NL standings on the Fourth of July, some 15 games in arrears of the first-place New York Giants. Incredibly they embarked on a remarkable tear and finished 10.5 games ahead of the Giants to win their first pennant of the twentieth century. While the Braves' underdog story was appealing to fans and writers alike, few observers gave the NL champions much chance against the supposedly invincible Athletics. Bender was obviously one of the unconvinced. He cavalierly skipped the scouting assignment and went fishing instead. Utterly unapologetic when he presented himself before his manager with no scouting report on the Braves, Bender told Mack that the vaunted A's had nothing to fear from the inferior NL upstarts from Boston.

Bender was not alone in thinking the A's would win in a cakewalk. In a World Series preview piece for the October 8, 1914, edition of *The Sporting News*, even Boston beat writer Tim Murnane openly expected the Athletics to emerge victorious.

> "What do you think of the Braves' chances with the Athletics?" is the important query now passing among baseball fans of the whole country. While I find very few will admit to the Braves having an equal chance with the Mackmen, I find several clever baseball men willing to predict the Series will go at least six games.
>
> I know the style of game put up by the Athletics and now have a fair line on the local surprise party. The Athletics look altogether the stronger batting team. As for pitching, I am inclined to think that Bender and Plank will outpoint their younger rivals.
>
> While I am not in the predicting business, experience, confidence, and baseball brains should pull the Athletics through, although you never can tell what might happen in a short series of games.

The 1914 World Series opened in Shibe Park on Friday, October 9, with the A's understandably the prohibitive favorites. The Braves shockingly won Game 1 easily, 7–1. Chief Bender lasted just 5⅓ innings before being relieved. It was the first time in his World Series career he had failed to throw a complete came. The A's managed just five hits off Boston's Dick Rudolph. Boston won Game 2 the next day, 1–0, when a misplayed fly ball in the ninth inning provided the only run of the contest. This time Bill James held the A's to two measly hits. A remarkable upset was in the offing.

As the series shifted to Boston, one member of the AL champs may have been distracted with off-the-field concerns. During the last two games of the

1914 World Series, outfielder Rube Oldring was persistently heckled by Braves fans about his personal life. They had learned a salacious tidbit: Oldring's upcoming marriage plans to a young lady named Hannah Thomas were being thwarted by Rube's common-law wife, Helen, who was suing him for nonsupport and abandonment. The messy matter was quietly settled out of court. After the Series, Oldring, who had just one hit in 15 at-bats, noted he did not play as well as he should have and attributed his lackluster performance to his marital troubles.

Game 3, played at nearly new Fenway Park on Monday, October 12, truly ripped the heart out of the Athletics. Philadelphia scored twice in the top of the tenth inning to take a seemingly safe 4–2 lead, but Boston rallied in the home half of the frame with a home run and a sacrifice fly off Bullet Joe Bush to knot the score. A wild throw by Bush in the bottom of the 12th handed the game to the Braves. Nothing could stop baseball's Cinderella squad now. The following day a two-run, fifth-inning single by ex–Cub Johnny Evers gave the Braves the necessary edge in a 3–1 win an improbable four-game sweep of the mighty Athletics.

Nobody had seen it coming. "Stunning" is a wholly inadequate adjective to describe the Braves' easy four-game triumph. Such was the enormity of the upset that some people wondered whether the Series was actually on the level. (Among some baseball historians, the suspicion lingers even to this day.) Be that as it may, Connie Mack's dynasty was abruptly over. Writing about the 1914 World Series 50 years later in an article for the October 1964 issue of *Baseball Digest*, journalist Herbert Simons giddily declared, "Someday, somewhere, a cow will kill a butcher, a mouse will marry an elephant, or Liz Burton [Taylor] will enter a nunnery. Until then, the most improbable happening of the twentieth century has to be the Miracle of the 1914 Boston Braves." The headlines in the October 15, 1914, issue of *The Sporting News* deservedly praised Braves manager George Stallings for orchestrating the upset, but also succinctly encapsulated in a subheading what had happened: "Athletics are to Blame for it All: They Thought the Braves an Easy Proposition." Catcher Wally Schang concurred. Years later he ruefully admitted that the A's went into the World Series too cocky and had lived it up too much in the preceding week.

In a 1932 interview with New York baseball writer Joe Williams, Mack discussed the famous World Series loss of 1914. Mack told Williams he wasn't surprised by the defeat and had given up on his team sometime in August! Mack explained that his team was riddled with dissention because half the players were dazzled by FL offers and were almost certain to jump leagues in 1915, while the other half wanted to remain in Philadelphia. The two factions could not see eye to eye.

The staggering World Series sweep loss to the Braves vexed Mack. He and

Ben Shibe were not in a celebratory mood and swiftly nixed a parade and dinner that the city of Philadelphia still wanted to hold in honor of the A's winning the 1914 AL pennant. Mack tersely told reporters there would be no banquet to celebrate the AL flag.

More unsettling were reports that several A's players had misbehaved during a post-season, all-star, goodwill baseball trip to Hawaii, apparently paying no heed to coach Ira Thomas, who had taken Mack's place on the tour once Mack had decided not to go. (Mack's daughter's wedding was coming up; it provided a plausible excuse for him to back out of a long trip he had no desire to make after losing the World Series in such a shocking manner.) After the World Series, *The Sporting News* commented on October 22, "It cannot be denied that not only the fans but the club management as well feel that some of the players have not shown the qualities demanded of members of the Philadelphia American League club."

Major changes were indeed afoot. By Christmas the story had broken: Mack had sold his superb second baseman, Eddie Collins, to the Chicago White Sox. The heart of the A's pitching staff—Eddie Plank, Jack Coombs and Chief Bender—were all gone by Christmas, with Coombs released outright, and Plank and Bender placed on waivers, with no takers. Some historians have termed the dissolution of the championship Athletics basically a salary dump by the cost-conscious manager, but it was more than that: It was a purging of elements that Mack had perceived to be destructive to team cohesion. Mack had willfully set the course for the A's to become the AL's bottom-feeders for years. In summarizing Mack's decision to break up the mainstays of the Athletics' pitching staff, *The Sporting News* declared in its December 10 edition,

> Neither Plank nor Bender would have been with the Athletics [in 1915] under any circumstances. Connie immediately announced after the close of the World Series that he was positively through with both pitchers. Bender started the Athletics on the start of their downfall at the hands of the Boston Braves last October. Great faith was put in his ability to start the White Elephants off with a victory. Instead Bender was knocked off the rubber. It was rumored afterwards that the Chief had incensed manager Mack by not obeying orders.

Mack put on the best possible public face before the first of his seven consecutive last-place finishes. "I am broke financially but full of ambition," he said. "It is like starting all over again for me and I love baseball and I love to build up teams. I have done it once and I will do it again."[4]

The 1915 version of the Philadelphia A's bore a slight resemblance to the pennant-winning team of the year before, but it was missing too many key pieces—especially on the pitching mound—to be competitive. Instead of Bender, Plank and Coombs, the A's relied heavily on Weldon Wyckoff, Joe Bush and Raymond (Rube) Bressler. It was a disaster. Wyckoff went 10–22. Bressler went 4–17, Bush 5–15. Newcomers Tom Sheehan and Tom Knowlson went 4–9 and 4–6 respectively. (The 1916 season would be far worse for Sheehan. Knowlson never played again in the majors after 1915.) Bob Shawkey and Herb Pennock showed promise, going 6–6 and 3–6. The A's infield still featured Stuffy McInnis at first base, while 40-year-old Napoleon Lajoie was brought back for a little bit of veteran stability—but mostly for old-times' sake—to play second base. Despite being ancient for a middle infielder, Lajoie batted a respectable .280. Shortstop Larry Kopf was an offensive albatross, though, hitting only .225. The longtime team mascot, a hunchback dwarf named Louis Van Zelst, died in Philadelphia just before spring training concluded. It was definitely a bad omen.

The real sore point for Mack in 1915 was the huge question mark at third base. Home Run Baker had just signed a three-year contract with the A's, but he was still unhappy with his salary and was actively pursued by the FL. Baker, in his prime at age 29, simply did not show up for spring training in Jacksonville. "Manager Mack does not appear to have been as successful as [Phillies manager Pat] Moran in picking up lively looking material to bolster his team," reported *The Sporting News* in its April 8 issue a week before the season began. "The third baseman to fill Frank Baker's shoes has not been found." Mack would try 14 different players at third base in 1915 with almost no success to show for his creativity. Mack's inability to replace Baker undoubtedly pleased the petulant holdout. Versatile Wally Schang, the A's catcher in 1914, ended up doing a fair chunk of the work at the hot corner for the 1915 Athletics, playing 43 games there and committing 18 errors. It was a position Schang had never played before in the majors—and only seldom would again after 1915—even though his MLB career lasted until 1931. Larry Kopf was also a semi-regular third-sacker for Mack, playing 42 games.

On Wednesday, April 14, in a fabulous display of chutzpah, Baker and his wife traveled from their Maryland home and conspicuously showed up at Shibe Park as spectators among the disappointingly small crowd of 9,000 fans at the Athletics' home opener! Incredulous, Mack greeted his AWOL third baseman's presence at the ballpark with nothing more than an icy stare. (Apparently no offer from anywhere was good enough for John Franklin Baker in 1915. He sat out the entire season, although he did play a few amateur games, much to the delight of his hometown nine in Trappe, MD. Baker also engaged in some lucrative semipro outings with teams in Atlantic City, Easton, MD, and Upland, PA, where he demanded and got handsome appearance fees. Baker's holdout became such an acute annoyance to Mack that, at one point during the frustrating campaign, he stated that he no longer wanted to hear Baker's name even mentioned.) Despite the distraction of Baker's unwanted presence in Shibe Park's grandstand and the general feeling of doom pervading the team's overall chances in 1915, the Athletics won their home opener, 2–0, over Boston on a nifty shutout by

Herb Pennock. "Maybe we'll surprise them,"[5] Mack optimistically said after the game.

The small turnout for the A's home opener shocked veteran Boston sports writer Tim Murnane, arguably the best baseball scribe of his time. "Why have the fans grown cold toward the Athletics here in the City of Brotherly Love?" he asked in a lengthy piece for the April 22, 1915, edition of *The Sporting News*. He proffered several theories, from the fans resenting the players who had jumped to FL teams, to the Athletics' complacency with success since 1910, to a general malaise about Connie Mack's team. Perhaps the Philly fans foresaw better than the Boston scribe what was going to happen over the course of that long summer. Murnane also reported, quite wrongly it turned out, that Home Run Baker would return to the Athletics' lineup when the A's played their first series at Boston's Fenway Park the following week.

About a month into the 1915 season, *Baseball Magazine* reported in its May edition on the Athletics' ongoing personnel woes: "Almost everybody has tried to play third [base], nobody of yet showing much of Baker's quality on the difficult station. With [Stuffy] McInnis out, there have also been sundry experiments on first [base]. The pitching staff has shown blamed little."

Baker remained holed up in Maryland throughout the 1915 campaign—and the defending AL champion A's wound up solidly in the AL basement with a horrible 43–109 record, accumulating 56 fewer wins than the 1914 A's had in an equal number of games. It set a record for negative win differential from one season to the next which remains unchallenged to this day. The dwindling number of home fans saw the White Elephants win just 19 games at Shibe Park all season. In 22 games versus the second-place Chicago White Sox, the A's were 3–19. The Athletics won just 4 of 24 games in August. As the team's prospects collapsed, so did morale. Mack parted ways with more unhappy players. After a public spat with Mack following a particularly dismal outing in Detroit, Herb Pennock wound up pitching for the Red Sox before the season was over. Many of the A's quite naturally lost their enthusiasm for being stuck on a hopeless team—and Mack got rid of them in short order. Jack Barry was sold to the Red Sox on July 2 for $10,000. Eddie Murphy and Jack Lapp were moved to the White Sox. Bob Shawkey was sold to the New York Yankees.

Bad baseball at Shibe Park was the inevitable result in 1915. On April 22, the normally sure-handed Lajoie made five errors at second base in a 7–6 loss to Boston. On June 23 rookie pitcher Bruno Haas walked 16 New York Yankees in a brutal 15–7 loss, becoming the only pitcher in the twentieth century to issue that many passes in a game. It was his only career decision. After 1915 Haas vanished from MLB forever with an 11.93 ERA. In its April 1916 issue, *Baseball Magazine* recalled Haas' horrific day. "Last summer Connie Mack sent Bruno Haas into a game," wrote J. C. Kofoed, "and Bruno proceeded to give sixteen or eighteen bases on balls. Whenever he did get the sphere over, it was usually slammed for a safe hit. Mack refused to take him out. 'He was learning something every minute he was in there. As we were out of the running anyway, it would have been foolish to put someone else in there.'" This tough-it-out style of pitching management during A's one-sided losses was routinely on display during the years when Mack's clubs were hopelessly in the cellar.

The 1915 A's were not much of a slugging threat. Rube Oldring, a holdover from the championship years, led the Athletics with a mere six home runs. That was three times as many as any other individual A's player could muster and three-eighths of the team's total of 16.

For a time Mack tried a raw 20-year-old named Sam Crane at shortstop. Crane was the stereotypical good-field-no-hit player. He played in only eight games over two seasons for the A's and did not attract much attention on the diamond. In 1929, however, Crane made quite a few negative headlines far outside the world of baseball for a twin-killing of a different sort: In a drunken stupor, Crane gunned down his paramour and another man in a Harrisburg, PA, saloon—the bloody end to a volatile lovers' triangle. The kind-hearted Mack steadfastly assisted Crane in his annual bids for freedom once he became eligible for parole. Furthermore, Mack promised Crane a job at Shibe Park upon his release from the hoosegow.

The Athletics staggered to the end of their 1915 schedule, hardly resembling a capable big league squad, especially on the mound. Particularly bad was a record-breaking September 29 doubleheader in Washington in which the Senators thumped the Mackmen, 10–2 and 20–5. The two defeats extended an A's losing streak to an ugly 11 games. Quipped *The Sporting News* in its October 7 edition, "Thirty runs in one afternoon is a major-league record that will stand for a while unless Connie Mack's pitching gets even worse than it has been." Mack employed 27 different pitchers in 1915. In contrast, the pennant-winning Red Sox used just 11 hurlers. The A's pitching staff issued the mind-boggling total of 827 walks in 1915—an average of 5.4 per game. The hurlers' penchant for delivering pitches high and far out of the strike zone inspired Ring Lardner to quip, "Connie Mack has a staff of simply unhittable pitchers, unhittable, that is, unless the opposing batsmen are permitted to take ladders up to the plate with them."[6]

Attendance at Shibe Park dropped dramatically in 1915. With such a poor product on the field compared to the recent championship years, only 146,223 fans passed through the ballpark's turnstiles all season. Meanwhile the usually woebegone Philadelphia Phillies drew more than three times as many paying customers to their home games—nearly 450,000—as they won the NL flag for the first time in the twentieth century, copping the pennant with a cushy seven-game advantage over the defending champion Braves. (The Phillies and their great star pitcher, Grover Cleveland Alexander, would lose the World Series to the Boston Red Sox in five games, though. The Red Sox had capably filled the void left by the Athletics and were on their way to becoming the AL championship dynasty for the remainder of the decade.)

The Frank Baker affair continued to drag on beyond the 1915 World Series. "There is scarcely a day that some yarn is not sprung about the former slugger from Trappe, MD," said the November 11 edition of *The Sporting News*, "but up to date manager Mack has been very uncommunicative." At one point the weekly newspaper had Mack and Baker talking out their differences secretly but amicably somewhere in Maryland, with Baker supposedly approving his sale to either New York or Chicago—as long as he was paid his full salary for 1915! The scuttlebutt in the very next edition of *The Sporting News*, though, had an entirely different twist. Rumor had it that Baker had a change of heart and he was certain to return to Mack's team for 1916. This bit of hopeful speculation for A's fans turned out to be utterly baseless. An editorial in the April 1916 edition of *Baseball Magazine* described Baker's holdout, with a scholarly allusion to the classics, thusly:

> Achilles sulked in his tent and gave Homer a theme for one of the world's greatest epics. Home Run Baker sulked likewise on his well-stocked farm and the epic which that act created isn't finished yet. Baker had a grievance, albeit not a strictly legal one. But he elected to forego the profits of a season in the big show to make a point.

In its November 25 edition, *The Sporting News* reported that the annual spring series of pre-season games in Philadelphia between the Phillies and the Athletics would likely not be held in 1916, as the pennant-winning Phillies were said to have made arrangements instead to play the Washington Senators at the time the intra-city games had normally taken place. Apparently a lack of interest by fans had made the games a losing financial proposition the past few springs. "There will be no regret here if the [pre-season] series between the White Elephants and the Quakers is called off," wrote William G. Weart, a local sports scribe who earned a few extra dollars on the side as *TSN*'s correspondent for both of Philly's MLB clubs. In recent years the City Series had failed to generate much excitement within the hearts of Philadelphia's baseball rooters, as the games were used—especially by Mack—to try out hopefuls rather than use his regulars. What was left unsaid, but probably tacitly understood by knowledgeable fans, was that any series between the formidable 1915 NL champion Phillies and the AL doormat Athletics would probably have been a horrible mismatch. The last thing Mack wanted was to have his team outclassed and embarrassed in Philadelphia in a meaningless set of pre-season games.

The glory days of Athletics baseball from just the previous year seemed like a distant memory. Surely things couldn't get worse in 1916 for the proud Philadelphia Athletics franchise and its dignified owner-manager. Could they?

Prelude to Disaster: Spring Training 1916

In the spring of 1916 the Old World's traditional imperial powers were dutifully slugging away at each other, absorbing horrendous casualties on the Western Front battlefields of the First World War. All the while, America hardly noticed the ceaseless bloodletting across the Atlantic. To the majority of Americans, it was a confusing European squabble amongst kaisers, czars, emperors, archdukes and their alliances—but most of all it was a costly and exceedingly bloody foreign entanglement that the average American wished to avoid completely.

As spring training approached and the professional baseball clubs prepared to head to southern destinations, the eyes of the rest of the world were turned to one of the most bloody and pointless engagements in the history of warfare. The Battle of Verdun, on the Meuse River, had begun with a surprise German assault on February 21 but was settling into another deadly Western Front stalemate that eventually involved 125 divisions and 2.4 million soldiers. Military historians sometimes refer to it as the "Meuse Mincer." By the time the carnage had reached its hellish conclusion in December, nearly 700,000 men had died in the muck and filth in a small section of northeastern France, a staggering average of 2,300 battlefield deaths per day. The end result was a Pyrrhic victory for the overtaxed French defenders over the advancing but exhausted Germans.

But in isolated America, far from the deafening roar of the ceaseless artillery barrages and the sickly stench of the rotting corpses in France's no-man's-land, March was here. In the springtime of 1916, every red-blooded American boy's fancy turned toward baseball, the unquestioned national pastime, not to a stagnating foreign war across the Atlantic. *The Sporting News,* the five-cent, self-proclaimed "Baseball Paper of the World," that, according to its masthead, had "all the best baseball gossip," had correspondents everywhere in the training camps to live up to its credo. It would thoroughly chronicle each move of every major league team during spring training, and disseminate most of the scuttlebutt around the plentiful minor league teams, too. It was a great time to be an American and a baseball fan. The awful scuffle in Europe was an entire ocean away. Life on this side of the pond was good, and major league baseball was part of it.

In a preview piece for the upcoming season published on March 9, *The Sporting News* asked each of the eight American League managers to assess his team's chances to take the pennant in 1916. Job security was apparently good for baseball managers that season, and they were only too glad to offer their opinions on the upcoming campaign. (All eight men who began the season as AL pilots ended the season in the same capacity. Only one NL manager, Cincinnati's Buck Herzog, whose team finished in the basement, got the ax in 1916.)

Detroit manager Hughie Jennings tactfully informed *The Sporting News* that six teams (all but Cleveland and Philadelphia) would be in the thick of the race. Boston's Bill Carrigan, fresh off a World Series triumph in 1915, confidently figured it would come down to his club and Jennings' outfit. New York Yankees manager Wild Bill Donovan, his lineup bolstered by his acquisition of the disenchanted slugger Home Run Baker for the princely sum of $37,500, envisioned a promising campaign for his team—especially with the Polo Grounds' right field

The Tall Tactician, Connie Mack, in a photograph taken circa 1916. The beloved Mack had already attained legendary status in Philadelphia and beyond by 1916. His team's pitiful performance that year did not seem to diminish Mack's stature in the baseball world very much (National Baseball Hall of Fame Library, Cooperstown, N.Y.).

fence being about 40 feet shorter for Baker than Shibe Park's similar wall. Clarence Rowland foresaw no reason why his Chicago White Sox should not accomplish great things, too. He thought his team was "feared." Clark Griffith warned that "the wise ones" who thought his Senators would be doormats would be fooled. Cleveland's Lee Fohl acknowledged that very few prognosticators had given his team much of a chance to make an impact, but cautioned the critics that his Indians might surprise those persons who figured his team would be "scalped by the contenders." New St. Louis Browns pilot Fielder Jones figured team speed would serve his club well and keep them in contention for the long run. The Browns' lineup had been bolstered by several refugees from the championship St. Louis Terriers of the now-defunct Federal League. Jones politely added, "And don't lose sight of Mack, for Connie might pull a surprise."

Connie Mack, in a skillful display of double-talk, presented an outwardly optimistic outlook about his Philadelphia Athletics, but hinted that fans should not expect too much from his green troops. "The season of 1916 is going to be an experimental one with the Athletics," Mack began. "When I sold [Eddie] Collins, [Frank] Baker, [Jack] Barry and the other performers, I declared that the Philadelphia team would be back in the American League pennant hunt a lot sooner than many persons anticipated. We may not be in the thickest of the flight this season, but I have a lot of players under contract, and quite a few prospects. I wouldn't be surprised if we show them a pretty strong team before the schedule is very old."

Most astute observers thought that Mack's optimism was merely public posturing. Nearly everyone figured the 1916 Athletics would be at the bottom of the AL heap at the conclusion of the season. W. A. Phelon of *Baseball Magazine* had the most generous assessment of the A's: He tabbed the Mackmen for a seventh-place finish. W. R. Hoefer of the same publication had a decisively more pessimistic outlook for the White Elephants: He wrote that Mack should be thankful "because there are only eight clubs in the American League and the misfits he commands can't finish twenty-seventh."[1] In the subsequent issue, the A's were pegged as 100–1 underdogs to win the AL pennant and 10–1 to finish even as high as fourth place. In fairness, the gamblers also assigned the same long odds to the Cleveland Indians—before they surprisingly acquired Tris Speaker from the Red Sox just prior to the start of the 1916 season.

In a piece in the July issue of *Baseball Magazine*, J. C. Kofoed wrote about the large number of raw players Mack would be using to assemble his 1916 version of the Philadelphia Athletics.

> His new crop consists of pitchers Crowell, Myers, [Bill] Morrisette, Nabors, Ray, Richardson and Voltz; catchers Myers [sic] and Murphy; infielders Witt, Crane and Pick; and outfielders Thompson and Stellbauer. A number of these boys have promise, but almost every one of them is lamentably green.
>
> There is absolutely no question that there is talent in the crowd, but it will not be brought to a point of real efficiency this season. Morrisette is the most seasoned of the pitchers, but Minot Crowell, "Chief" Myers, and Jack Nabors, the lanky Talladega star, excel him in sheer ability. This quartet, with [Joe] Bush, [Weldon] Wyckoff and [Rube] Bressler, is expected to make a respectable showing for the boxmen.
>
> Carl Ray, a lefthander, has murderous speed and a good curve, but his control and

fielding ability (or lack of it) is wretched. Richardson is a giant whose arm did not round into shape as rapidly as it should, while Voltz has not yet had a thorough trial.

It is doubtful if shortstop Sam Crane ever wins a regular big-league berth. He is a player who came up from Richmond touted as a second Jack Barry in fielding skill. Though brilliant at times, he was erratic, and his hitting [was] far below the average. Lawton Witt, the collegian, has more talent than any man in the squad.... A splendid ground-coverer and a natural hitter, Witt should hold the shortstop berth without difficulty. At the far corner, Charley [sic] Pick, a more experienced man than any of the others, will doubtless play the position for the better part of the season. He is a steady if not a particularly brilliant player.

The new catchers, [Billy] Myers [sic] and [Mike] Murphy, though still leagues and leagues removed from the class of Schang and Lapp, are boys with sufficient promise to hold positions with the Athletics for quite a while to come. Myers in particular has shown great skill. Connie is rather chary of boosting recruit maskmen since Jim McAvoy disappointed him so sadly, but he thinks well of Myers [sic] and Murphy.

In my opinion, "Shag" Thompson is too good a man to keep indefinitely on the bench, and he is slated to succeed [Rube] Oldring or [Jimmy] Walsh. [Bill] Stellbauer, the newest outfield recruit, who hit .300 in Peoria, is more or less of an unknown quantity.

The 1916 baseball season was a return to normalcy in the majors. Peace had resumed in the upper echelons of the professional game. The Federal League had flamed out amid a mountain of debt after its second and final MLB season in 1915. Fans generally stayed away from FL ballparks the previous summer despite a terrific five-team pennant race—arguably the best in MLB history—and enticing, bargain-basement, ten-cent admission prices. Those players who had jumped to the FL for untold riches had to swallow their pride and return humbly to their old clubs, if they'd still have them. Most FL players were accepted back into the fold of the NL and AL with few hard feelings, although they often found their salaries had reverted back to the pre-1914 levels that had so bothered them two seasons earlier. However, the ghosts of the FL still surfaced in 1916. Some were significant news items, such as the $500,000 antitrust lawsuit launched by the Baltimore Feds against "organized baseball" (i.e., the AL and NL). Others FL news tidbits were esoteric, such as the one about the unfortunate landlord of one FL ballpark futilely trying to collect the back rent owed to him by the now-defunct Kansas City Packers.

One player who was returning from the FL under a sizable cloud of suspicion was 33-year-old Hal Chase, a genial, gifted, and oddly charismatic first baseman—perhaps the best of baseball's entire Deadball Era. "Prince Hal" Chase had played the last half of 1914 and all of 1915 with the FL's Buffalo franchise. He led the circuit in homers with 17 during the latter season, making him one of the more desirable FL refugees. Unfortunately, Chase had a penchant for running around with the wrong crowd, especially a coterie of gamblers who frequently supplemented his income with payoffs to throw games.

Chase's associations and misdeeds were well known to professional baseball's owners, management, fans and reporters, but they were seldom discussed freely in the press. In *Baseball America*, Donald Honig's excellent history of the game published in 1985, the author wrote about the gambling problems that plagued the highest levels of the sport in the 1910s but were largely ignored.

> Not every man who drew on a big league uniform in those days was immune to the thrills of temptation. A ballplayer, knowing that little mounds of money were being exchanged because of his performance on a given day, could get to indulging in secret reveries. Many did, and some began acting them out—how many, we cannot be sure. The sportswriters of the day certainly weren't telling; they had taken a vow of silence when it came to staining the image of the fantasy world Americans found so clean-limbed and inspiring. Those writers who did mention their suspicions were told to let it pass. [Baseball's] blemishes were better glossed over. The escapist dreams of apple-piety Main Street had to be protected.[2]

A see-no-evil approach was the preferred norm. During the 1916 season, *Baseball Magazine* strongly rebuked a fan whose letter dared to question the honesty of some MLB games and players. The publication toed the party line in its June issue, assertively (and naively) declaring,

> As for a player throwing a game, he couldn't do so even if he wanted to. It would take at least nine men and an umpire to deliver a game, and even then it would be a risky proposition. It is an absolute fact that no game has ever been thrown in either Organized Baseball [NL and AL] or the Federal League within the present generation without delving into ancient history. There is absolutely no call for such argument, or rather lack of argument at this stage of the game.

Despite assurances from baseball's chroniclers that the national game was above reproach, spectators were not so certain. Fans were known to taunt Chase with "What's the odds, Hal?" Still, the idea that America's national pastime could be corrupted by gambling was too taboo a topic to address openly in 1916. Criticism of Chase and his ilk came more subtly. Detroit manager Hughie Jennings, in a startlingly strong rebuke in *The Sporting News* on March 23, admitted that any MLB team would benefit from Chase's skillful glove play at first base and his obvious speed and daring on the base paths. "Yet for all his ability," declared Jennings, "I would not have him on my club, and I do not believe any other major league manager will take a chance with him. He will not heed training rules and he has a demoralizing influence on the younger players. When he was manager of the New York [AL] club, instead of trying to keep his players straight, he used to lead them astray."

Despite Jennings' dire warnings, the talent-strapped Cincinnati Reds did take a chance on Chase in 1916 and used him as their regular first baseman. Years later, in *Baseball America*, Donald Honig theorized on why the Reds decided to sign Prince Hal. "The notorious Hal Chase was a scintillating talent, so magical around first base that one team after another was willing to risk hiring him, probably figuring that a Hal Chase that gave you his all even 80 percent of the time was preferable to anyone else."[3]

The Athletics got off to a shaky 1916 season long before they played even one exhibition game. Long-time Shibe Park groundskeeper Joe Schroeder died in January. It was another bad omen, a harbinger reminiscent of the previous spring when the A's hunchback mascot breathed his last just before the season began. Bad weather and miscommunications delayed the club's pitchers and catchers from arriving promptly at the Athletics' spring training camp in Jacksonville, FL. For most players, a steamship leaving New York City was the preferred way of arriving in the sunny south. Things didn't work out so well, though. "Manager Mack's pitchers and catchers got away to a bad start," wrote William G. Weart, *The Sporting News*' Philadelphia beat writer, in the March 16 edition. "The storm which the Phillies passed through crippled the steamship on which Connie's battery candidates were to have started for the south a few days later. In consequence, there was a mix-up in steamship arrangements, the boat leaving a day later than expected. Then the steamship lost several hours on the journey, and instead of practice starting on March 10, it was not possible to get things moving in the camp at Jacksonville until Sunday, March 12." Weart further noted, "It was unusual for manager Mack to start his season's work on a Sunday, but he did so in order to partly make up for two days lost."

Further reports from spring training give hints that the Athletics would not threaten to win the AL pennant once the regular season got rolling. "Connie and [coach] Ira Thomas, who is in charge of the battery candidates, have been trying a lot of new wrinkles with the twirlers," it was reported in *The Sporting News*. "They will insist that any hurler who remains with the Athletics must be able to field his position and keep base runners close to the sacks as well as something in ability to fool batsmen. Hard work is the slogan in the Athletics' camp this spring, for Connie realizes he must pull a 'comeback' very soon. He is supremely confident that he has the raw material for another combination that will win American League pennants and world's championships."

Ira Thomas, 35, had been a favorite utility player of Mack's from 1909 through 1915, often splitting the club's catching duties with Jack Lapp during the A's pennant-winning heyday. He was considered huge for his day, measuring 6'2" and tipping the scales at 200 pounds. He also had rather prominent ears. Thomas' busiest season came in 1911 when he appeared in 103 games as a catcher for Mack's AL pennant winners. He had stayed with the A's in a coaching role, although he did appear in one game as a player as late as June 1915. Now Thomas' playing days were done. Mack liked Thomas; he admired his baseball smarts. Thomas would be Mack's bench coach—a second set of eyes and ears—in 1916. Harry Davis, a fixture with the club, also served as a coach and would be used once in 1916 as a pinch-hitter.

On March 23 *The Sporting News* updated the goings-on with the A's in Jacksonville: "The Athletics' outfielders and infielders left New York last Friday [March 17] for Jacksonville and were due to start their training today. During the latter part of the week the Athletics' first squad will go to Palm Beach and Miami to play the Boston Braves." The spring training news brief mentioned that the A's were not depending upon a heavy schedule of exhibition games to prepare them for the season ahead. "Connie has booked only eight games with major league teams in Florida this year. In addition to the trip to Palm Beach and Miami, he will send a team to Daytona for a couple of games with the Brooklyn Dodgers, and the latter and the Braves will stop at Jacksonville on their way north for games against the Mackmen."

One of those infielders making his first trip south via steamship was a rookie of Polish descent, Lawton (Whitey) Witt, a shortstop who had last played for the Goddard Seminary team in Vermont. Baseball writer Fred Lieb years later would accurately describe Witt as "green as grass." Witt, a 20-year-old Pennsylvanian originally from Orange, MA, had never seen a major league city before he arrived in New York City's harbor to board the Athletics' southbound steamship. Lieb continued, "The boat ride down the coast was as much of an adventure for the kid as though he had sailed on Columbus' *Santa Maria*. He never knew when the liner would sail right off the ocean."[4] Witt would show enough promise as an infielder in Jacksonville to win the spot as the Athletics' regular shortstop—and have a truly memorable 1916 season, mostly for the wrong reasons.

Among its March 23 baseball briefs, *The Sporting News* also reported this quirky and wholly inaccurate fact: "The Athletics may present Myers and Myers as a battery. Myers is a pitcher recruited from the North Carolina League, while Myers, the catcher, comes from the Three-I League." Pitcher Elmer Myers had actually been on the 1915 A's roster, tossing a complete game victory in his only start. He would be a reliable regular in Mack's pitching rotation in 1916. There was no catcher named "Myers" at the A's spring training camp. His name was actually Billy Meyer—his surname had an extra "e" and was without an "s." (*Baseball Magazine*, in its preview, had made the same error in discussing the new catcher.) Before latching on with the Athletics, Meyer's resume showed precisely one game of MLB experience, that coming with the Chicago White Sox in 1913 when he got a single in his lone at-bat for a 1.000 batting average to that point in his nascent career. Meyer would appear in 50 games in 1916 before a bout of appendicitis sidelined him during a July road trip. Fans cagey enough to read between the lines of *The Sporting News'* reports could sense that the 1916 A's would be very much a patchwork outfit and an ongoing work in the making.

On March 30 *The Sporting News* reported that Mack's squad was operating in near anonymity during this preseason.

Not a lot of news has come out of Jacksonville, where Connie Mack is drilling a new team of Athletics and starting practically all over again to get a place in the sun of baseball. Mack is all but overlooked.... Last week his team played a [three-game exhibition series] with the Boston Braves and was soundly trounced, and fandom laughed derisively. They can laugh at his rookies now, and he admits his new team does look bad, particularly the pitchers. But Connie promises to have the last laugh, and those who believe in him rather think he will have it too.

Mack's A's may not have been garnering much publicity compared to the perceived AL front-runners, but they did get plenty of ink in a lengthy and fawning March 25 Associated Press article with a Jacksonville dateline that described the work ethic that Mack was trying to instill into his raw charges.

> It's an easy road down but a hard pull up. This truth is impressing itself on Connie Mack, who is down here in training camp working as he has never worked before in an effort to do a comeback. Changed conditions with the Athletics have meant a marked departure in Mack's methods, and the railbirds who have watched the Tall Tactician in previous springs hardly recognize him as the same man, so different has he become, not in appearance but in manner.
>
> Never before has manager Mack driven a squad so hard as he is working his men this year. In other seasons when there were plenty of veterans in the lineup, the work consisted mainly in conditioning the talent. Little was said about tactics. The tall manager would stroll up and down and study the form of young pitchers, but he bothered little with the veterans, being content to let them shape up in their own way.
>
> This year, with the problem of building a new team before him, the leader seems to be a different man. He is taking charge of everything himself. [Coaches] Thomas and Davis naturally give him some help, but the bulk of the direction is being assumed by Mr. Mack, and he is almost as much of a martinet as [John] McGraw himself in his manner of driving the men.
>
> An early start is made. Each player is called at 8 o'clock. By 9 he is due on the field. Practice is underway at 9:30. All of the pitchers have to take a systematic warm-up with the catchers. Then they work in the box, so as to get the distance right. Each man must pitch in the manner the leader specifies. His form must be right.
>
> After each pitcher finishes his work in the box, he must go to short or second to handle grounders and perfect his fielding. No slovenly work will be pardoned to pitchers at Shibe Park this year.
>
> Even then the work is not done. There is batting practice, and those not at bat have to chase grounders in the outfield.
>
> When all this is done, those players who are overweight are sent for a 15-minute jog around the outfield, a kind of drudgery not hitherto much favored by manager Mack.
>
> The same program is repeated in the afternoon, though by way of relief a ballgame is played. The players enjoy taking part in this game, and manager Mack has always liked to study players in a contest as a measure of getting a line on what a man will do when in action.
>
> In other years there was considerable liberality in letting the men get away for a

little golf and other similar amusements. But this year there will be leave of absence for none. Even manager Mack is giving up his golf in spite of the fact that he is very fond of the game.

The whole impression carried by the work is one of great earnestness. It is as though the famous winner of six pennants had felt that he must get from his material its ultimate.

He is determined to produce an effective pitching staff and is sincere in the belief that he has the men. Whoever might be moved to raise the objection that these candidates have no special class is met by the reply that the greatest products of the Mack system were the men who came to Philadelphia unknown and were developed under the lean Cornelius.

The winner of six pennant and three world's championships keenly realizes that it is on the pitchers the success of his team must depend.

In the old days of the great teams, the Mackmen always had wonderful pitching. It is true that they had a goodly proportion of hitting also. But in the various successful seasons Waddell, Plank, Bender, Coombs, Morgan, Henley, Coakley, Dygert, Krause, and one or two others were largely responsible for the triumphs registered.

Last year the collapse of the team was entirely the fault of the pitchers. It might have been possible to put a pretty fair club on Shibe Park if the hurlers had demonstrated more stuff, but when they went, everything went, and the result was a year of disaster.

Now manager Mack is starting all over again. He is out to build a new staff. Bush, Bressler and Wyckoff have no better chance to make the team than the rawest recruit. It is going to be a fight all the way. These three veterans last year fell far short of what was hoped of them. Now they must battle for their places. If they are good enough to win games, all right. If not, other men will get their billets.

Joe Bush, winner of a World Series game that made him one of the most talked about pitchers in 1913, seems to appreciate the seriousness of the situation. He is showing an earnestness that was lacking before. He wants to stay. He has promised to work at his top notch. He was more eager than any of the youngsters to get out on the field for the first practices, and his mental attitude seems totally changed.

Bush, Bressler and Wyckoff all have the stuff of which great pitchers are made, and yet not one has ever lived up to his reputation. Hence, none are being counted on in the plans for 1916. The dependence and the hope will be placed on the newcomers.

Two of these newcomers—Myers and Morrisette—Mack is banking on strongly. He contends that both are great pitchers right now. Myers demonstrated big-league class last year when he shut out Washington in one of the final games of the season and won the admiring comments of the Washington players.

Other members of the staff will, in the opinion of the manager, demonstrate a most amazing development. Last year the conditions were all wrong for good work. Most of these pitchers did not report until the team was hopelessly out of the race and demoralization had set in.

This year they will start with the slate clean.

Some of the men have grown and filled out. This is notably true of Sheehan and Richardson. The latter needs only experience. He has admitted stuff. Sheehan gave flashes of form last year. For both men there is a good chance.

[Jack] Nabors was only a big country boy last year. He knew nothing. He has more speed than any pitcher in the squad. He has learned much in the time that has passed since he joined the club. He is the tall slender type of [Cy] Falkenberg pitcher liked by big league managers.

These are the men from whom the most is hoped. There is also a good gamble that someone will come through of the following: Ray, a left-hander from North Carolina; Mellinger, another southpaw from Cedar Rapids; and Weaver, a Philadelphia boy.

There are three new catchers, a couple of whom will be retained to help out Wally Schang. All of them did a lot of work last year, Murphy, Myers and Perkins each catching a hundred games in his league. Most is hoped for from Murphy, of Binghamton, in the New York State League. He is an all-around star in the opinion of manager Mack. There is nothing he cannot do.

The infield and outfield present no present problem. There is enough good material to take care of both.

Pitchers and catchers, especially pitchers, will make manager Mack extend himself as he has seldom been called upon to do in many years. The men who are being tried out here are giants in stature. They have shown much in the minors. The best judge of material in the game thinks that out of them it will be possible to produce two stars and two good, dependable twirlers.

Less than this—two good pitchers, to be exact—made the Red Sox a pennant winner last year.

In the company of tall, husky youngsters working for slab positions in Jacksonville now may be the men who will put the Athletics back in their old winning stride.

To that end, a certain lean, wrinkled, sharp-featured gentleman is keeping a close watch on their movements. He knows better than any of his critics the problem that he has to face, but he has the confidence born of past achievements, and he bends himself to the task at hand, deaf to sneers and doubts, believing in not only himself, but in the youngsters he has gathered. True, few of them will be Collinses, Barrys, Bakers, Benders or Planks, but some of them may be.

While *The Sporting News*' correspondent may have hinted at a degree of optimism on March 30, the front page of the following edition of the publication—Thursday, April 6—predicted nothing but cloudy skies and a dangerous dearth of alacrity for the Athletics, who were less than a week away from the 1916 lid-lifter. "Rankest Gloom in Camp of Mackmen," blared the ominous front-page headline, along with two equally dreary subheadings: "Failure of Pitchers Depresses all Members of Team" and "Connie Admits His Plans Have Failed, But Still Has Hope His Comeback is Merely Postponed."

The article, penned by William G. Weart, who would cover both the A's and Phillies all season for both the *Philadelphia Evening Telegraph* and *The Sporting News,* confirmed the baseball newspaper's report from late November that there would be no pre-season series in Philadelphia between the Phillies and the A's for the first time since 1902—which was probably just as well because of the dismal, rainy spring weather in Pennsylvania and the prevailing opinion among just about everybody connected with baseball that the defending NL champion Phillies would have thrashed their AL cousins with very little difficulty. Weart continued,

> There is a lot of gloom in the camp of the Athletics. Manager Mack expected far better results from his training trip than he has been able to discover. Connie arranged for a late start for his pitchers and catchers this year and a very late start for his outfielders and infielders. The latter were in training camp in Jacksonville for only a few days, nearly a week being spent on a trip to Miami and Daytona, where games were played with the Boston Braves and the Brooklyn Dodgers.
>
> Unfortunately, Mack's pitchers developed sore arms a few days after they started work. They apparently started off at too swift a pace and they had to pay the penalty. This resulted not only in a setback to the twirlers and the efforts to develop their talents and to still further take advantage of the instructions which many of them had received last season, but it also had an effect upon the spirits of the veterans. The latter are eager again to become members of a winning combination, but they were discouraged by the poor showing of the pitchers in Florida.
>
> Wyckoff and Bressler, whom manager Mack was confident would make good this year, looked almost hopeless in Jacksonville on account of sore arms. They failed to improve and Connie decided to leave them at Jacksonville until they could get into condition. Whether it will be confident for Wyckoff and Bressler to get into form in time for the opening of the championship race is doubtful. If they do not come along that fast, chances are they will be left in Jacksonville for an indefinite period.
>
> Getting together a pitching staff that will prove to be reliable has been about the toughest proposition that Connie Mack ever had. A year ago, he was confident that Wyckoff, Bush and Bressler would take the places of Coombs, Bender and Plank. All three of these men failed to deliver the goods last year and served to wreck the hopes of their manager and the other players. This year it looks as though Connie would only have Bush to depend upon for the opening of the American League campaign. There is some good material among the young twirling recruits, but the have been unable to show it, owing to sore arms.
>
> Without good pitchers, no team can succeed and the effect of the failure of the twirlers to make a good start has been bad on the entire team. This could be seen in the spirits of the other players. There has been little pepper in the White Elephants this spring. Team spirit, which was once such a big asset for the Athletics, is lacking for the time being. This will return when Mack's pitchers start to make good. But twirling was a big source of discouragement last season and it is still the anchor which is holding down the team this spring.
>
> Manager Mack, after sizing up his team this spring, admitted that it would take him longer than he thought to put together another winning combination. Connie hoped to get his new machine oiled up by the middle of the championship race. Now he cannot predict when the uplift will really get underway.
>
> Behind the bat, Mack has four good men in Schang, Murphy, Meyer and Perkins. First base and second base will be well taken care of, with McInnis in one position and Lajoie to fill in if [Lew] Malone should fail to make good. There is nothing wrong with the outfield with Strunk, Oldring, Walsh and Thompson to take care of the positions.

In Witt, a schoolboy who played third base before joining the team, Connie has a likely looking candidate for shortstop. Witt appears to be a natural hitter and he is now being tried out at Jack Barry's old station and doing good work. Pick is holding own the third base position, but if McConnell could hit as well as he could field, he would have a good chance to make the place.

At the present time there is a lot of gloom among the Athletics, but this writer believes he has seen enough natural ability in the Athletics' players, veterans and youngsters, to be of the opinion that the outlook is not so dark as it has been painted by some writers. The entire situation depends upon when the twirlers get going right. When they do, the clouds should lift in a hurry.

For A's fans searching for something to cheer about amidst all the pre-season negativity, if one looked deep enough through the April 6 edition of *The Sporting News*, one could find a glowing report about 41-year-old Napoleon (Larry) Lajoie's apparent renaissance as a second baseman for the White Elephants:

> The biggest surprise, and one of the most pleasant ones, that has been sprung in the Athletics' camp this spring is the vast improvement and rejuvenation of Lajoie, writes Jim Nasium in the *Philadelphia Inquirer*. Larry is going better now than he has for three or four years and has every appearance and the speed and dash of a youngster. This is no springtime "bull," but is on the level and our tip is that Larry, and not a youngster, will be seen out there playing second base when the season opens. Larry is covering more ground and putting more dash into his work than we have seen him showing since the old days when he was king, and he is humming that pill in the same old way, which means about as good as it can be done. As [Lew] Malone, who can field that position as well as anybody would want it done, gives every evidence of being decidedly weak with the old slapstick, we look for Larry to be in there at the keystone sack again this coming heated term and we would not be a bit surprised if he had one of his old-time seasons. They have been counting Larry out for several seasons now. Perhaps he doesn't cover as much ground as he did in his heyday, but he still gets them in a manner to make many other second basemen envious and we still fail to lamp [sic] any of them who are less welcome by a pitcher than the veteran Frenchman.

In the April 13 edition of *The Sporting News*, which came out a day after the A's played their first game of the season against the Red Sox in Boston, Philadelphia correspondent William G. Weart stuck by his earlier refrains: The remaining veterans from the A's pennant years were discouraged by the weakness of the youngsters, especially the pitching corps, and their demoralization was hurtful to the squad as a whole. Weart opined that perhaps Mack would have been better off to drastically cut loose all his remaining veterans and start afresh without any links on the roster to the Athletics' former greatness. Weart did mention that a team of A's rookies, "yannigans" as the baseball writers of the day liked to refer to rookie outfits, had done reasonably well playing against assorted minor league and amateur teams in Virginia and Tennessee under the guidance of coach Ira Thomas. Nevertheless, Weart concluded,

It is certain, however, that the Athletics will go into the championship race with a pitching staff that looks very bad considering the kind of twirlers Connie had in previous campaigns. Bush is looked upon as certain to start the race at Boston next Wednesday, but when Wyckoff and Bressler will report for duty is not known. This means that Connie will only have young pitchers to depend upon after he sends Bush to the mound. It would not surprise me, though, if Mack's pitchers developed faster than the fans expected.

The early and unwarranted optimism that began in the A's spring-training routine in Jacksonville was over, having given way to a more realistic approach that the upcoming season would be a challenge every step of the way. Understaffed as far as quality pitching went, and led offensively by the aging Nap Lajoie and 25-year-old Stuffy McInnis, the first of 154 games in the 1916 American League schedule was next on the agenda for the woebegone Philadelphia Athletics. The defending World Series champion Boston Red Sox awaited Connie Mack's last-place club from 1915 at Fenway Park on Wednesday, April 12. The Red Sox were not without their share of problems. In a move that surprised baseball fans everywhere, the team had just resolved its nasty salary dispute with stellar center fielder Tris Speaker by unceremoniously dealing him to the unfashionable Cleveland Indians for two players and $55,000. Speaker himself was as shocked as anyone by the move. But the champion Red Sox were cocky and awash with talent. Even losing a player the caliber of Speaker, a future Hall of Famer and a true all-time great, did not seem to hurt Boston's chances of repeating as AL and World Series champions in 1916 all that much. In contrast, the youthful and largely inexperienced A's were just hoping to get by, improve on their shabby 1915 record, and not be too badly outclassed in the upcoming baseball season. Even that humble goal was wishful thinking.

April: Despair and Hope

The Opening Day lineup that Connie Mack submitted to plate umpire Bill Dinneen at Fenway Park on April 12, 1916, was vaguely reminiscent of the one he had written two years before in New York City on April 14, 1914, when his A's came into that opener as the defending World Series champions. There were four names that appeared in both lineups: Strunk, Oldring, McInnis, and Schang. There could have been a fifth common name. Joe Bush, who had started the 1914 season on the mound for Mack's team, was still on the Athletics roster in 1916 and would prove to be their most reliable pitcher throughout the miserable campaign. He did not get the assignment to start on Opening Day, though. Jack Nabors, who had shown some promise towards the end of the difficult 1915 campaign, got the call instead of Bush.

Philadelphia Athletics Starting Nine, April 14, 1914

Eddie Murphy RF
Rube Oldring LF
Eddie Collins 2B
Frank Baker 3B
Stuffy McInnis 1B
Amos Strunk CF
Jack Barry SS
Wally Schang C
Joe Bush P

Philadelphia Athletics Starting Nine, April 12, 1916

Jimmy Walsh RF
Amos Strunk CF
Rube Oldring LF
Nap Lajoie 2B
Stuffy McInnis 1B
Wally Schang C
Charlie Pick 3B
Sam Crane SS
Jack Nabors P

That Wednesday afternoon the Athletics were pitted against a solid Boston Red Sox team, the defending World Series champions from 1915. Although the Red Sox no longer had Tris Speaker patrolling center field (Tillie Walker occupied that position), they did have reliable Harry Hooper in right field and Chick Shorten in left field. Everett Scott, baseball's "iron man" of his day, was at shortstop. Larry Gardner, a hero from the Red Sox's 1912 World Series squad, was at third base. Dick Hoblitzell was at first base. Jack Barry, the shortstop from Connie Mack's formidable but now long-dismantled $100,000 infield, was the Boston second baseman. Pinch Thomas was the Red Sox catcher.

The starting pitcher for Boston was a Baltimore southpaw named George Herman (Babe) Ruth. Had there been a Cy Young Award in 1916, Ruth almost certainly would have won the AL version. Ruth would start 41 games in 1916 and complete 23 of them. He wound up with a 23–12 record and an impressive 1.75 ERA, the best in the AL. He struck out 170 batters, threw nine shutouts (another mark that led the league), and even saved a game in one of his three relief efforts that year (although saves would not be an official statistic until long after Ruth was dead). Ruth was only beginning to show the makings of a slugger. Entering this game Ruth had walloped only four of his 714 career home runs.

So, how did the Athletics fare on Opening Day? Not too badly. The Red Sox won the game by a slim 2–1 margin and had to endure a harrowing top of the ninth to do it. Boston managed only five hits while the A's got just four. Two of them were doubles by Stuffy McInnis. Lajoie got a single as did Charlie Pick. All five Red Sox hits were singles. About 5,000 fans were in attendance at Fenway Park.

The game was scoreless until the bottom of the sixth inning when the Red Sox manufactured a single run to take a 1–0 lead. By that time, though, Nabors was finished. He had been lifted in the fifth inning for a pinch-hitter, Bill Stellbauer, who promptly struck out in his MLB debut. Joe Bush went the rest of the way for the Athletics and gave up both Red Sox runs. (The Red Sox added another run in the seventh inning.) Neither run was earned. The Mackmen were their own worst enemy on Opening Day, committing four errors to Boston's one. Bush himself was responsible for two of the A's defensive gaffes. The A's did turn the game's only double play. Nabors looked good in his outing, allowing no Red Sox runs, three walks and two hits. The Red Sox scrounged for runs, scoring them the hard way. They laid down four sacrifice bunts, including one by Ruth. The Athletics were compelled to use two catchers on the day, beginning with Wally Schang and finishing with rookie Billy Meyer after Schang hurt his hand. The injury was serious enough to keep Schang out of the Philadelphia starting lineup until the first week in May, although he did make seven pinch-hitting appearances in the interim—all of them unsuccessful. In fact, the bulk of the team's catching duties fell to Meyer (until he himself was lost to the team with appendicitis after playing 50 games) as Mack opted to use Schang mostly as a left fielder for the rest of the season.

Philadelphia made things interesting with a ninth-inning rally. Jimmy Walsh drew a walk and later scored on Larry Lajoie's RBI single. Ruth was lifted from the mound with one out and replaced by Rube Foster. Foster retired both

McInnis and pinch-hitter Whitey Witt (making his MLB debut) to preserve the win for the home team. The A's were now 0–1 and a game behind St. Louis, Boston, Detroit and Washington in the AL standings. They would never be as close to the top of the heap again as they were on Opening Day.

The next day's game at Fenway Park would be typical of the struggles faced by the Athletics all season long. Poor pitching resulted in the Athletics digging themselves into a hole early in the game and never being able to climb out of it. Carl Ray, a hopeful left-handed prospect from North Carolina who had been called up to the majors late in 1915, was given the start. He lasted a mere one-third of an inning, giving up a hit and two walks and throwing a wild pitch, before getting the hook from Mack. Ray took the loss. Replacing Ray on the mound was another 1915 late-season call-up, a 23-year-old right-hander named Jack Richardson. He managed to retired the side, but not before the Red Sox had jumped out to a 4–0 lead. Richardson faced four batters, gave up two hits and a walk, struck out one man and committed a balk. Richardson never again pitched in the majors. His 1916 ERA was a gigantic 40.50. Elmer Myers went the rest of the way for the A's.

The home side was up 7–0 before Mack's team scored twice in the sixth. The Red Sox won the game handily, 8–2. Ernie Shore pitched seven strong innings for the defending champs, allowing just three hits. Herb Pennock, who had left the A's under bad terms partway through the previous year, mopped up the last two innings with some difficulty, allowing four walks and a hit. None of them came around to score, though. If there was any bright spot for the Athletics in the game, their pitchers had surrendered nothing but singles again. The Red Sox did take liberties on the base paths, stealing five sacks. Philadelphia was almost as daring, swiping three bases. Two of them were stolen by Stellbauer, who pinch-hit for catcher Billy Meyer in the ninth inning, and drew a walk. At the end of the day only the Cleveland Indians and the A's were 0–2 in the AL.

Cold, rainy weather greatly affected the attendance in Boston that first weekend. "The Sox drew 5,000 on Opening Day," wrote Ralph E. McMillan, the Boston correspondent for *The Sporting News*, "which would remind you of the afternoon when [Admiral] Peary sighted the well-known pole. The next day a frapped Scotch mist kept the attendance down to 3,000. Why any sane person outside a baseball scribe should want to watch baseball on days of this sort is more than we can understand. Maybe there aren't any sane people outside of baseball scribes."

After a day off, the A's and Red Sox concluded their three-game series at Fenway Park on Saturday, April 15. Philadelphia put up a game struggle. They parlayed Whitey Witt's first career hit into an unearned run as they took a 1–0 first-inning lead—their first lead so far in 1916. Joe Bush pitched a complete game for the Mackmen, scattered ten hits, but came up a tough 2–1 loser. He was now saddled with two losses in the Athletics' first three games. Rube Foster went the distance for the winners, giving up just four hits, two of them to Amos Strunk. Foster helped his own cause with a hit and an RBI. The Red Sox scored the go-ahead run in the eighth. Mack used two pinch-hitters in the top of the ninth—Shag Thompson and Stellbauer—but came up empty. Stellbauer's strikeout ended the game. The A's were off to an ominous 0–3 start to the 1916 season. They had been outscored 12–4 in their three-game set with the Red Sox, and they were the only winless team in the AL. Conversely, the Red Sox were the only undefeated team in the league and held a half-game advantage over the Chicago White Sox atop the standings.

The April 20 edition of *The Sporting News* made no specific mention of the Athletics' poor start to the season. Its only note on the team was a flattering tidbit on the youthful newcomer playing shortstop. "One of Connie Mack's real finds is said to be [Whitey] Witt, his young shortstop who hails from Germantown, PA. He is a free-swinging, left-handed hitter, and in the preseason games batted well over .300."

The A's moved from Boston to New York to face the Yankees on Tuesday, April 18. As in two of the three losses to the Red Sox, the Athletics put up a stern fight at the Polo Grounds but lost, 4–2. The Yankees outhit the A's, 11–6. Whitey Witt, in his second outing at shortstop, got two of them. Philadelphia committed three errors. Jack Nabors went six innings and took the loss—the first of many on his 1916 ledger. Tom Sheehan and Cap Crowell pitched the final two innings for the Mackmen. Crowell would be given his walking papers by the middle of June. Bob Shawkey, whom Connie Mack had dealt to the Yankees in the middle of 1915, got his first victory of the season. With Sam Crane temporarily sidelined with a charley horse and permanently disadvantaged with an uncorrectable weak batting form, Witt became the Athletics' regular shortstop from this point onward. Crane spent many seasons in the minor leagues as an excellent defensive infielder, but his inability to hit MLB pitching at an acceptable rate prevented him from re-attaining a regular job in the big leagues. The A's were now 0–4 and had led in only one of those four games.

The Athletics' fifth outing of the season was an excruciating 2–1 loss to the Yankees on April 19. Whitey Witt scored a run for the visitors in the top of the first inning. The Yankees scored two unearned runs in the bottom of the same inning. That accounted for all the game's scoring. The Athletics generated just three hits off winning pitcher Cliff Markle, a righty. Crowell had fared decently in relief the day before, so Mack gave him the starting role the very next day. He gave up four hits, four walks and no earned runs. Four A's errors did him in—two by shortstop Witt, his first miscues of the season, but far from the last. The scorekeeper's "E6" would be a common note in the game logs for the Athletics. The A's had opened the season on the road and had gone 0–5, living up to the naysayers' pre-season predictions that Connie Mack's 1916 crew would be no better than his cellar-dwellers from 1915. They had been trounced only once, though, giving the fans, players, and manager of the last-place club some measure of hope and confidence, albeit a small dose, as they headed home to face the Red Sox at the Shibe Park home opener. *The Sporting News*' New York correspondent, Joe Vila, in that same April 20 issue, reported that Connie Mack was not at all discouraged with his team's start, saw every reason to remain optimistic, and predicted he would show the public a vastly improved team. Vila wrote, "Connie Mack's Athletics played two games with the Yankees, and though defeated in each combat, they played pretty good baseball."

On Opening Day at Shibe Park, the front-running Boston Red Sox dampened the already subdued spirits of the Athletics and their supporters on Thursday, April 20, with a four-run outburst in the first inning off Joe Bush. As in the shellacking the Red Sox administered at Fenway a week earlier, the A's lacked the guns to fight their way back into the game. They could muster only five hits—all singles. The Red Sox, powered by 12 hits and another terrific complete game by Babe Ruth, won in a romp, 7–1. Bush was awful. Facing just seven Red Sox hitters, he allowed four hits, a walk, and four runs. He also threw a wild pitch. Manager Mack, fully cognizant that he had no pennant contender in 1916, was more than willing to experiment on the fly. Accordingly, Bush got the hook after just one inning and was replaced by 24-year-old Harry Weaver. Weaver lasted through six innings and allowed three further runs to the defending champs. Carl Ray pitched the last two innings and escaped unscathed. Bush was tagged with another loss, his third of the young season, as the A's dropped to 0–6. Every other AL team had won at least twice already in the 1916 season.

It had to happen—and it did on Friday, April 21: The Philadelphia Athletics won their first game of 1916! It was a 3–1 win over the Boston Red Sox, but it was much closer than it should have been. The A's outhit Boston, 12–4, but had to hang on in the ninth inning to prevent a late Red Sox rally. Elmer Myers was superb on the mound for the victors. He went the distance and allowed just four Red Sox hits. He had a shutout going through eight frames. Babe Ruth entered the game as a pinch-hitter in the sixth inning for pitcher Herb Pennock but failed to do any damage. (Ruth was batting .091.) The Athletics finally got some extra-base hits in quantity for the first time all season. Myers helped his own cause with a double and a single. Amos Strunk contributed two doubles and a sacrifice bunt. For the first time in 1916, the A's played an error-free game. Their first victory of the season put the Athletics just one game behind the Cleveland Indians, who were sitting at 2–5 despite the positive presence of the recently acquired Tris Speaker and his .450 batting average in center field.

The following day, Saturday, April 22, the A's made it two straight triumphs with an even more impressive win over the visitors from Boston. Jack Nabors got the complete-game, 6–2 win. (It would be both memorable and noteworthy for him, but he did not realize why at the time.) Both Red Sox runs were unearned. The A's jumped out to a 3–0 lead in the first inning and never looked back. Philadelphia got just five hits to Boston's eight, but four of the A's safeties were doubles. The Athletics' two-game winning streak would be the longest of 1916, although it would be matched several times. The win lifted the A's half a game closer to seventh-place Cleveland, who played a 15-inning, darkness-concluded, 1–1 tie game that afternoon at St. Louis. The Red Sox, thanks to two unexpected setbacks against the Mackmen, were now sitting in third place. The New York Yankees were perched atop the AL standings.

Any good news from the Athletics was magnified in the press. *TSN*, a publication that regarded Connie Mack as nearly a saintly figure in the national pastime, happily reported in its April 27 edition that the A's now had a number other than zero in the win column of the AL standings. Two front-page stories heralded the A's breakthrough achievement and renewed confidence, fostering the hope that the Athletics would be at least a competitive squad the rest of the way.

> As a rule, fans count results only in the number of victories and defeats, and few of them could see much hope for the Athletics when they lost their first six games of the season. Day after day Mack's young pitchers gave good performances, but erratic fielding and failure to hit offset the effectiveness of the twirlers. Last Friday the Mackmen broke the ice and now the entire situation has changed. Following an opening day game at Shibe Park, when conditions looked very bad, the Athletics pulled themselves together and 5,000 fans on Friday saw for the first time a flash of the skill of the new combination...
>
> Connie Mack has made more real progress in the building up of his new team than few knew or suspected. No all-round better exhibition could have been given by any team than Mack's combination gave in scoring their first win of the season.
>
> Elmer Myers, a rookie twirler, got what Crowell, Nabors and Sheehan, other young twirlers, failed to get when they pitched splendid ball. There was perfect support in the field and the assistance of a lot of base hits by his teammates. The excellence of the pitching, fielding and hitting gingered up the White Elephant outfit and put them on their toes for the first time this season. The insight that the fans secured of the real strength of the combination sent them away from Shibe Park greatly encouraged and with the belief that the Athletics are going to give more than one pennant aspirant some hard jolts in the present pennant fight. That they are not to be mistaken was shown when Mack's team repeated over Boston Saturday, with Nabors pitching. The Athletics hit splendidly, waited out the wild [Rube] Foster like veterans, and did brilliant work on the defensive. From this time on, look for Mack's team to win its share of games.

Sunday baseball was outlawed in Philadelphia in 1916, so the Red Sox and A's had a scheduled day off before resuming hostilities at Shibe Park. Things got back to normal for the champions from Boston with a 4–0 victory on Monday, April 24. Both clubs managed eight hits, but the visitors made theirs count.

A sizable chunk of the offensive damage and all of the Boston runs came from their 5-6-7-8 hitters: Duffy Lewis, Larry Gardner, Jack Barry, and Bill Carrigan. Cap Crowell was the losing pitcher; Dutch Leonard picked up the win. Crowell also committed the A's lone error.

The topic of Sunday baseball reached the highest court in Maryland, where the wise men finally decided to strike down the prohibition of pro games on the Sabbath. The decision was applauded in an editorial in *Baseball Magazine*'s July 1916 edition:

> The Court of Appeals in Maryland, the highest tribunal of the state, has made a profound discovery: It has decided, in its august wisdom, that Sunday baseball should not be ranked with murder, arson, and highway robbery. In fact, it is not even a misdemeanor. Sunday baseball in Maryland is declared legal.
>
> The European war to the contrary not withstanding, civilization as a whole may be said to progress. There is no more hopeful sign of that progress than the communal attitude toward the observance of Sunday. The rigid observance of this day, in many states, is one of a few relics of an intolerant era of the past when religious beliefs were imposed and enforced by law.
>
> Why the Blue Laws, which would make of the first day of the week a season of cheerless gloom, should have survived all these years is one of life's mysteries. "We hold these truths to be self-evident," to quote a historic document, that all persons have an unchallenged right to hold whatever religious beliefs they choose and to allow other persons a similar right. It is the latter part of the statement that provides a stumbling block for the Blue Laws' advocates. The sour Puritanism of former generations, which saw in anything pleasing an element of sin, still survives in opposition to Sunday baseball. A clean, healthful sport that takes the masses into their open air on their one day of freedom is opposed neither to logic nor common sense, however it be opposed to the bigoted views of the hard-headed minority. The conservative minority is not obliged to attend Sunday games. Why in the name of reason and tolerance should it oppose an equal liberty to those who see no harm in such pastimes? Some day New York will become as enlightened as Maryland. Some day, in the next two or three hundred years, Pennsylvania will follow suit. And while it staggers the imagination, it is not too much to hope that future millenniums may yet witness big league baseball in that stronghold of conservatism—Boston.

On Wednesday, April 26, the A's were back on the road, playing at Washington's Griffith Stadium. They made it three wins in four tries with a gutsy 3-2 triumph over the hometown Senators. Joe Bush went the full nine innings to notch his first win. Rube Oldring was the offensive hero for the visitors, driving in two runs, one with a triple. Whitey Witt scored twice on Oldring's hits. The winning run crossed the plate in the eighth inning off reliever Joe Boehling, the third Washington pitcher of the day. Despite the win, the A's 3-7 record still placed them in the AL basement. On a positive note, they weren't statistically the worst team in MLB. The NL New York Giants had only one win in seven outings so far.

Washington evened their account with the A's on Thursday, April 27. Rube Bressler was a tough-luck loser, getting tagged with the 4–2 loss. Bressler was already on the bench in the eighth inning when the Senators broke a 2–2 tie with a pair of runs off Elmer Myers. Under the scoring rules of the day, though, it was Bressler's game to lose. Three Athletics' errors did not help, although none resulted in runs. Whitey Witt made his third of the season. Third baseman Charlie Pick made his fifth. Harry Harper went the full nine innings for the win. The Athletics, now 3–8, seemed to be on the cusp of respectability despite the setback. Their losses were generally close. To date, blowout defeats had been rare.

The first mortifying loss of the year for the Athletics came on Friday, April 28, as they ended their three-game trip to Washington. The A's scored six times in the fifth inning to take a comfortable 6–1 lead. The Senators bounced back to score twice in the home half, but the score remained 6–3 until the bottom of the ninth inning—at which point the wheels fell off. Jack Nabors, who had been cruising along nicely, suddenly couldn't get anyone out. Cap Crowell was summoned to the hill, and he did no better than Nabors. Crowell faced four Senators and gave up three hits. A 6–3 win had quickly morphed into a 7–6 loss. By today's standards, Crowell, who was responsible for the seventh run, would be saddled with the loss. Fairly or unfairly, it went to Nabors by the standards of 1916, and it dropped his record to 1–2. Witt and Pick each made another error, both occurrences becoming more and more commonplace as the season moved along. The ugly defeat dropped the Athletics to 3–9 after 12 games.

The following day, Saturday, April 29, featured another late-inning A's collapse. This time it occurred in front of the home fans at Shibe Park in a game versus New York. It was the first of 19 consecutive home dates for the Athletics. The Yankees tied the game with a run in the top of the ninth inning and won it on two in the tenth inning. Myers went the distance and was tagged with the loss. Whitey Witt made error number five on the year. The A's were now showing a telltale sign of a bad team: They were losing games they should have won. If there was any bright spot in the game for Mack, Frank Baker, now playing third base and batting clean-up for New York, went hitless in four at-bats in his return to Shibe Park. With Sunday baseball outlawed in Philadelphia, that was the A's last contest in April. They were at 3–10, in last place in the AL, 5.5 games out of first—just about where all the pundits had figured they would be. They did, however, have a long stretch of home games ahead of them and the hope that some promising collegiate players would be on their way to Shibe Park to help the floundering team's chances.

William G. Weart, in *The Sporting News*, tried to paint the Athletics' woes in the best light possible, noting that the defending NL champion Phillies were struggling too, in a manner of speaking. (They had started the campaign 6–1, but had fallen from first to third place after dropping four of five games.) A subheadline in a *TSN* piece from May 4 stated, "Mack can only report he's still trying." The story said,

> Manager Mack and his lieutenants have been greatly encouraged by the work of the team this spring and better things appear to be in store. The Athletics will be at home until May 25 and it is expected that Connie will be able to make a great deal of progress in developing a winner. The team has been badly handicapped this spring. The training schedule was not one which turned out well. The chief regret was the fact that the pitchers, with one exception, got sore arms down in Florida, despite the excellent weather, and all hands became dispirited in consequence. Since the pitchers have been doing better work and rounding into form, the spirits of the entire combination have been improved, and there is now a lot of ginger in the work of White Elephants.
>
> With more than three weeks at home, Connie will be able to give his men all of the work that they require. The White Elephants were very hard to beat at Boston, New York, and Washington, where they won a lot of praise, and they should be even better able to give a good account of themselves when they again hit the road.
>
> Reports continue to come in of various college stars being signed by manager Mack for tryouts here after the colleges close. If one-half of the stories are true, Connie must be having enough athletes coming here in June to start a college of his own. Almost any college ballplayer of any prominence is said to have been signed for the Athletics or to have been given an offer by the leader of the White Elephants. Among these lads are said to be a wonderful infielder at the University of Maine named Lowry, pitcher Johnson of Ursinus who has a long string of strikeouts, and Fahy, a pitcher of the Catholic University, who fanned 11 batsmen in a game this spring.

In that same *TSN* column, Weart wrote about a noteworthy April 28 NL game between the Phillies and the Dodgers "which would have been thought impossible two years ago." The contest was played in cool, cloudy, and sometimes rainy conditions at Philadelphia's Baker Bowl, located not too far from Shibe Park on Lehigh Avenue. It was significant for the fans of Connie Mack's squad because it featured two former Athletics superstars from the team's not-so-long-ago heyday—Chief Bender and Jack Coombs—facing each other on the mound for the first time ever. Bender, who had toiled for the Baltimore Terrapins of the Federal League in 1915, was now plying his trade for the Phillies; Coombs was in his second NL season with Brooklyn. It was Bender's first start in the NL. "Neither looked like a star," declared Weart, a negative comment that may have pleased their former supporters. Coombs got credit for the win in a sloppily played game where the wet field and four errors by the home team played a significant role in the final outcome.

Nevertheless, the perception that the old, absent A's stars from the glory years were now in decline provided little consolation to the typical Athletics fan. Perhaps May would bring brighter days to Shibe Park.

May: Hope and the High-Water Mark

Connie Mack
There is a man in Quakertown
And he is wondrous wise.
Each year he jumps into the bush
And gathers bush league guys.
And after he has sold his stars,
With all his might and main,
He tries with every trick he knows
To make new stars again.
—W. R. Hoefer *Baseball Magazine*, May 1916

    May started with a bang for the Athletics. One Monday, May 1, the A's got all the runs they needed in the bottom of the first inning for a 4–2 win over the New York Yankees. The Athletics backed Joe Bush's solid effort on the mound with a three-run first frame. The key blow was Amos Strunk's two-run homer—the first four-bagger the Athletics had hit all season, and his first ever in major league competition. Bush struck out five and allowed only a single earned run in going the distance and collecting his second win. Three Philadelphia errors did not harm the home team too much. The defensive blunders were committed by the familiar culprits. Whitey Witt made his sixth error at shortstop; third baseman Charlie Pick made his seventh. Even Nap Lajoie committed an error at second base, his third of 1916. Allen Russell went the full eight innings in a losing outing for the visitors. The swift-moving game took just 107 minutes to complete. Perhaps the long home stretch would indeed do Mack's club a world of good.
    The positive work emanating from the home club's dugout on May 1 did not carry over to May 2. The Yankees exacted a measure of revenge by pounding the Athletics, 9–4, in a game that was never close. The Yankees led 9–0 at one point and racked up 14 hits to Philadelphia's five. Every Yankee in the lineup got at least one hit. A late A's rally made the score sound more respectable than it really was. Wally Schang did, however, knock his first homer of the 1916 cam-

paign for the A's, bringing the team's seasonal total to two. Rube Bressler was ineffective, allowing six runs in five innings before giving way to Bill Morrisette. In his 1916 debut for Connie Mack's squad, Morrisette struggled in the last four frames for the A's, allowed three more runs—and was summarily dropped from the team. Morrisette did not play another MLB game until he resurfaced on the pitching staff of the 1920 Detroit Tigers. He had pitched four games for Mack in 1915 and obviously had not done much to convince his manager he had big-league stuff.

The following day, Wednesday, May 3, the topsy-turvy A's-Yankees series continued. This time the hard-luck Jack Nabors battled New York's Ray Keating in a terrific pitchers' duel. The score was knotted 1–1 after seven innings. Mack brought in the seemingly inexhaustible Joe Bush to finish the game. Mack's move paid dividends. The A's score twice in the eighth—courtesy of a two-run homer by Napoleon Lajoie off reliever Urban Shocker into Shibe Park's left-field bleachers—and then staved off a promising ninth-inning rally by the visitors. Mack's side hung on for a 3–2 victory. Bush picked up win number three; he alone had accounted for 60 percent of the team's wins. Instead of making errors, Witt contributed with a triple and Pick with a double. The A's played an errorless ballgame, while the Yankees committed three errors. With the win, the 5–11 A's were still occupying the AL cellar, but they had moved to within half a game of the seventh-place St. Louis Browns. The A's were not the worst team in the majors, though. The New York Giants—the A's World Series foes in 1905, 1911 and 1913—were off to an abysmal 2–10 start in their NL schedule. Things would get considerably brighter for McGraw's bunch as the 1916 season progressed, however.

Thursday, May 4, saw the first-place Washington Senators arrive at Shibe Park, which meant the home team had to face the formidable right arm of Walter Johnson. The flame-throwing Johnson was dominant in a 5–1 win for the visitors. The A's mustered just six hits off the Big Train, who whiffed seven Mackmen while walking zero. In contrast, Philadelphia reliever Harry Weaver gave up three runs, six hits, and a walk in just one inning of work to ruin a fine eight-inning effort by starter Tom Sheehan and turn a close game into a comfortable victory for the Senators. Weaver's days with the club were numbered. Witt and Pick were up to their unreliable infield defense again, each committing an error.

There was no game on May 5, but the A's rebounded with a win on Saturday, May 6. Joe Bush, easily the Athletics' most valuable asset so far in the season, pitched a complete-game, 4–1 victory for his fourth win of the season. The A's got six hits off Harry Harper and Doc Ayers, but three of them were doubles. Senators manager Clark Griffith was not around for the conclusion of the contest. He was ejected by plate umpire Dick Nallin, marking the first time in the 1916 campaign that any player in an A's game had been given the boot by the men in blue. The loss dropped Washington into second place behind Cleveland, which probably did not help soothe Griffith's surly mood.

Both teams took Sunday off to observe the Sabbath, but were back in action on Monday, May 8. The A's continued to play surprisingly good baseball as they had an excellent game against Walter Johnson. Maybe, just maybe, Connie Mack's collection of newcomers supported by a handful of veterans was going to pay dividends. The Senators' Big Train was tagged for 13 hits over eight innings in a 4–2 loss. His teammates' five errors did not help Johnson, nor did their meager output of only four hits. One was a home run by Turner Barber off winning pitcher Elmer Myers. Whitey Witt led the A's attack with two doubles and a sacrifice bunt. Philadelphia was 7–12 after 19 games.

The Athletics, despite being nowhere near the top of the AL standings in the first week of May, were having an adverse effect on the league's leaders. Philadelphia beat writer and shameless cheerleader William G. Weart reported in *The Sporting News* on May 11 about the A's newfound respectability:

> It doesn't look as if the western teams of the American League would have any soft spots during their first eastern trip of the season. The westerners may win the majority of their games in this city [Philadelphia], but if past performances are kept up, they will have to be on their toes at all times to get away with the victories. The Athletics already have distinguished themselves this season by knocking Washington and Boston out of first place.
>
> The White Elephants are tail-enders but they are hard to conquer. Manager Mack is not only showing a brand of pitching that was not looked for so early in the race, considering the conditions in training camp, but Connie has also succeeded in reawakening the spirits of his veterans and the combination is giving a snappy exhibition day after day which must sooner or later tell in the percentage table.
>
> Recently the team has been hitting the ball much better than it did in the first couple of weeks of the season. This has been due to the fact that the players have recently been able to get all of the batting practice that they desired, whereas, for a long time, they were able to do little club swinging before a game.
>
> Long-distance hitting has been quite a feature of Athletics' recent games. Home runs at Shibe Park are usually rare, and for a long time Frank Baker had a mortgage on drives of this character. Last week, however, three of the Mackmen came through with four-base drives on successive afternoons. First, Amos Strunk sent the ball over the right-field wall for the first hit of that character during his career. The next day Wally Schang duplicated Strunk's feat.
>
> On the third day Lajoie came to time with a drive into the left-field bleachers for a four-bagger which won the game from the New York Highlanders. It was the first hit for the circuit made at Shibe Park by Lajoie while wearing the uniform of the White Elephants. The day previous, Lajoie came near to putting the ball in the bleachers, but Lee Magee reached up and kept the horsehide from going among the spectators.
>
> Three home runs in successive games by members of the Athletics is something practically unheard of, and no jealous rival can set up a claim that they were due to "short fences."

Wally Schang got back into the game last week and once more the Athletics have things working smoothly in the catching department. Schang had his right hand hurt in the first game of the season [in Boston], and Billy Meyer stepped into the breach. For a youngster, Meyer certainly acquitted himself in a splendid manner. This applied not only to his work behind the bat but also to his hitting.

Another hopeful sign in the White Elephants' camp is the improvement in the playing of Witt and Pick. Neither has been exactly a weak brother this year. Pick has played steady ball at all times and he has hit fairly well. Witt's inexperience cost some games, but that was to be expected. Recently Witt has been hitting the ball well and his fielding has been much steadier, thanks to the coaching of Lajoie.

There is no doubt but that the long stay at home of the Mackmen is going to bear excellent fruit. Victories are not coming fast, but day after day the fans who go to Shibe Park have been seeing a class of baseball playing by the home team which is far superior to the listlessness of certain veterans and the crudeness of the youngsters who wore the team's uniform last season. The hard work done by manager Mack and his lieutenants has begun to tell.

Two players were released last week, pitcher Morissette and shortstop Sam Crane being sent to Jack Dunn's Baltimore club. Morissette did poor work in his last game here, but a couple of days later he appeared in a Baltimore uniform, went in to pitch in the second inning, and did not allow a hit for eight innings. Crane had been suffering this spring with a charley horse which prevented him from getting the chance to keep the job at shortstop.

Any remnants of the recent good showings against the front-running Washington Senators totally vanished on Tuesday, May 9, when the Detroit Tigers made their first appearance of 1916 at Shibe Park—and walked away on the winning end of a 16–2 laugher. It was the most runs the Athletics would allow all season. "Walked away" is an appropriate description. There were a remarkable 30 bases on balls issued in the game—an MLB record unchallenged to this day—which some charitable observers blamed on high winds ripping through Shibe Park. Eighteen of the walks were courtesy of three A's pitchers. Twelve of them were surrendered by the Athletics' third pitcher, Carl Ray. This game got out of hand quickly with an eight-run Tigers outburst in the second inning. Jack Nabors gave up five runs in one inning pitched. Harry Weaver, another pre-season favorite to stabilize the pitching corps, gave up four more runs in one inning of work in what would be his Athletics' swansong. (Weaver would resurface in the NL with Cincinnati in 1917.) It was also the final game for Ray in the uniform of the White Elephants or any other MLB team. The A's had more errors (five) than hits (three). Whitey Witt made two fielding gaffes, putting him at double digits for the season. Detroit starter George Cunningham did not get out of the third inning, but got credit for the win under the scoring regulations of the day. Bernie Boland went 6⅓ innings in relief. Ty Cobb had two doubles for the visitors. The awful game lasted 150 minutes, a nine-inning marathon by 1916 standards. Plate umpire Silk O'Loughlin was undoubtedly relieved when the last man was retired in the bottom of the ninth inning.

The next day, Wednesday, May 10, with umpire Ollie Chill behind the plate, the A's and Tigers' pitchers marginally improved, combining for "only" 18 bases on balls in Detroit's 9–3 win. Mack's hurlers, Tom Sheehan and Jack Nabors, accounted for 11 of them. Whitey Witt picked up two more errors to raise his unflattering season's total to 12. The A's made a total of five. On the brighter side, Amos Strunk got three of the A's five hits off winning Tigers pitcher George Boehler. Philadelphia was now 7–14 after 21 games.

On Thursday, May 11, the Tigers and A's played something more akin to a major league-caliber game than they had played in either of the previous two days. The A's pushed a run across the plate in the home half of the ninth inning to win a thriller, 3–2. Elmer Myers went the distance for the A's but walked ten Tigers in doing so. Two double plays got Myers out of a couple of jams. He only gave up three hits—all of them were by Detroit first baseman George Burns. Bill Stellbauer got three hits in three at-bats for the winners. Jean Dubuc was tagged with the loss in relief of Harry Coveleski. The A's 8–14 record made them look almost respectable.

The Tigers-A's game on Friday, May 12, may have been the most entertaining contest the Athletics played all season, although accounts suggest that it was far from a thing of aesthetic beauty. In an ebb-and-flow affair, the visitors from Detroit prevailed, 8–6, in 11 innings. The Tigers held a 3–0 lead until the bottom of the seventh, only to see the Mackmen score three times to level the contest. Each team scored a single run in the ninth inning to send the game past regulation. The Tigers scored four runs in the 11th inning, only to have Philadelphia score twice in the home half, but the rally fizzled. Detroit used four pitchers. Jean Dubuc, the losing pitcher in the previous day's game, threw three innings and picked up the win. Athletics starter Cap Crowell went nine innings and gave up ten Tigers hits, but it was reliever Tom Sheehan who gave up seven more hits in two innings for the loss. The defeat dropped Sheehan's record to a discouraging 0–3.

In his coverage of the crazy Tigers-A's series in its May 18 edition, William G. Weart of *The Sporting News* was rightly fixated on the vast number of bases on balls issued and runners left on base by both teams.

> During the four games with the Tigers, the Athletics' twirlers handed out 49 bases on balls while Detroit's pitchers gave out 36 passes and two hit batsmen. This made a grand total of 87 batsmen who walked to first base. In one game there were 30 passes issued and in another 26. In the four games, the Athletics had 45 runners left on base and Detroit 47, a grand total of 92 runners stranded. In the final contest of the series, an 11-inning affair, the Athletics had 20 runners left [on base] and Detroit 16.

The odd part about it was that Mack's pitchers have not been wild this season. They had been getting the ball over the plate in a manner which caused congratulation, and their control was far superior to that which they displayed last season. Various excuses were made for the hurlers, one of which was the high wind that blew across the grounds from left field to right shoved their fastballs out of the course intended or just enough to make it clear the plate time after time.

That Detroit got away with the series by three victories to one was nothing for the Tigers to crow about. They looked to be about the weakest team that appeared here this season—until the Browns came. Only for numerous pieces of bad judgment on the part of the Mackmen on the bases, the result of the series in the matter of victories and defeats would have been reversed. After it was all over, Manager Mack declared that the final game was the dumbest exhibition of baseball on the part of his players that he ever witnessed.

Coming on top of the success of the Athletics in beating the Senators two games out of three and knocking them out of first place, the work of the home team was certainly surprising and disappointing. As for the Tigers, we had looked for them to show much better form than they did. Jennings' men make a lot of noise, but they do not look anything like the powerful, confident combination that Hughie has been accustomed to bring to this city. However the season is still young and Jennings may get his team going.

Saturday, May 13, was a red-letter day for Connie Mack's club—after defeating the St. Louis Browns they were no longer in last place in the American League. That spot was now occupied by the Browns, who lost 4–3 at Shibe Park. The A's took a 3–0 lead into the seventh inning only to have the visitors from St. Louis score three unearned runs to tie the game. Two errors by Whitey Witt (bringing his season's total to a ghastly 14) and another by Nap Lajoie almost spoiled an excellent outing by pitcher Elmer Myers. The Athletics showed some resilience by retaking the lead in the bottom half of the seventh and not wavering from that point onward. Myers went the distance, giving up no earned runs and striking out six Browns. Impressively, it was the third win in just six days for Myers. (Mack would tell the *Philadelphia Inquirer* early in June that he considered young Myers to be one of the greatest pitchers ever developed in many years, and that he would make history.) Witt made up for his shabby fielding by getting three of the A's seven hits, including a triple, although he didn't score a run. The win vaulted the A's and their 9–15 record into the lofty altitude of seventh place in the AL standings, half a game ahead of the cellar-dwelling Browns, although they were still 7.5 games in arrears of the front-running Cleveland Indians, whose 18–9 record was tops in the majors.

After taking the Sabbath off, as was required by the municipal Blue Laws in Philadelphia, the Browns and Athletics resumed their series on Monday, May 15. Forty-year-old Eddie Plank, one of the A's pitching heroes from the glory days of yesteryear, was on the mound for the visitors while Bullet Joe Bush had the honors for Mack's team. Both pitchers went the distance, but it was Plank who faltered. Carrying a 4–1 lead into the bottom of the seventh, Plank surrendered four runs to end up on the losing side of a 5–4 decision. Plank allowed nine A's hits, including two by Whitey Witt. (One was a triple, his third of the year—and again he was stranded on third base.) St. Louis managed just five hits off Bush, one a double by Plank. Two of the hits came off the bat of swift-footed left fielder Burt Shotton, who would later manage 11 seasons in the NL, including pennant winners in Brooklyn in 1947 and 1949. The hard-fought win opened up more space in the AL standings between the suddenly respectable Athletics and the sagging Browns. Philadelphia, 10–15, was now just half a game behind the sixth-place Chicago White Sox, who were idle.

Baseball Magazine, in its July 1916 edition, ran an article that commented on and lamented the new trend of relief pitchers entering AL games and not coming to bat very much. It also asked the age-old question about the anemic batting skills of MLB pitchers.

> In the olden days before pitchers could be shifted at will and pinch hitters thrown into the gap, the hurler hit (or tried to hit) nearly as often as the other fellows.
>
> The one [statistic] that would set the old-time scorers craziest, would be that of [Bernie] Boland, the Detroit pitcher. Mr. Boland, up to May 16, had worked in ten games and yet had been at bat exactly one time.
>
> Why is it that nearly every pitcher can bat enormous fungo hits, and yet nearly every pitcher is a miserable hitter when it comes to batting in an actual game? It's one of the mysteries of the game, and it always has been. Almost any pitcher can toss a ball in the air, then swipe it with tremendous power, sending it clear to the farthest fences—and yet when he has to face a fast pitch later on, he'll fan like a windmill. Queer old stuff, this baseball, isn't it?

No game was played on Tuesday, and the day off from the diamond seemed to rejuvenate the Browns from their doldrums. St. Louis cruised to a fairly comfortable 7–4 win over the Athletics on Wednesday, May 17. The visitors put up crooked numbers in both the second and third innings off A's starter Cap Crowell (who lasted just two innings) and Tom Sheehan, who stuck around for four frames. The Athletics tried to make a game of it with three runs in the home half of the sixth and narrowed the Browns' lead to 6–4, but they never threatened again. Dave Davenport went the distance for the Browns and got the win. Rube Bressler, a holdover from Mack's 1914 World Series pitching staff, mopped up the final three innings for the defeated home team. Three A's errors didn't help matters much. One was committed by third baseman Charlie Pick who, with his 13th error of 1916, was rivaling shortstop Whitey Witt in fielding miscues. Shag Thompson, a reserve outfielder who failed to get a hit for the A's in a pinch-hitting role, was dropped from the squad after the game. He had amassed a startling .000 batting average by getting no hits in 17 at-bats. Thompson was a huge disappointment to Mack, having been hailed in some pre-season forecasts as a natural-born hitter and future outfield fixture for the Athletics.

Next to foray into Shibe Park were the Chicago White Sox, who were considered by many fans and baseball writers to have been underperforming—and manager Clarence Rowland was feeling the heat that always comes with unmet expectations. On Thursday, May 18, White Sox leadoff batter Happy Felsch got a hit in his first time at bat and scored a run, but that was it for the visitors. Elmer Myers did a masterful job of keeping the Chicago Southsiders at bay for the remainder of the game in the Athletics' solid 5–1 victory. Stuffy McInnis' three-run homer in the seventh inning—his first of 1916—salted things away for the Mackmen. The A's 2–5 hitters, Schang, Strunk, McInnis and Lajoie, accounted for most of the offensive damage on the afternoon, scoring four runs and collecting six hits. Myers was now 5–1 on the season. Red Faber took the loss for the visitors and was yanked after the McInnis home run. The victory vaulted the A's into a sixth-place tie with the White Sox, each club trailing Cleveland in the AL standings by eight full games.

Fans of pitching duels enjoyed the contest at Shibe Park the following day, May 19, as Chicago's Eddie Cicotte and Bullet Joe Bush put up zero after zero through ten innings. A two-out base hit by Charlie Pick drove in Amos Strunk with the game's only run in the bottom of the 11th inning. Bush allowed only three White Sox hits, all singles, two of them by Shoeless Joe Jackson. Bush was 6–3 on the season. The win lifted the Athletics alone into sixth place. It would be the seasonal high-water mark for the Mackmen. The White Sox, fancied by some pundits as a pennant contender, embarrassingly fell into the AL basement, as St. Louis surprisingly won in Boston for the second straight day.

With the Athletics' confidence at a high, Chicago finished its three-game set in Philadelphia by shellacking the home team, 11–0, on Saturday, May 20. Cap Crowell was hit hard again. Two White Sox runs in the top of the first inning and a six-run outburst in third inning put the game out of reach quickly. Crowell was in the showers after the third inning. Six of the eight runs he allowed were earned. Whitey Witt's 18th error helped keep the White Sox rally going. Tom Sheehan was called upon by Connie Mack for a stint of long relief, and did well until surrendering three Chicago runs in the ninth inning when the game was hopelessly out of reach. For the visitors, ex–Athletic Eddie Collins, who was now playing second base for the White Sox, got three hits in his old stomping grounds and scored two runs.

In its May 25 edition, *The Sporting News* hyped the upcoming four battles the Athletics would have when the visiting first-place Cleveland Indians made their initial appearance in 1916 at Shibe Park. "Connie's Kids Fear No Team on Earth," declared the hopeful headline. "Actually Eager for the Chance at [Lee]

Slick-fielding first baseman Stuffy McInnis had his hands full in 1916 with his error-prone fellow infielders. His remarkable .992 fielding percentage in 1916 is a testament to his stellar defensive skills. McInnis also batted .295 (National Baseball Hall of Fame Library, Cooperstown, N.Y.).

Fohl's Indians" said the subheading above William G. Weart's optimistic story that heaped praise upon the Athletics' recent pitching heroes.

Cleveland is the last American League team to make its appearance here [in Philadelphia] in the first round of the season, the Indians arriving Monday at the top of the organization's percentage table for a four-game series. They found the Mackmen fit to cope with them, for recent successes have given Connie Mack's players the necessary confidence and fighting spirit. The two teams—the Indians and the White Elephants—are the season's surprises of the American League circuit. Those who doped the probable outcomes before the season opened didn't give either a chance for anything above seventh place.

Then came the deals which bolstered up the Indians and they have been a sensation. Connie Mack did not spring any deals. He merely kept on polishing up the youngsters he had accrued from various channels. The Athletics got off to a bad start by losing six games in a row. Since then they have won a majority of their games. The long stand at home has been of vast benefit to the entire combination. That it has the fighting spirit and the confidence is shown by no task being too hard to tackle or accomplish.

Already this spring the Mackmen have toppled Boston and Washington out of first place. They beat St. Louis and shoved the Browns to last place. Then they tackled Chicago and two straight victories, with a couple of victories by St. Louis, caused the Athletics to move into sixth place and the White Sox to drop into the cellar.

Under these circumstances it can be believed that the White Elephants were not afraid of any visit from the Indians, especially with Joe Bush and Elmer Myers pitching unbeatable ball. When the books were closed last Saturday night, Bush had a string of six straight victories and Myers five victories in a row. No pitchers in the country, except [Fritz] Coumbe of Cleveland could show such winning streaks this season.

Myers success has been of such a wonderful character that Connie Mack is on record as saying that while Elmer does not know as much baseball as his former stars Plank, Bender and Coombs, he is right now a better pitcher than any of these men were in their primes. Think of a compliment like that coming form Connie, who is seldom enthusiastic about the work of a youngster. Furthermore, Connie predicts that Myers will be ranked with Walter Johnson and Grover Alexander before the season of 1916 is over.

Connie is not making snap judgment either on the young man from York Springs, PA. For more than three years manager Mack has had Myers under his eye. It was in the fall of 1912 when Connie picked up Myers. The next spring Connie sent him to the Raleigh, NC club where Earle Mack, Connie's son, was manager. That spring a certain club stopped at Raleigh to play Earle's team. Earle asked the manager of the opposing club to look over his youngsters and tell him what he thought of the players. The manager said that Earle had some promising lads, but he didn't think any of them would make the big league.

"That manager was mistaken," said Connie.

Myers was one of the players looked over in March 1913. He was big and green, but all these years Connie kept watching his progress and getting reports from Earle. In 1915 Myers was taken to the [Athletics'] training camp in Jacksonville. Then he was turned back to Raleigh for another season. Last fall he started to show what he could do by holding Washington down to a couple of hits and blanking the Senators. This spring his work has been the talk of the country.

Myers is a big right-hander with the easiest motion imaginable, so easy in fact that the best batsmen in the league have been fooled by his wonderful speed. What is more is he has a cool head and he knows how to field his position, and he has a habit of getting in base hits when they will do the most good.

Bush has shown this year the class that was expected of him two years ago. His latest achievement was the shutting out of the Chicago White Sox in 11 innings and allowing only three hits—one by [Eddie] Collins and two by [Shoeless Joe] Jackson.

Now watch out for manager Mack to trot out another star twirler. Several weeks of hard work were put on the young pitchers last season and many more weeks this spring. The crop of hurlers is beginning to be harvested and it should be one to surprise the fans.

Manager Mack has been weeding out his staff of pitchers, an indication that he is satisfied he has right now, or will have when the colleges break up, the kind of pitchers that he has been looking for for more than a year. Harry Weaver, a right-hander, was sent to New Haven last week and at the same time Johnny Ray, a southpaw, was shunted to Newport News. Later Rube Bressler, a left-hander who looked for a little while as though he would develop into another Eddie Plank, was sent to Newark with third baseman [Thomas] Healey, formerly of the University of Pittsburgh. In addition, outfielder Shag Thompson, from the University of North Carolina, who, like Bressler, failed to make good his early promise, was sent to Omaha.

These changes have pared down the Athletics' staff considerably, but when the team comes back from the western trip, there will be a number of new faces, the additions being collegians, for Connie still has a lot of faith in the "high-brow" players.

The series with the Cleveland team will wind up the home stay for the White Elephants.

In summarizing the MLB pennant races through May 21, *Baseball Magazine* was pleasantly surprised in its June issue that the Athletics were not languishing in the AL's basement.

A surprise party has been furnished by the Athletics. After Cleveland was reinforced by [Tris] Speaker, it was taken for granted that Connie Mack's comical crew would flop to the bottom and remain right there for keeps. But the Athletics, weak at the bat, ridiculously shaky in the field, a misfit crowd in every imaginable fashion, nevertheless succeeded in getting over the .400 mark, and in climbing over the fizzling Browns as well. Inspection of the details shows that pitcher [Elmer] Myers has been largely responsible, his individual record of victories being enough to hoist the Athletics over the Browns, while Joe Bush, pitching grandly against handicaps, has done a lot to hold the club in seventh position. Aside from these two, the Philadelphia pitchers have been steady losers. Fine batting by Stelbauer [sic], Strunk and the good old Lajoie have brought the club along, and, with such pitching as Bush and Myers can give, the Athletics are not to be lightly regarded.

Cleveland's Fritz Coumbe, who merited special mention among Joe Bush and Elmer Myers in William G. Weart's gushing article in *The Sporting News* for his early-season pitching heroics, was put to the test in the opening game of the Indians-Athletics series at Shibe Park on Monday, May 22, against the red-hot Myers. Spotted a 3–0 first-inning lead, Coumbe was battered by Mack's boys for four runs in the bottom of the first inning, the key blow being a three-run homer by Jimmy Walsh. After facing just seven A's batters, Coumbe was given the hook by manager Lee Fohl and replaced by Jim Bagby. The Indians regained the lead with two runs in the top of the second off Elmer Myers, who was having a shaky outing. Bagby held a 6–4 lead into the bottom of the eighth inning only to see the A's push six runs across the plate to assume a 10–6 lead. Things got a little bit dicey for the home side in the top of the ninth when Braggo Roth smashed a two-run, pinch-hit home run to narrow the A's advantage to just 10–8, but Myers held on for a less-than-stellar, complete-game victory. The win was powered by a 14-hit outburst by the home team. The ten runs would be the most the Athletics would score in a single game all season, although the total would be matched on September 30 in a wild game versus the Washington Senators. The victory gave Philadelphia a 13–17 record 30 games into the campaign, and elevated them into fifth place in the AL standings, ahead of Detroit, St. Louis and Chicago. The A's had seemingly turned a corner.

After a rainout on Tuesday, the series resumed on Wednesday, May 24, and saw Cleveland eke out a hard-fought 5–4 win. Both losing pitcher Joe Bush and winning hurler Guy Morton (who quietly raised his record to 8–1) went the distance. Cleveland got more walks than hits (a 6:5 ratio) in their win. Five errors—three by the Indians—figured in the majority of runs. Only three of Myers' five runs were earned, while just one of Morton's four runs counted against his ERA. Philadelphia had a 2–1 lead after the first inning, but Cleveland chipped away and took the lead for good with a two-run fifth inning. Doubles by Tris Speaker and Braggo Roth did the most damage to the home team's hopes. The loss dropped the A's back into sixth place. Amos Strunk, who picked up two hits, could be found near the top of the AL's batting and slugging average leaders, while Charlie Pick's nine stolen bases ranked him third in the league. A rain-shortened contest occurred the following day, with the Indians leading 3–1 when it was called in the fifth inning, so the game did not count. Thus the series ended with the clubs having completed just two of their four scheduled games at wet Shibe Park, each team managing a single victory.

On Friday, May 26, the A's embarked on a long road trip beginning with a stop in Washington. The Mackmen lost a tough one, 2–1. Elmer Myers got the loss despite striking out six Senators, issuing no walks and allowing just five hits. Myers did hit two Senators batters, though. The A's clung to a tenuous 1–0 lead until the bottom of the seventh when the home team scored twice. George Dumont, the winning pitcher, had a superb outing, allowing only three hits (although two of them were doubles) and no walks to the visitors. He allowed no earned runs. Whitey Witt, who was among the punchless hitters for Philadelphia, was charged with his 18th error of the season.

On Saturday, two more losses to the Senators in a Griffith Stadium doubleheader extended the Philadelphia losing streak to four. The scores of the Washington triumphs were 5–3 and 3–1. Joe Bush went the distance in the first game but was significantly hurt by two errors. Jack Nabors pitched decently in the second game, but he did not get much offensive help from his A's teammates. Weldon Wyckoff, who had posted an 11–7 record for Connie Mack in the pennant year of 1914 but fell to 10–22 in the disastrous 1915 campaign, made his 1916 pitching debut in relief of Nabors in the bottom of the eighth. He did not look especially daunting, allowing two walks and a single, but he got through the difficult frame without surrendering a run to Washington. Walter Johnson took a shutout into the ninth inning for the home team, allowed a single A's run, and ran his record to an impressive 9–3. The pair of Athletics' losses dropped them into seventh place, a mere half-game ahead of the cellar-dwelling St. Louis Browns.

On Monday, May 29, an inconclusive 5–5 tie game was played between the two clubs. It was the only "official" tie game the Mackmen had in 1916. Hard-luck A's pitcher Jack Nabors seemed poised for a rare win against Walter Johnson, who had entered the game in relief of Sam Rice. (Rice would abandon the mound and become a full-time outfielder for Washington in 1917. He would enjoy a lengthy Hall of Fame career, falling just 13 short of 3,000 career hits.) The A's led 5–3 entering the bottom of the ninth inning. The home team scored one run off Nabors and chased him to the bench. Mack sent in reliable Elmer Myers to close the door, but he allowed an unearned tying run before retiring the side, at which point the spirited contest was halted. In accordance with AL rules, since five innings had been completed, the game's stats counted, but the tie had no bearing on the AL standings.

With the sudden reversal of the A's fortunes, *The Sporting News*'s Philadelphia correspondent William G. Weart's June 1 report was considerably far less rosy in its outlook for the Athletics' prospects than his previous week's column had been. In fact, he focused more on the success of the NL Phillies than on the fading A's, a rarity for a writer who was an unabashed Connie Mack booster. Weart pointed out that beyond Myers and Bush, it was plainly obvious the Athletics had very little going for them in the pitching department and were suffering accordingly.

> Will Connie Mack drive his present team this season or will he again resort to experimenting? The answer to this question will probably be delayed until the team goes on its western trip. The Athletics are just about at the turning point of their career for 1916. Without another pitcher or two who can go in and win a fair share of games it will be impossible for the Athletics to land a first division berth this season.

Connie has two splendid hurlers in Joe Bush and Elmer Myers. There the pitching possibilities have stopped. Two swell twirling bets—and then nothing. At least that has been the way of this spring. In the meantime, other pitchers have been experimented with, and it is time that one or two of the holdovers should show. In June there will come the college reinforcements. Much is expected of them, and it will be necessary to flash another pitcher of merit by the middle of June for the team to have a chance to cope with the leading teams.

The Athletics have done so much better than anticipated that naturally the fans are eager to see them do more. If Connie could get some help for Bush and Myers in the twirling department and an outfielder could come up to the mark, there is no telling how high the White Elephants might climb this season.

Only one of the American League teams has been able to take the measure of the White Elephants at Shibe Park this year. This team was Detroit, and the Tigers owed their three victories out of four games to wildness on the part of Mack's hurlers. Boston and New York could only break even in four games, and Cleveland got an even break in two games with the third stopped by rain when the Indians had a 3–1 lead in the fifth inning. Chicago, St. Louis and Washington each lost two games out of three played. This was better than an even break for the White Elephants at home. Now the big test comes with the long road trip.

Weldon Wyckoff made his 1916 debut against Cleveland here and lasted only part of one inning, during which seven batsmen faced him, two of whom went out, two singled, and three received bases on balls. From this it does not look like Connie could count much on Wyckoff this year. Rube Bressler, who also shattered some of Mack's hopes for the future, was sent to Newark, where he got into three games and was then sent back to the Athletics.

The Athletics found New York and the suddenly surging Yankees to be a severe challenge. On Tuesday, May 30, the Yankees romped to an easy 7–2 win in the first game of a doubleheader. The A's did not score until the top of the ninth. A's starter Cap Crowell made things easy for New York by walking 11 Yankees. His record fell to 0–5. Three Philadelphia errors, including Whitey Witt's 19th of the young season, further hurt the visitors' cause. Ray Fisher picked up the win for New York.

The second game was a complete-game masterpiece by Elmer Myers, a 1–0 gem. Philadelphia scored an unearned run in the top of the seventh to make an unlucky loser out of ex–Athletic Bob Shawkey. New York managed just four hits off Myers, all singles. The Athletics were 14–22 after the much-needed win, and Myers' record was elevated to 7–2.

The Athletics ended May with another doubleheader at the Polo Grounds, losing both ends. The first tilt was one that got away from Mack's squad, an ugly 8–7 loss to the Yankees, a game in which Philadelphia led 5–1 at one juncture. Starting pitcher Jack Nabors was yanked for a pinch-hitter after three innings. Weldon Wyckoff came on in relief and was undeniably bad. He faced two batters and gave up a hit and a walk. Both runners scored. Joe Bush looked far from spectacular in relief of Wyckoff, allowing five runs in five innings. The game's devastating blow was a grand slam by Yankees right fielder Frank Gilhooley, occurring after the side should have been safely retired, with two outs in the bottom of the eighth inning. It was Gilhooley's only home run of 1916. It was a catastrophic eighth frame for Philadelphia. In the end, the Yankees scored five runs to assume the lead. Bush was tagged with the loss and now had a mediocre record of 6–6. Shortstop Whitey Witt hit a double, but he was no help defensively. He made three errors to run his yearly total to an unsightly 22. On a positive note, Athletics catcher Billy Meyer hit his only career home run in the first inning off Yankees starter Nick Cullop.

The second game of the twin bill was a comfortable 9–5 win for the New Yorkers. Connie Mack apparently figured Weldon Wyckoff had not exerted himself much by facing just two Yankees in the opener, so the manager penciled him in to start the second game. Wyckoff managed to endure for a complete game but was roughed up considerably throughout the contest. The loss was Wyckoff's only decision of 1916 and the last decision he would record in his spotty six-year major league career. By mid-season he would be dealt to Boston. Wyckoff began his starting assignment shakily, giving up a two-run blast to Hugh High (the only home run High would hit in 1916), and quickly fell behind 3–0 after just one inning. Philadelphia tried to make a game of it, but their eight hits could not offset their four costly errors. Witt committed another gaffe at shortstop and now had 23 errors in 39 games in 1916. The loss of these two games dropped the A's into a tie at the bottom of the AL heap with the St. Louis Browns, each club having a 14–24 mark. Thus the Athletics would enter June as a co-cellar-dweller.

June: Reality Tramples Optimism

The first day of June, a Thursday, brought another day of A's-Yankees baseball at the Polo Grounds. In arguably their finest outing of the 1916 season, Philadelphia thumped New York, 5–0, on the strength of 16 hits. Joe Bush had a magnificent outing, limiting New York to just four hits for the complete-game shutout. Bush himself got two singles and a run batted in to help his own cause. Ray Caldwell endured the pasting for the full nine innings in a losing effort for the home team. With St. Louis splitting a home doubleheader versus Cleveland, the A's decisive win put them back into seventh place all by themselves.

Friday was a travel day for Connie Mack's club—a long train trip westward to St. Louis. During the A's off-day, the Browns beat Cleveland and moved back into a seventh-place tie with Connie Mack's club. By the end of Saturday, June 3, the Browns occupied seventh place by themselves thanks to a ninth-inning comeback triumph that turned a 2–1 defeat into a 3–2 victory. The A's had mustered only two hits off Dave Davenport and reliever Ernie Koob but were three outs away from a gritty victory. Tom Sheehan, looking for his first win of the season, could not close the deal, though. Del Pratt and Armando Marsans both got hits and scored runs in the bottom of the ninth inning. Whitey Witt's ongoing subpar play at shortstop—he made his 24th error of the season—was costly as two of the Browns' runs were unearned. St. Louis won despite committing five errors. The loss dropped the Athletics into last place in the AL—a position they would retain for the rest of the 1916 season.

Sunday baseball was a legal activity in St. Louis, so nothing prevented the A's and Browns from taking to the diamond on Sunday, June 4. The visitors jumped out to a quick 2–0 in the top of the first inning, sending Browns starter Ernie Koob to the showers before he retired a single Philadelphia batter, but they were unable to maintain their advantage. St. Louis responded with a single tally in the home half of the third inning and three more runs in the sixth off Elmer Myers, who went the distance. The A's got one run back in the ninth, but came out on the wrong end of a 4–3 score. Bob Groom got the win for the home team in a long relief stint—8⅔ innings. Groom needed a smidgen of relief help from Carl Weilman, who retired the last Athletic to preserve the win. The loss dropped Philadelphia, now 15–26, to eighth place, 10.5 games out of first place, not that it mattered. The A's and their fans were no longer entertaining the possibility of winning the AL pennant.

Bad weather and travel meant that the A's got nearly a full week off before taking the field again. The last game of the series versus the Browns and an entire four-game series at Comiskey Park in Chicago were washed away by unrelenting storms.

On Saturday, June 10, in Cleveland, the Tribe manhandled the well-rested A's, 10–1, at Dunn Field on the strength of 16 hits, four of which were doubles. Cleveland also laid down four sacrifice bunts for good measure! A strong outing on the mound was turned in by Stanley Coveleski, Cleveland spitball master, who pitched a complete game for the victorious home team and was 7–3 on the season. The Athletics' pitching was horrendous. Tom Sheehan lasted just one inning and gave up three Cleveland runs. Sheehan took the loss and was now 0–5. Cap Crowell relieved Sheehan in the second inning and he too got pounded, giving up five runs. For Crowell, a one-time heralded prospect from Brown University, it was his last MLB appearance. He ended his 1916 season 0–5 with a 4.99 ERA. Weldon Wyckoff was substituted for Crowell in the third inning and put in a respectable outing. He allowed only two further Cleveland runs over the next six frames. Whitey Witt added to the misery by committing two more errors at shortstop to bring his season's total to 26.

The A's were in a freefall. Even the always optimistic William G. Weart had little to praise the Athletics for in his report for *The Sporting News* on June 8, though he did manage to note that Rube Oldring had recently put together a commendable 12-for-19 streak at the plate. The Athletics' pitching woes dominated Weart's thoughts.

> Manager Mack has announced that there will be eight college players join [sic] his team when the White Elephants return home the third week of this month. Nearly all of these men are pitchers. They will be greatly needed unless some of the twirlers that Connie has been experimenting with get going right during the western trip. Crowell, Nabors and Sheehan failed in game after game.
>
> It certainly has been a peculiar situation in the Mack camp. Connie has had two of the best pitching bets in the country in Myers and Bush. The others have shown practically no class. Still they must have merit or Connie would not be sending them to the mound so regularly. A victory or two may be the making of any one of these young men. Certainly they can never complain that manager Mack did not give them enough chances to make good. The next two weeks should decide their fate.

There was no law prohibiting Sunday baseball in Cleveland either, so the A's tried to put their losing ways behind them on the Sabbath. It did not happen.

Cleveland rolled to an easy 7–2 win on June 11, scoring six runs in the first two innings. The recently ineffective Elmer Myers was responsible for six runs (all earned), six hits and two walks before giving way to Jack Nabors, who did well in his five innings, allowing just a single Indians run, but was hopelessly in arrears. Tom Sheehan retired all three Cleveland hitters he faced in the eighth. Guy Morton, an Alabamian, looked very strong for the home team in collecting his 11th win of the 1916 campaign. He allowed nine A's hits, all singles, but he minimized the damage they caused. Philadelphia plated two runs in the top of the eighth but no more. The Athletics' record was now 15–28, and they were surely looking more and more like the hopeless bunch that many had predicted they would be coming out of spring training.

Monday, June 12, added another loss to the Athletics' ledger. This time Cleveland prevailed, 3–1. Again, the damage was done early. The Tribe scored twice in the bottom of the first off starter Joe Bush, who was now 7–7. Bush surrendered another run in the fourth and was removed from the mound by Mack after five innings. Tom Sheehan finished the game for the Mackmen, going the final three frames without allowing another Cleveland tally, as long relief was now Sheehan's specialty. The A's got a run back in the top of the sixth, but could muster no further scoring. Of the Athletics' six hits, Charlie Pick got three of them, including a double. Pick, whose fielding was improving and who was on a bit of a recent batting tear, scored the A's lone run.

It was more of the same on Tuesday, June 13. The A's fell behind early and could not recover as the Indians romped in a laugher, 11–2. To be accurate, Philadelphia actually jumped out to a 2–0 lead in the top of the first inning as Cleveland starter Jim Bagby looked beatable. The home team responded with 11 runs in the next four innings—all off battered A's starter Elmer Myers, who gave up 13 hits and seven walks. Myers was mercifully yanked after five innings in favor of Jack Nabors, who was unscathed in the final three innings. Things were definitely getting ugly for Philadelphia who, with their 15–30 record, had now lost twice as many games as they had won. Mack's crew had scored the fewest runs among all MLB teams (138) while allowing the most (221). They had also lost six consecutive games and eight of their last nine. Optimism in the A's clubhouse was becoming a rare commodity.

The June 15 edition of *The Sporting News* had little positive news to report about the A's recent woeful run of losses, so instead correspondent William G. Weart dwelt on how the plentiful rainouts were hurting Connie Mack's team in the wallet.

> The storm king pocketed the Athletics last week. Connie Mack's players were idle for five days in succession, which looks like a record for the club. The first postponement was at St. Louis and the other four at Chicago. There was a time it seemed as though good weather followed Connie and his team around the circuit and at home.

It seldom rained or was even cloudy when the Athletics had a big game to play or a doubleheader carded.

This year things have been entirely reversed. Only once this season were the Athletics favored with good weather on a big occasion. This was on Memorial Day in New York. It was thought the Athletics had a choice date when they were assigned to open the season at Boston against the world's champions. Instead, the weather conditions were very bad. It was the same way for opening here [in Philadelphia] against the Red Sox.

The climax was reached last week when for four days the Mackmen watched the rain fall at Chicago during the Republican convention. It will take a mighty fine brand of weather during the remainder of the season to enable the Athletics to come anywhere near offsetting the heavy losses already incurred by the bad weather conditions this year.

Several of the college players that manager Mack will give tryouts here this month have already reported to Shibe Park. They are practicing daily and will be given a looking over when Connie gets home next week. Some of them were under instruction there last summer and the first thing that Connie will want to know is whether or not they have profited by their early lessons.

The next stop on the Athletics' unproductive road trip was Detroit's Navin Field. On June 15, the A's put forth a more competitive effort than in the last few games, but the result was still the same—a seventh consecutive loss. Detroit emerged with a 5-1 win in a game that was not truly decided until the bottom of the seventh inning when the Tigers padded their 2-1 lead with three more runs. Joe Bush was the losing pitcher, hindered once again by two costly errors by the usual infield suspects: Whitey Witt and Charlie Pick, who now had 27 and 18 errors respectively. Bush did himself no favors by walking six Tigers. The loss dropped his record to 7-8. Hooks Dauss, who would win 223 games in a career spent entirely with the Tigers, went the distance for his ninth win of 1916, allowing just five Philadelphia hits, none for extra bases. With a 15-31 record, the A's were now clearly in the AL cellar, five games out of seventh place.

Connie Mack's club reached a new low defensively on Friday, June 16, by committing six errors in their 4-3 loss to Detroit. Amazingly, none came at the hands of shortstop Whitey Witt, although Charlie Pick was responsible for two to up his seasonal muff total to 20. The tough-luck loser was Jack Nabors, now 1-6, who gave up no earned runs in seven innings, but he did commit one of the A's errors. Philadelphia outhit Detroit, 9-8, and collared Ty Cobb with an 0 for 4 day at the plate. Cobb made up for his unusual lack of offensive punch with two outfield assists. Jean Dubuc tossed a complete game for the victors. Philadelphia had now lost eight straight games and was becoming a laughingstock.

On Saturday, June 17, the A's defensive play improved only marginally. This time five Philadelphia errors were largely responsible for a 7-3 loss to Detroit. Whitey Witt had his worst defensive outing of the season by committing three of the gaffes. Catcher Wally Schang had the other two. Of the seven Tigers runs, only two were earned. Elmer Myers, who went the full eight innings for Mack's charges, was hardly blameless. He walked nine Tigers and allowed eight hits in the 37 batters he faced. In picking up the victory, George Cunningham threw nine strong innings for Detroit and allowed only one earned run. Philadelphia had jumped into a 2–0 lead in the second inning, but trailed 3–2 after three frames and never regained the lead. It was the ninth consecutive setback for the discouraged A's.

It was more of the same on Sunday, June 18. Sabbath baseball was permitted without restriction in Michigan, thus the Tigers were permitted to drub the dismal Athletics once again, this time 8–2. The Athletics racked up five more errors, three of them by Wally Schang in their tenth loss in a row. Predictably, one more gaffe was added to the defensive ledger of shortstop Whitey Witt. Tom Sheehan endured the defensive debacle and went the distance in absorbing his sixth loss of the season without a win. He allowed 14 hits. The winning pitcher for the Tigers was Earl Hamilton, who had been acquired from the St. Louis Browns at the end of May. He gave up no earned runs in his complete game despite allowing seven hits and five walks. Hamilton had a knack for inducing ground balls in this game as he recorded seven assists. Apparently this effort, his only win in five starts for Detroit, failed to impress Tigers management. Hamilton was put on waivers and reclaimed by St. Louis shortly thereafter. Somewhat ironically, Hamilton's first pitching assignment upon his return to the Browns was against the Tigers—which he lost.

With even less positive news to report in *The Sporting News* than he had the previous Thursday, on June 22 William G. Weart, in a lengthy and unusually light-hearted piece for the weekly baseball newspaper, only reluctantly mentioned the A's doldrums in the final two paragraphs. Instead Weart cast a hopeful light on the youthful prospects flooding into Shibe Park from the schoolyards and college campuses for tryouts in hopes of crashing the A's roster.

New School Term Opens at Shibe Park
Prof. Mack Figures to Turn Out Another Class
Institutions of Learning Everywhere Scoured for
Talent to be Developed for Future Athletics

Pick up almost any newspaper these days and there is nearly certain to be found on the sporting page an item head like this: "Schoolboy Wonder for Connie Mack." Sometimes the word "schoolboy" is changed for "college." In a recent interview Connie said he didn't know how many players he would have for tryouts when he got his team back to Shibe Park [in] the middle of June. This undoubtedly meant that Connie had lines out for a large number of youngsters in the schools and the colleges, and from the reports that have been coming in over the wires about 50 percent of the school and college players who are deemed fit for a major league tryout and who would like to turn professional have been landed by Connie and his scouts.

One noticeable thing about the stories is that the majority of the lads appear to be 17 or 18 years of age. Connie certainly likes to get his players in the first flower of youth. It is just possible that when manager Mack sends Harry Davis, Ira Thomas, Mike Brennan or any of his other scouts out to look over a youngster, his first instruction is: "Inquire if he uses a razor. If he does, don't bother with him."

From the alleged ages of Connie's 1916 crop of juveniles, any salesman who tried to sell safety razors to them would starve to death. That's Connie's way of building up a team, however. Other managers build for one or two years. Connie builds for five years. He really built his 1910 team for ten years, only some of the stars that Mack made got to thinking that they were bigger than the master and the wonderful machine had to be torn apart when it still had many years of first-class service in sight.

There was a suspicion this spring when Myers and Bush turned in victories at a steady clip that perhaps manager Mack would start his big drive early in the present championship race. The lack of another pitcher who could win occasionally and weakness in the outfield and infield, though, proved too big a handicap.

Now the time has arrived when the big work starts. Connie has weeded out players who have failed to come up to expectations or whom he cannot use at this time. He has sent Minot [Cap] Crowell, formerly of Brown University, to a team Down South. Crowell came here with a big college reputation. Efforts were made to cure him of certain pitching faults and he was sent in to start numerous games. Usually he lasted about two innings.

Another player let go is second baseman Lewis Malone, formerly of Mt. St. Mary's College, who looked very promising in his early career here last season, but has not been playing this season owing to [Nap] Lajoie doing such excellent work. Malone and [Bill] Stellbauer, an outfielder from Peoria in the Three-I League, have been sent to St. Paul of the American Association. Stellbauer hit well, but fell down in the field. He lacked aggressiveness and seemed to be all at sea at times. A few months in the minors should help him a lot, as he is young and appears to be a natural hitter.

For a couple of weeks past, players have been arriving at Shibe Park and getting in daily workouts pending the arrival of the Athletics' squad from the West. One of the players from whom much is expected is an infielder named [Otis] Lawry from the University of Maine. For several months, Lawry has been highly touted. The University of Maine team was coached this year by Monte Cross, former shortstop of the Phillies and the Athletics. Monte has already put the "OK" mark on Lawry, whom he declares is the fastest man he has ever seen in baseball. Monte says that Lawry can beat any of the noted sprinters of the present or past, and he doesn't bar Harry Bay, Ty Cobb, George Sisler, or Burt Shotton when he makes the remark.

The Athletics are now home from their disastrous trip to a couple of the eastern cities and the West. Before going away the White Elephants were doing good work and more than holding their own. It was expected that the trip would make or break the team's chances of getting out of last place this season. The answer is "break." The pitching did not come up to expectations and the fielding was bad, with the result that game after game was lost and the team became more firmly entrenched in last place.

The Athletics will resume business at Shibe Park tomorrow. Each American League box score sent out from this city from now on can be expected to contain the name of a player who is not known to the fans. It is expected that manager Mack will give many of the youngsters a chance to get into the games. Others, however, will only be used in the morning contests. If they do not come up to the mark, they will be quietly shipped away to some minor league club. For the next two months Shibe Park in the mornings is likely to be the busiest baseball field in the country. The bell has rung. Mack's Baseball School is in session and the professors are ready to give their pupils their hardest examinations.

With the dismal road trip over, Mack's club returned to the familiar confines of Shibe Park where the Washington Senators were waiting for them on Tuesday, June 20. Joe Bush gave up a mere three hits in eight innings but still managed to lose the hard-fought game by a 2–1 count. The Athletics were held to six hits by the Senators' Bert Gallia, a right-hander from Texas. Gallia held the A's off the scoresheet until the ninth inning when a late rally by the home team came up just short. Wally Schang's triple drove in Amos Strunk, but when the final out was made, Schang was still standing at third base. Gallia helped himself defensively by starting two rally-squelching double plays. Bush had been removed from the batting order in the eighth inning for a rookie pinch-hitter, a 21-year-old from Illinois named Lester Alfred (Red) Lanning, who failed to get a hit of Gallia in his MLB debut. Lanning was hailed as a promising collegiate outfielder and pitcher, but ended up doing neither effectively for Mack before being released after 19 games. Jack Nabors, who continued to pitch well whenever Mack called upon him—but had precious little to show for it—retired all three Senators he faced in the top of the ninth to give the A's a fighting chance. It mattered little, though, as the Athletics fell for the 11th straight time. They had lost 70 percent of their contests in 1916 and were now 15–35. Things would get considerably worse instead of better for Connie Mack's outfit during the remaining two-thirds of the schedule.

Rain prevented play on Wednesday, so the Senators and A's played twice at Shibe Park on Thursday, June 22, to make up for the lost game. Lo and behold, the A's broke their awful losing streak with a 4–2 win in the first contest. Unlike the previous 11 games, the A's managed to score late to take a close affair rather than having their opponents do it to them. Philadelphia jumped out to a 2–0 lead with a pair of unearned runs off Sam Rice. Washington resolutely got the two runs back in the top of the fifth. Bert Gallia, Tuesday's pitching hero for the Senators, could not replicate his efforts in long relief of Rice. Doubles by Amos Strunk and Nap Lajoie proved to be the key blows as the home team scored twice in the eighth inning for the win. Elmer Myers got the long-awaited win for the Mackmen. His seven strikeouts were offset by ten bases on balls, but the defense held the fort. The A's turned three double pays and refreshingly committed only one error. Ancient Nap Lajoie, approaching his 42nd birthday, earned a rousing cheer by stealing both second and third base in the rare win.

The game proved to be the last with the A's of 1916 for 32-year-old left fielder Rube Oldring, who batted second and went hitless with a walk in two at-bats. Oldring was one of the few remaining links to Mack's pennant teams. Following the World Series championship of 1913, Oldring had been voted the most popular ballplayer in Philadelphia by the fans and had received a new Cadillac automobile as a prize. But nearly three years later, Oldring had become disillusioned with the downward direction the Athletics were headed in and asked for his release. Mack, now committed to a full-fledged youth movement, obliged. For a short time Oldring would reside at his farm in New Jersey. He would resurface with the New York Yankees before very long, though.

Alas, the A's winning streak lasted just one game, as the Senators were victorious 6–1 in the second game—a game which clearly illustrated to the home crowd their team's obvious flaws. Jack Nabors got the start but he was ineffective, walking three of the eight batters he faced in 1⅔ innings. Nevertheless, Nabors allowed no runs. Joe Bush was not as fortunate, however, allowing five runs in 5⅓ innings before giving way to mop-up man Weldon Wyckoff in the eighth inning. Wyckoff was less than impressive as well, allowing four bases on balls and a run in two innings. Errors once again hurt the Athletics. Whitey Witt's 32nd of 1916 was one of three the team made. George Dumont, the best pitcher on the hill that day by far, got the win for Washington. Lajoie duplicated his stolen-base feat of the first game by again nabbing second and third base, raising his season's total to five. (From all accounts, a bad call by base umpire Brick Owens deprived Lajoie of another steal of third base later in the game.) By only

The futility of playing for the hapless 1916 squad weighed heavily on brooding outfielder Rube Oldring, who was once voted the most popular member of the A's during their championship years. He abruptly retired during the A's longest losing streak—only to resurface shortly thereafter as a member of the pennant-contending New York Yankees (National Baseball Hall of Fame Library, Cooperstown, N.Y.).

splitting the twin bill against their lowly adversaries, the surging Senators prevented themselves from claiming a share of the lead with the Cleveland Indians in the AL pennant chase. At the other end of the standings, the win and loss had made the A's a 16–36 team and increased their winning percentage from .300 to .308. The Athletics were a distant 14.5 games out of first place and, more tellingly, six games out of seventh place.

The Athletics' home stand was brief as they traveled to Boston's Fenway Park after the doubleheader split versus the Senators. On Friday, June 23, Whitey Witt—"the towheaded shortstop of the Mack Mobilization School"—was honored as a returning local hero by citizens of Winchendon, MA, who turned out at Fenway in sizable numbers for the occasion. According to Ralph E. McMillan, the Boston correspondent for *The Sporting News*, Witt was presented with "a gold watch and sundry other tokens of esteem." Once the game began, though, Witt made a horrendous and costly baserunning blunder, described by McMillan in *TSN*'s June 29 edition: "Witt played a nice game after the presentation, and tore off a regular three-bagger, only to lose the hit altogether by neglecting to touch the first cushion en route. Over-anxiety to please the home folks probably had something to do with the fatal omission."

Tom Sheehan certainly could have used Witt's nullified triple. The A's right-hander had an excellent but disappointing outing versus the defending World Series champions. He allowed just one run and two hits, but still managed to lose the game, 1–0, and fell to 0–7. In the epitome of a tough loss, Dick Hoblitzell scored the game's only run in the bottom of the seventh inning without the benefit of a Red Sox hit or an RBI. A walk to Hoblitzell, a sacrifice bunt, a ground out, and a wild pitch brought home the winning tally for the home side. Ernie Shore, Boston's 6'4" right-hander, harmlessly scattered six Athletics hits for a complete-game shutout. Twenty-year-old Harland Rowe of Springvale, ME, one of Connie Mack's youthful hopefuls, got the nod to play third base instead of error-prone Charlie Pick. He was credited with two assists. Rowe also got one of the A's six singles off Shore.

The A's and Red Sox played two games in balmy conditions before a terrific crowd on Saturday, June 24. It was "the first real Saturday of the year [for fine weather in Boston]," according to the June 29 edition of *The Sporting News*. For the Athletics, the first game of the twin bill was excruciatingly similar to Friday's loss to Boston. Hard-luck Philadelphia starter Jack Nabors took a 2–1 lead into the bottom of the ninth only to have two unearned runs turn what should have been a sweet victory into a teeth-gnashing defeat. This game that has gone down in Athletics' lore as the prototypical loss for the hapless 1916 club, and it produced a marvelous anecdote. Like many sports yarns, the truth has been twisted and embellished over the years, but here are the facts based on the game's official box score, the account published in *The Sporting News*, and a bit of detective work.

The Red Sox managed just three hits in the entire game, two by leadoff hitter Harry Hooper and one by Hal Janvrin, who batted second. Hooper and Janvrin scored all three of the home team's runs. Going into the bottom of the ninth, Nabors had given up just one hit, a spectacular pitching feat against the defending World Series champions. Hooper singled to lead off the inning. Janvrin then hit a tricky ground ball to Whitey Witt, who could not corral it. The play was generously scored an infield single. Both runners advanced a base on an infield out. Dick Hoblitzell hit a fly ball to short left field that was caught by strong-armed Wally Schang for the second out. Hooper recklessly tried to score after the catch. Schang unleashed a perfect throw to catcher Mike Murphy, who had Hooper dead to rights by about 15 feet—had he held onto the ball. Instead the ball popped out of Murphy's glove, allowing Hooper to score the tying run and Janvrin to move to third base. With Tilly Walker batting, Nabors cavalierly chucked the very next pitch well over the head of Murphy. It crashed high atop the backstop and Janvrin trotted home with Boston's winning run.

Nabors' teammate and hotel roommate, the equally luckless Tom Sheehan, was certain Nabors had thrown the horribly wild pitch on purpose. Sheehan, who had valiantly and cruelly lost a 1–0 heartbreaker the day before, curiously asked Nabors why he had deliberately thrown a wild pitch to the backstop. Nabors supposedly replied something to the effect of, "Look, I knew those guys wouldn't get me another run—and if you think I'm going to throw nine more innings on a hot day like this, you're crazy!"[1]

Submarine-style pitcher Carl Mays was the lucky winner of the first game. He was in the right position at the right time to benefit from Nabors' largesse, having thrown just a single inning in relief of Dutch Leonard before the Red Sox rallied for the improbably wacky win in the bottom of the ninth. Mack experimented with a new third baseman for the second day in a row: Lee King of Waltham, MA, played the first of his 42 games for the 1916 A's and got two hits, laid down a sacrifice bunt, and handled two chances flawlessly. King was the son of 19th-century hurler Silver King, one of baseball's first sidearm throwers, who won 203 games in his MLB career. He would be a handy utility player for Mack in this troubling season. As well as guarding the keystone sack, King would play shortstop, second base, and all three outfield positions before the season concluded.

Hardly having worked up a decent sweat in winning the first game versus the snake-bitten A's, Carl Mays threw a complete game in the second half of the doubleheader to pick up two wins in a single day. The score of this one was 7–3. Boston had to overcome a deficit again, but this time they did it with plenty of time to spare. The Red Sox scored four runs in the bottom of the fourth inning to overcome Philadelphia's short-lived 2–1 lead. Mays gave up three earned runs and seven hits, but Athletics hurler Joe Bush was more generous, giving up nine hits and five earned runs. Four A's errors did not help the visitors' cause. The two losses dropped Philadelphia to 16–39. The rest of the AL clubs were collectively opening up a sizable gap on the hapless Mackmen.

Boston's civic "blue laws" prevented a Sunday game from happening at Fenway Park, but it was worth the wait until Monday, June 26, for Connie Mack's crew as they played their best game in weeks. The result was a convincing 8–5 victory over the hot Red Sox in which the A's outhit the defending champions, 14–6. Tom Sheehan finally got his first win of 1916 to raise his record to 1–7. Five Athletics had multiple hits. Whitey Witt, whose obvious defensive shortcomings were tolerated because of his bat and his speed on the basepaths, got three of them. Rookie Harland Rowe got a timely pinch-hit double and scored the A's go-ahead run. Sheehan's win was actually in relief of Weldon Wyckoff, who was removed for pinch-hitter Rowe in the top of the fourth. Philadelphia played error-free baseball for a change. Boston used five pitchers to no avail. Rube Foster, a righty from Oklahoma, took the loss for the home team and dropped to 4–6. The win upped the Athletics' record to 17–39, but they were still 16 games off the pace set by the AL-leading Cleveland Indians.

Two more newcomers made their MLB debuts with the A's at Fenway Park on Tuesday, June 27: twenty-one-year-old right-handed pitcher Russell Conwell (Jing) Johnson, a Pennsylvanian; and 24-year-old catcher Ralph Arthur (Doc) Carroll, a Massachusetts lad. Carroll would not make much of an impression on anyone—with perhaps the exception of Tom Sheehan, who remembered him anecdotally decades later—and his MLB career would be limited to just ten games. On this date Carroll found big league pitching tough to handle, striking out twice in four at-bats versus left-handed sensation Babe Ruth. Johnson was spotted a 2–0 lead heading into the bottom of the first inning, courtesy of a two-run single by Stuffy McInnis, but could not take advantage of Ruth's lone lapse of excellence. Boston got one run back in the bottom of the first inning and three more in the fourth en route to a comfortable 7–2 win. Ruth fanned ten A's. It was Ruth's 11th win of 1916, a season in which he was the most dominant pitcher in the American League, outshining even the great Walter Johnson. Ruth also got one of the 11 Red Sox hits, a single. Johnson managed to linger for 6⅔ innings before giving way to reliever Weldon Wyckoff. Wyckoff's outing, lasting 1⅔ innings, was his last appearance for the A's. Johnson, though, proved to be the ultimate journeyman pitcher. He managed to yo-yo his way in and out of the majors, playing portions of five MLB seasons through 1928, but he could always proudly boast that his AL pitching debut was against Babe Ruth. The loss was the A's 40th of the season, four more than any other MLB team had and five more than the seventh-place Browns.

In his report on the Athletics for the June 29 edition *The Sporting News*, William G. Weart discussed the progress of Mack's hopeful newcomers, the sneaky speed and steady reliability of a familiar old hand at second base, and the bad luck that had occasionally befallen the Athletics' pitchers in games when they seemingly deserved to have better results.

Connie Mack has started to experiment with some of the collegians who reported to him here [in Philadelphia] last week. The first of the 1916 class to get a chance was a lad named Lester Lanning. Lanning is a pitcher and an outfielder and he was sent to left field when [Rube] Oldring hurt his leg. The lad throws and bats left-handed and has shown signs of promise. [Harland] Rowe, a third baseman from the University of Maine, got his first chance in a game against the Boston Red Sox last Friday. Connie has a bunch of more young talent that will break into the box scores soon.

There is one player on the Athletics, though, who is not going to be displaced in a hurry if he can help it. This is Napoleon Lajoie. In a double-header here [at Shibe Park] last week with Washington, Lajoie not only batted and fielded in wonderful style, he also stole bases like a Ty Cobb. In each game that day, Lajoie made clean steals of second and third. It really looked as though he had twice stolen third base in one game [but for a controversial out call]. However, a record of four stolen bases for a man of his age was certainly a wonderful performance.

Things certainly have not broken right for the Athletics lately. They have been getting a lot of defeats that have been deserved, and they have been getting some defeats because of the breaks. In two games last week, Mack's hurlers held their opponents down to a total of five singles and yet both games were lost. Washington got only three hits on one game off Joe Bush and [Jack] Nabors, but two of these singles came with runners who had started around the circuit on passes. These runs were enough to win the contest.

At Boston on Friday, [Tom] Sheehan gave his best performance since joining the Mackmen. Sheehan held the Red Sox to just two hits and neither of these figured in the scoring of the only run of the afternoon. Sheehan lost the game because a man he gave a base on balls got within scoring distance on outs and scooted home on a wild pitch.

Wednesday, June 28, brought the New York Yankees to Shibe Park, and they literally ran their way to a 9–7 victory that was more one-sided than it appeared in the box score. The Yanks managed eight hits of losing pitcher Elmer Myers, who was far from sharp. Four Athletics errors, nine stolen bases (by five different players), one hit batsman, and five bases on balls also helped the visitors in their triumph. Catcher Billy Meyer seemed utterly unable to corral the fleet-footed Yankees. Right fielder Frank Gilhooley was especially daring on the basepaths, swiping four bags. Hugh High and Wally Pipp each got timely triples to pace the New York attack. One Philadelphia error was Whitey Witt's 34th. Newcomer Harland Rowe made two of them in four chances at third base. The A's actually outhit the Yankees, 11–8, but were trailing 9–2 going into the bottom of the seventh inning. A five-run outburst drove Ray Keating, the eventual winning pitcher, from the mound. Allen Russell pitched finely in relief for the final two innings, facing the minimum six batters, to seal the Yankees' win. Otis Lawry, the A's college-bred rookie hyped in William G. Weart's report in *The Sporting News*, made his MLB debut as a pinch-hitter in the bottom of the ninth inning—and promptly struck out. The game also featured a bizarre incident in which Yankees manager Wild Bill Donovan sent Joe Duggan, the team's trainer, into the upper reaches of Shibe Park's grandstand to physically silence a heckler who had clearly gotten under his skin. AL president Ban Johnson, who was having more than his fair share of nasty episodes to deal with in 1916, ended up fining Donovan $100 and suspending Duggan.

On Thursday, June 29, the Yankees won with pitching instead of stolen bases. Ex-Athletics hurler Bob Shawkey tossed a complete-game gem, winning 5–0, and allowing just four hits, a walk, and a hit batsman. In contrast, Jack Nabors was ineffective as the Philadelphia starter, allowing three runs on three hits and a walk in the first inning to put the home side in a hole from which they never escaped. Tom Sheehan pitched seven strong innings for the hapless home team, allowing only one additional run. Twenty-one-year-old George Hesselbacher, a 6'2" right-handed local boy, another of Mack's collegiate hopefuls, came in for mop-up duties in the ninth inning. Hesselbacher gave up a walk, a hit, and an earned run in the four batters he faced. Only two Yankees stole bases. The lone extra-base hit by the visitors came courtesy of ex–Athletic Frank Baker, who rapped out a double in his old stomping grounds. The A's were now a miserable 17–42.

Friday, June 30, brought the A's disastrous month to an appropriate end with another shutout loss at Shibe Park at the hands of the New York Yankees. This time the Yankees won, 7–0, propelled by 11 hits (two of them triples) and three walks surrendered by Joe Bush, who fell to 7–12. Four New Yorkers recorded two hits in the onslaught. Yankees hurler Ray Fisher gave up eight hits to the home team—three of them to Amos Strunk, including a triple—but no Athletic managed to touch home plate, thanks to a pair of timely double plays. Fisher, who raised his record to 6–4, struck out five Mackmen and walked no one. The first two Philadelphia batters were collegians Otis Lawry and Lee King, who each got a base hit. Newcomer Harland Rowe fared poorly batting in the seventh slot, going 0 for 4 with two strikeouts.

Sixty games into the 1916 season, the A's were an embarrassing 17–43. With just 175 runs scored, they were the only AL club that hadn't scored at least 205 times. With 299 runs against, they were the only MLB club remotely close to allowing 300 opposition runs. Everything that could go wrong for Connie Mack in June had gone wrong. They had won a paltry three games and absorbed 19 confidence-draining losses. Rookies, for the most part, were not panning out as planned. The club's two aces were struggling, victims of poor offensive support and their own pitching and defensive blunders. Runs were becoming more and more difficult to score for the A's, and all the while their defense was becoming increasingly porous. They endured an 11-game losing streak, lost 15 out of 16 games in one awful stretch, and sank hopelessly and irretrievably into the AL basement. The Athletics ended June on a four-game losing skein. Somehow July would cruelly prove to be even worse for baseball's grand old patriarch and his once-proud White Elephants.

July: The Depths of Ineptitude

> The college-boy pitchers became sacrificial lambs. While an entire generation of Europe's youth was being decimated in the trenches of France, an entire generation of college baseball players seemed to be parading across the pitching mounds of the American League, wearing Athletics uniforms and giving up walks.—George Robinson & Charles Salzberg, *On a Clear Day They Could See Seventh Place*

The authors of the above passage were correct: When the 16 MLB teams and dozens of minor league teams took the field on Saturday, July 1, most of the players and fans were caught up with nothing more than the importance of baseball's place in the fabric of American culture. Players, owners, and fans alike were isolated by distance and politics from the catastrophe that had enveloped most of the western world since August 1914. They were blissfully unaware that history's bloodiest battle had begun that very morning along the banks of the Somme River in northern France.

After a week of steadily bombarding the German trenches and defensive redoubts with the greatest artillery barrage in history, at 7:30 a.m., some 80,000 British troops marched out of their trenches in waves into no-man's land in an orderly, unhurried gait. Their goal was to relieve the German pressure on Verdun by forcing the enemy to re-locate some of the troops to the Somme River basin. They had been optimistically told that the only Germans they would encounter would surely be wounded, dead, or too shell-shocked to put up any meaningful resistance. They were badly misinformed. When the British Tommies—many of whom were civilian recruits who had cheerfully enlisted to serve alongside their pals and were experiencing their first taste of combat—got within range of the German positions, deadly machine gun fire poured down on them. Thousands died as entire divisions were mowed down. Nearly 20,000 Brits were killed that first morning in three separate waves of suicidal attacks. Most who fell between the trenches never even saw a German. Total British casualties numbered more than 57,000, or 20 percent of the entire British forces stationed in France. It was easily the worst day in the history of the British Army—and it was only the beginning. The Battle of the Somme would last until mid–November and eventually claim more than a million casualties on both sides. In the end, the enormous Allied sacrifices were rewarded with the insignificant advance of about six miles into German-held territory.

In America, the 1916 presidential election campaign churned onward. Democratic incumbent Woodrow Wilson campaigned against Republican challenger Charles Evans Hughes with the slogan, "He kept us out of the war!" But deep down Wilson knew that if he were re-elected in November, circumstances would probably force him to enter the conflict despite the overwhelming public desire for retaining neutrality. In the meantime, life was good in America. Jobs were plentiful and the economy was humming along nicely. The last season of baseball before the Great War rudely intruded on the national pastime was moving into its summer glory. Already though, the pitiful Philadelphia Athletics had been reduced to the role of also-ran. Their prospects were as bleak as their horrible record, but 94 more games still had to be played by Connie Mack's club before the schedule mercifully ended one of the most dismal seasons ever endured by an MLB outfit.

The Yankees-A's series continued at Shibe Park on Saturday, July 1. New York overcame a 4–1 deficit and scratched out a tough 5–4 win in a game in which neither team stood out. Both teams got seven hits, and both committed four errors. The two usual error suspects for the A's, Whitey Witt and Charlie Pick, could not be blamed on this day. Both had been benched in favor of Connie Mack's collegiate hopefuls, as had Nap Lajoie. The Yankees proved too resilient for the home team. They pushed their fifth run across the plate in the top of the ninth to break a 4–4 deadlock. Elmer Myers took the defeat and fell to 8–8, but went the distance. New York used two pitchers, Allen Russell and George Mogridge, to subdue the A's bats. Mogridge, a 6'2" lefty from Rochester, NY, was the pitcher of record when the Yankees took the lead in the top of the ninth inning and was thus credited with his fourth win of the season. New York had three extra-base hits (two doubles and a triple) to the Athletics' zero. Philadelphia tried to play small ball, using the sacrifice bunt five times. The four runs plated by the Mackmen all came in the fourth inning off Russell. They were all unearned thanks to the plentiful defensive miscues. Philadelphia now had 17 wins and 44 losses on the season and were becoming the objects of derision in the professional baseball world. They were nine games out of seventh place and in the midst of a five-game losing run. With no hope of the A's fielding even a competent team, Shibe Park attendance dropped sharply.

Monday, July 3, brought the Boston Red Sox into Shibe Park. Much like the Yankees did on July 1, the champs from Beantown struggled mightily but in the end eked out a 6–4 victory that was not truly decided until the last Philadelphia rally was squelched in the bottom of the ninth inning. The A's outhit the Red Sox, 12–11, but led only once, 2–1, after three innings. Boston responded with two runs in the top of the fourth and never relinquished the lead thereafter. Jack Nabors pitched decently over eight innings for the Mackmen, permitting just two earned runs, but still lost his eighth game of the campaign after starting 1916 at 1–0. After Charlie Pick unsuccessfully batted for Nabors in the eighth inning, Tom Sheehan had a poor ninth inning on the mound, allowing two insurance runs courtesy of two hits and a walk. The A's got one run back in the home half of the ninth to keep things close, but not close enough to avoid their sixth straight defeat. Ernie Shore got the win for the visitors, but needed relief help from Carl Mays, who retired the last two A's. Catcher Billy Meyer whiffed to end the entertaining contest. The game saw the MLB debut of utility player Lee McElwee for the A's. He would play 54 games for the Mackmen in 1916 at third base, first base, second base, shortstop, and right field and then disappear from the big leagues forever. In this game McElwee batted seventh, hit a double in five at-bats, and scored a run. The loss dropped Philadelphia to 17–45. The Athletics' defeats seemed to be accruing at a breakneck clip with no relief in sight.

Tuesday was a big day on the baseball calendar, as it was the Fourth of July. Every MLB team was scheduled to play a traditional holiday doubleheader. In Philadelphia, the Boston Red Sox celebrated Independence Day by throttling the hometown Athletics twice, 11–2 and 5–2. The first game showed the A's at their defensive worst as they committed the horrendous total of seven errors. Three of them were committed by third baseman Charlie Pick, whose return to the lineup was truly forgettable. Pick now had 25 errors on the season, still ten fewer than shortstop Whitey Witt's 35. Witt, of course, also committed one of the A's fielding gaffes. Boston rolled up 16 hits against local boy George Hesselbacher, scoring three times in the first inning for all the runs they would need. The Red Sox added two more runs in the third inning and three runs in both the eighth and the ninth innings. Every starter in the Boston lineup managed at least one hit. Mack permitted Hesselbacher to go the full nine innings despite the thorough shellacking. Dutch Leonard went the distance for the visitors, allowing just eight hits. One, though, provided the offensive highlight for the Mackmen: Nap Lajoie connected for his second home run of the season in the seventh inning.

The second game of the doubleheader was more closely contested but still ended in a decisive 5–2 Boston victory. Carl Mays allowed just three hits by the home team, although one was a solo home run in the seventh inning by Wally Schang, his second of 1916. Joe Bush was the losing hurler for the A's. He allowed nine hits. This time the Athletics committed a paltry four errors. Three of them were at the hands of newcomer Lee King, who had made seven errors in ten games. King was Mack's shortstop in the second game as Whitey Witt was given the game off. The two losses dropped the Athletics to 17–47 and extended the club's latest losing skein to eight games.

In the July 6 edition of *The Sporting News*, William G. Weart discussed Connie Mack's youth-based initiative at length and how it was not paying immediate dividends. Weart also praised the excellent play he saw from the visiting New York Yankees that put them in front in the chase for the AL pennant. He also gave passing notice to the sudden retirement of A's outfielder Rube Oldring, which he was taking with a large grain of salt.

> More work is being done these days at Shibe Park than at any baseball field in the United States, but the harvest of victories is very small. Every morning manager Mack and captain [Harry] Davis have a large squad of youngsters on the field going through their paces. For two hours there is no let up. Then comes an intermission for lunch and the juveniles go at it again until time for the teams to take the field to practice for the afternoon contest. Shibe Park is a real beehive of activity. Visiting clubs have been gathering in victories, but there is no telling at this time when results will show and the tide will turn from defeat to victory for the home team.
>
> Mack has not yet passed final judgment on any of his 1916 college recruits, for he wants to give every one of them a thorough test. He has been playing [Lee] King, [Harland] Rowe and [Otis] Lawry in the infield, although none of them is up to the mark expected. These youngsters all come from New England colleges and they got out of condition by reason of the fact that they had to take their final examinations during June and then took a little vacation. King appears to be destined for a trial in left field later and he is not really counted as infield material. He is the son of [19th-century MLB pitcher] Silver King, and hails from the Massachusetts Aggies. Rowe and Lawry come from the University of Maine.
>
> There were games last week when the Athletics' infield was comprised entirely of New England youths, with McInnis on first, King or Lawry on second base, King or Witt at shortstop, and Rowe at third base. It is probably a record for a major league team to take the field with its entire infield composed of players who live in the same section of the country. The combined age of the infield that Mack has had performing at Shibe Park recently is 82 years. Probably never before has a manager of a major league team had the courage to put such a youthful quartet together.
>
> Of the youngsters tried out, Lawry, although just getting over an attack of tonsillitis, has made the best showing. Lawry got into the game because [Nap] Lajoie was forced to let up, owing to an infected toe. Lawry impressed the fans and the players the first day he got a chance at second base by his speed, his ground covering ability, and his ease and grace in handling grounders and making throws.
>
> In Mack's opinion, Lawry is a "smart" player. That is, he does not play the game mechanically, but uses good judgment and knows something about inside playing. Lawry came here highly touted. He is not yet proven that he is the fastest man ever seen in baseball, as [his collegiate coach] Monte Cross and others have claimed, but he has shown enough, considering his lack of physical condition to convince the fans that Connie has picked up a youngster of more than ordinary merit.
>
> It looks as though Mack's new infield will be made up of McInnis at first base, Lawry at second base, and King at shortstop, with third base still open. King may be

the youth to land the left field job. There are others coming, though, for tryouts for the positions, but who they are and where they come from manager Mack declines to state.

The young pitchers will probably get a chance to show this week. Jingling [Jing] Johnson, who was a strikeout artist at Ursinus College, got a chance against Boston last week. The Red Sox could not hit his delivery to any great extent, but he was wild and Boston easily won the game. Johnson has been under Mack's eye for about three years and he will get more chances to prove that he is fit for a major league job.

In the meantime Ira Thomas is out scouting. Ira is supposed to be on the lookout for pitchers, as he has charge of the twirling staff of the Athletics. Thomas is a hard man to suit, and a pitcher must show a lot of stuff to cause him to send a favorable report to manager Mack. Where Ira has been looking for talent is a mystery.

The New York Yankees looked very good during their series here last week. Manager [Wild Bill] Donovan has his combination going in great style and both [Frank] Baker and Lee Magee, who were late in starting, hit the ball hard. [Frank] Gilhooley did wonderful work on the base paths, and in one game stole four bases. Donovan not only has a well rounded out aggregation, but he also has a lot of reserve material which may come in handy later on. The Yankees took the lead in the race the first day they were here and they increased it before leaving for Washington.

Another of Mack's players who figured in the World Series splits of the team is no longer on the roster. Rube Oldring has voluntarily given up his job. Rube resigned and then was given his unconditional release. He has been ill and he has taken a dislike to the national game. Oldring is now on a farm in New Jersey. It would not be surprising if he got over his distaste for baseball in a few months, for he threatened to quit last fall and again got the fever in the spring.

Thursday, July 6, saw the return of the Detroit Tigers to Philadelphia. As usual, Tigers center fielder Ty Cobb was in the news. His temper had gotten him into trouble twice in the past week. In a fit of anger during a game in Chicago on June 30, Cobb flung his bat into the grandstand after striking out. A few days earlier, in an act remarkably reminiscent of his infamous 1912 stunt at Hilltop Park in New York City when he beat up a crippled man, Cobb climbed into the grandstand in St. Louis to combat another heckler, although *TSN*'s Chicago correspondent opined that the heckler likely deserved to be rebuked for his nasty comments. AL president Ban Johnson, who was judge, jury, and executioner for all disciplinary matters, suspended Cobb for a few days to let him cool off, but the feisty Georgian was back in the Detroit lineup when his team took the field to begin a series at Shibe Park.

The rest did wonders for Cobb. On this day, Cobb was well behaved and the standout offensive spark plug for the visitors. He got two hits and a walk, stole three bases, and scored three runs in Detroit's relatively easy 9–4 victory over the Mackmen. The Tigers smacked 12 hits off three A's hurlers. Starter Tom Sheehan was rocked for three runs in two innings. The other two Athletics' pitchers who finished the game were youngsters from Massachusetts who were making their MLB debuts. Neither would pitch another game in the big leagues. Michael Driscoll, a right-hander, gave up five runs in five innings and picked up the loss. Walt Whittaker, another righty, mopped up the last two innings, giving up a run. The A's defense was typically horrid. They made six errors, three by catcher Billy Meyer. Charlie Pick committed two blunders and Lee King had the other. Willie Mitchell got the start for Detroit, but he was yanked one out into the third inning. George Cunningham went the rest of the way for the win, his fifth of the season against eight losses. The setback was Philadelphia's ninth in succession.

On Friday, July 7, two more graduates from the A's collegiate talent pool made their MLB debuts. Ralph Mitterling batted seventh and played center field. Marshall (Marsh) Williams pitched two innings of relief. Williams was a biochemistry student from the University of South Carolina. Neither did much to help the struggling Athletics avoid their tenth straight defeat, a 9–2 loss to the Tigers. Detroit pounded 14 hits off A's starter Elmer Myers in seven innings and had a 6–0 lead in the fifth inning before Philadelphia put anything on the scoreboard. One of the Tigers' hits was a rare home run by Ty Cobb, just his second of the season. It was a two-run dinger that opened the scoring in the first inning. George Burns got a homer for the visitors as well, his first of the year. The A's managed ten hits themselves, but had trouble bunching them together for runs. The home side also hit into two double plays. Newcomer Mitterling went 0 for 4 at the plate with a strikeout. In his only defensive chance of the game, Mitterling made an error, one of three Connie Mack's crew committed. Williams did not allow a run but gave up two walks. Harry Coveleski, the 30-year-old, left-handed brother of Cleveland's Stan, went the distance and got his 11th win of the season. He whiffed five A's and walked just one. Philadelphia was now 17–49. With 193 total runs scored, the Athletics were the only MLB team that had not scored at least 200 runs. In contrast, Detroit had scored 309 times. The A's now trailed seventh-place St. Louis by 11 games. It hardly mattered now, but they were a distant 24 games behind the AL-leading New York Yankees.

The Athletics played one of their better games on Saturday, July 8, but still came out on the wrong end of a 3–2 decision to Detroit. George Burns got his second homer in two games in the fifth inning off Jack Nabors to give the visitors a 2–1 lead. Both teams scored in the ninth to end the scoring. Despite striking out six Tigers and walking just one, Nabors extended his personal losing streak to nine games as the A's matched their earlier 11-game losing streak. Bill James went the distance for his second win of the season for Detroit. The two bright spots for on the day for Philadelphia were Red Lanning and Jimmy Walsh, who each got two hits. One of Lanning's hits was a double, his first. Nap Lajoie, the team's elder statesman, slapped a double of his own, his tenth of 1916. Nevertheless, the Athletics reached the 50-loss plateau and now had a winning percentage of just .254.

Next into Shibe Park were the St. Louis Browns, who played a doubleheader versus the A's on Tuesday, July 11. Recent form stayed unchanged as the Browns rolled to an easy 8–3 win in the opener. St. Louis amassed an 8–0 lead after four innings, scoring four runs each off two of Mack's pitching hopefuls: George Hesselbacher and Marsh Williams. Tom Sheehan pitched the final five frames and kept the Browns from administering any further damage. The A's managed another ten-hit effort and scored three times in the third inning off Browns starter Ernie Koob, and rookie Ralph Mitterling had a three-hit game, but it was not nearly enough. For backup catcher Mike Murphy, who appeared in 14 games for the White Elephants in 1916, his final MLB contest was the opening-game loss. Jimmy Walsh, who wasn't even in the lineup, was ejected by plate umpire Clarence (Brick) Owens for "bench jockeying." (Owens, whose astonishing record of causing riots is probably unsurpassed in baseball history, got his nickname after being struck in the head with a brick while umpiring a Missouri Valley League game in Pittsburgh, KS, in 1904. The arbiter said he did not mind the nickname as it was more acceptable than many other pejorative names he had been called.) Connie Mack's belief that his players should always comport themselves as gentlemen apparently had the desired effect. Walsh would be the only A's player to be ejected all season—and it would happen twice in consecutive days. The Athletics' latest losing streak had hit an even dozen.

The faithful in the dwindling Shibe Park crowds got a rare reward in the second contest as Philadelphia finally put one in the win column. Joe Bush pitched a sparkling five-hit shutout in the A's 3–0 victory, but it was not without controversy. St. Louis manager Fielder Jones believed that Walsh's ejection in the first game also disqualified him from the second game. Jones was ejected for his unceasing complaints, and the game was put under protest by the Browns. Small ball won the game for the home team as Connie Mack's club supplemented their six hits with five sacrifice bunts. Four St. Louis hurlers took part in the game, with starter Earl Hamilton assigned the loss. For at least one game, the A's looked like a respectable MLB team, although their desultory campaign was evident in their awful 18–51 record.

A headline in the July 13 edition of *The Sporting News* blared, "Alibis Offered for Mack's Collegians," along with the horribly ungrammatical subheading, "Too Much Exams Put Them to the Bad Physically." William G. Weart was only too happy to make excuses for the lackluster play of his favorite AL team and its saintly manager. He also discussed the details of the odd incident in a Yankees-A's game at Shibe Park two weeks before which resulted in New York manager Wild Bill Donovan being fined and team trainer Jimmy Duggan being suspended by AL president Ban Johnson.

For ten days the fans of this city have been watching Connie Mack's college recruits play in championship games and they have had no reason to become wildly enthused. Defeat after defeat has been chalked up against the Athletics, and up to date, not one of the youngsters tried out by manager Mack has showed form which would cause anyone to believe he will develop into another Eddie Collins, another Jack Barry, or a second Frank Baker. The collegians have not shone in the field and they have not shown that they possess the punch when they go to bat. Nevertheless, it is believed that some of the recruits will yet develop into major league class.

It must be remembered that practically none of them has yet reached the voting age and that none of them ever played even in a minor league, unless he did so under an assumed name. Their youth would indicate that their only violation of the amateur code was in playing for seashore or mountain resort teams during their college days. It must be remembered, too, that Connie was not looking for them to do anything wonderful during the first couple of weeks that they played at Shibe Park. The reason for this was that all of them reported either actually ill, or out of condition, caused by the fact that they had been compelled to forget baseball for a time and take their examinations.

Accidents to men who had been playing all season and the resignation of [Rube] Oldring resulted in manager Mack being compelled to put the boys into the game much sooner than he had anticipated. This has probably resulted in the failure of any of them to play up to his mark. Better things are looked for from them when they get into condition and get over their stage fright. In the meantime Harry Davis has gone out into the underbrush in search of more talent and Ira Thomas has been on the skill hunt for a couple of weeks. Mack has also done some sleuthing on Saturday and Sunday.

While manager Mack said down South during training that it would take him longer to put together his new team than he had figured and he realized that little short of a miracle could give the Athletics a chance to finish better than last, this has been a season of disappointment for the club, barring one flash in the spring when the White Elephants climbed to sixth place. [Actually, they had briefly attained fifth spot in the AL standings.] Connie could not figure on [Rube] Oldring doing such poor work and then quitting when he needed his services most. Neither could he have anticipated Stuffy McInnis, who had always batted over the .300 mark, falling down and hitting at a .180 clip. Connie also counted upon [pitchers] Rube Bressler and Weldon Wyckoff doing good work.

The failure of these four players cut deep into Connie's plans and expectations for the 1916 season. There is no sign of gloom about the White Elephants' camp, however. Nearly everyone is hustling all the time. Connie has uncovered a splendid backstop in Billy Meyer, while Lawton [Whitey] Witt, a raw recruit without minor league experience, who was shoved from third base to shortstop, has developed in good style. Then Connie showed that he has another great pitcher in Elmer Myers. The latter has lost a lot of games, but it must be remembered that he has not got the old machine to help him out.

One or more new players are introduced to the public nearly every day. Last Friday Connie sent in a lad named [Marsh] Williams from the University of South Carolina to twirl the last two innings against the Tigers. Not a hit was made off the southerner in two innings and his work was the most impressive done by any of the twirlers tried out by the Athletics this season. Like all the pitchers who get a chance nowadays with the White Elephants, Williams is a right-hander and he is a big fellow.

During the visit of the New York Yankees here [on June 28] there was an incident out of the ordinary which resulted in manager [Wild Bill] Donovan being fined $100, and the trainer of the Yankees, Jimmy Duggan, being suspended. A fan in the upper deck of the grandstand yelled remarks at Donovan and called Wild Bill a "park sparrow." The fan evidently stung Donovan with some of the remarks during an inning in which the Athletics scored four runs and took the lead.

Donovan is said to have instructed Duggan to go into the upper deck and make the fan keep quiet. Duggan did so, putting his hand over the rooter's mouth and acting as if he intended to choke the man. An usher dragged Duggan away from the fan, who later accepted an invitation from the New York team's bench to come downstairs and get what was coming to him. Donovan and two other players of the New York team left the field and entered the grandstand to meet him. The fan explained to Donovan that he formerly played with Wild Bill in Fairmount Park here and that he was merely kidding him. Duggan apologized to the fan for his rough treatment, but the latter was plenty sore and was dead willing to have it out with the New York team's trainer.

An old-timer like Donovan certainly deserved censure for paying any attention to the fan's remarks, and it is not likely that Bill would have done so but for the fact that the Athletics for a few minutes made the Yankees look like a bunch of "lot angels."

On Wednesday, July 12, the Browns and Athletics met for another doubleheader at Shibe Park for the second day in a row. This time the visitors from St. Louis won both games. The opener was a laugher, as the Browns parlayed a big first inning into a comfortable 8–3 victory. Newcomer George Hesselbacher got the nod from Mack in the first game. He was tagged for three quick runs, courtesy of a three-run blast off the bat of George Sisler, and did not make it to the second inning. Mack replaced Hesselbacher with Marsh Williams, who pitched the final eight innings and allowed five more St. Louis runs. Philadelphia's defense again proved substandard, committing four errors. Three were made by Otis Lawry at second base. Eddie Plank, not quite the pitcher he was during the A's glory days, got the win for the Browns despite allowing ten Philadelphia hits.

The second game simply got away from the home side. The Athletics led 1–0 heading into the ninth inning, only to see the Browns tie the score and then win 2–1 in ten innings. Elmer Myers was the tough-luck loser. Two errors, including one by Whitey Witt, who was back at shortstop, and one by Myers himself proved critical. The game featured what appeared to be a Philadelphia triple play on an attempted bunt by St. Louis' George Sisler. However, base umpire Brick Owens ruled that only two men were retired on the play, turning it into a rare 2–8–6 twin killing (catcher Meyer to center fielder Mitterling to shortstop Witt). Right fielder Jimmy Walsh, who had been ejected during the previous day's doubleheader by Owens, was enraged at the call. He gave Owens an earful, and was promptly given the thumb by the arbiter. Dave Davenport started the game for the Browns, went seven innings, and was on the hook for the loss until the ninth-inning rally. Earl Hamilton pitched three shutout innings to get his second win of 1916. Myers dropped to 8–10. The Athletics were now 18–53, a full 13 games out of seventh place. The Browns, at 34–43, were the only other AL team under .500.

The Athletics' five-game series with the Browns concluded on Thursday, July 13. The visitors from St. Louis continued their winning ways with a 7–3 triumph. The A's were once again their own worst enemies, making four errors. Offensively they mustered only five hits. Jack Nabors lost his ninth decision in a row, although he gave up just two runs in five innings. Tom Sheehan surrendered three runs in just one inning of relief. George Hesselbacher finished things up for the Athletics with three innings of relief in which he gave up two runs. In an interesting tidbit of strategy, Connie Mack sent in Elmer Myers to pinch-hit for Nabors in the bottom of the fifth inning, and Myers responded with a base hit (although he did not score). Mack's punchless college boys could have taken batting lessons from pitcher-turned-pinch-hitter Myers as they were a combined 0 for 14 at the plate. Carl Weilman, a huge 6'5" lefty, got the complete-game win for the Browns and was now 10–10 on the season. Third baseman Charlie Pick had to leave early in the game after being spiked. Harland Rowe replaced him at the keystone sack. Connie Mack was probably neither amused nor impressed when he heard about the only MLB player transaction of July 13: Recently retired Athletics outfielder Rube Oldring, as predicted by William G. Weart in the pages of *The Sporting News*, suddenly unretired when the contending New York Yankees offered him a free-agent contract.

The Chicago White Sox arrived in Philadelphia on Saturday, July 15, for a series at Shibe Park. The White Sox manufactured four runs on seven hits, more than enough to hand the discouraged A's another loss, this time 4–1. The White Sox scored single runs in the first, second, third, and fifth innings. Four sacrifice bunts augmented the Chicago offense, which was limited to two doubles and five singles off Tom Sheehan, now 1–8, who went the distance for the loss. Only three of the White Sox runs were earned as Whitey Witt's 38th error of the season factored into the scoring. Chicago right-hander Jim Scott proved tough to figure out. He struck out ten Mackmen. The Athletics only managed only four hits, all singles, two of them by Wally Schang. Schang also drove in Witt with the A's only run in the first inning. Mack's college boys went a combined 0 for 10 at the plate, and after dropping the second game of a doubleheader, 1–0, the Athletics sunk to 18–56–1, 25 games behind the front-running New York Yankees.

Years later Tom Sheehan recalled an incident from what must have been the July 15 game at Shibe Park versus the White Sox, as it was the first time he pitched to Doc Carroll. (Sheehan misremembered it as a game in New York's Polo Grounds versus the Yankees.) Nevertheless, the incident is worth repeating, despite its inaccuracies, as it illustrated the A's difficulties in the catching position in 1916.

> Once we were playing the Yankees at the Polo Grounds and I'm pitching. [Val] Picinich warms me up, but as the first hitter steps in, Val goes back to the bench and takes off the tools.
>
> Another guy comes out, a guy I've never seen. He comes out to the mound and says, "My name is Carroll. I'm the catcher. What are your signs?" I tell him not to confuse me and to get the heck back there and catch. He stuck around for about a week and nobody ever saw him again.[1]

With no baseball permitted in Philadelphia on Sunday, and rain washing out Monday's game, the White Sox and Athletics played a doubleheader on Tuesday, July 18, to make up for their inactivity. In the opener, Philadelphia scored two runs in the bottom of the first inning off Eddie Cicotte for a 2–0 lead, but nothing afterwards as Chicago rolled to a 9–2 triumph. Most of the damage came late in the game. Red Lanning, one of Mack's rookie hopefuls, was given his first pitching assignment and fared not too badly even though he got the loss. He gave up three runs in five innings, although only two were earned. Jack Nabors gave up six runs in the final four innings. Hoping to exploit Otis Lawry's speed, Mack batted him first and stationed him at second base, shifting Nap Lajoie to first base. Lawry got two of the A's seven hits, but stole no bases. The most memorable moment of the game was a horrendous one. Wally Schang, the A's first-string catcher who was fleet of foot enough to play the outfield occasionally when called upon by Mack to do so, was stationed in left field. Midway through the game, Shoeless Joe Jackson hit a foul fly ball near the concrete wall of the grandstand. Schang made a running catch but was apparently oblivious to the wall he was approaching. He crashed headlong into the barrier, breaking his jaw and knocking himself senseless. The collision elicited shrieks and groans from the Shibe Park patrons. Players from both teams were enlisted to haul the unconscious Schang to the Athletics' clubhouse. The better part of half an hour elapsed before he regained his senses. Ralph Mitterling replaced the woozy Schang in left field. Schang, one of the A's best hitters and one of the few contented veterans remaining from the team's pennant years, would be absent from the Athletics' lineup for a month.

The second game of the twin bill was typically frustrating for Philadelphia. Elmer Myers struck out ten White Sox and walked none, but still lost 3–2, all the runs being unearned thanks to four A's errors. Lajoie and Lawry each made a defensive gaffe. Chicago scored one run in the fourth inning and two more in the sixth. Philadelphia did not make a dent on the score sheet until the bottom of the ninth inning—enduring a streak of 16 scoreless innings in the course of the doubleheader—when they scored twice to raise the hopes of the Shibe Park faithful. Jim Scott was fit enough to throw another complete game for the White Sox, his second of the series. At the mathematical halfway point of the season, the A's were 18–58 (with one tie game). They had scored just 213 runs—2.77 per game. The White Elephants' run total was 63 fewer than the next lowest-scoring AL team, the Boston Red Sox, who were presently residing in second place with a 46–35 record.

William G. Weart's lengthy report in the July 20 edition of *The Sporting News* focused on how graciously the A's and their manager were accepting loss after loss during the horrendous season—and how badly some of the visiting AL managers behaved when the expected win at Shibe Park either did not materialize or was much more difficult to obtain than anticipated. Weart also apportioned space to grumble about the should-have-been triple play versus the Browns on July 12 that was denied by umpire Brick Owens, and questioned the arbiter's general abilities to officiate in the AL. The correspondent also discussed the progress of Mack's collegians and took a verbal shot at the carpetbagging Rube Oldring's retirement and unsurprising quick reversal that put him into the lineup of the pennant-contending New York Yankees.

> It's an awful, awful thing to be a loser! With the exception of one period of prosperity, lasting for about three weeks, the Athletics have been a regular football for the other teams of the American League this year. They have lost an average of three games out of four and not one member of the Athletics' outfit, whether owner or player, has made the slightest complaint. Team after team has been coming here [Shibe Park] lately and winning every game of a series. Occasionally the Athletics have looked as though they were going to win a game. Yet some break or piece of bad playing caused the opposition to nose out a winner. Still no complaint by the Athletics.
>
> The same cannot be said of the managers of the other teams. It looks as though every manager has counted each game his club is scheduled to play the Athletics as a victory in advance of the game being played and cannot bear the thought he might be beaten. One day, Bill Donovan, manager of the New York Yankees, sent the trainer of his team into the grandstand to thrash a man who dared to root for the Athletics and tried at the same time to get the goat of Wild Bill and his players.
>
> What probably incensed Donovan more than anything else was the fact that the White Elephants scored four runs in one inning and looked like a winner.
>
> Last week [Fielder] Jones brought the St. Louis Browns here for a series of five games. Fielder's team got four victories. The Athletics won one game, and if Jones can have his way, that victory will be taken from the home club. As the Athletics only had about three victories for about six weeks of play, it certainly would be tough luck to have that one taken away from them. Here is Jones' point and the one on which he based his protest of the game:
>
> In the first game of a doubleheader, Jimmy Walsh, who was not in the contest, was sent off the Athletics' bench by Umpire Owens [for bench jockeying]. When the

batting order was announced for the second game, Walsh was slated to play right field. Jones claimed Walsh was out for the afternoon, but Umpire Connolly ruled that Jimmy had a right to play in the second contest. Jones argued the point so vigorously that he was sent off the field. Then the Athletics, with Walsh playing, went out and beat St. Louis 3–0. That night Jones protested the game. According to manager Mack, the Browns' manager has not the slightest chance to get away with the claim.

The next day another doubleheader was played and the Athletics pulled off a triple play on [George] Sisler's bunted fly to Meyer. Umpire Owens, however, got badly mixed up over the play and only allowed a double play. There was a big argument during which Jimmy Walsh was sent off the field by Umpire Owens and the next day Jimmy got notice of an indefinite suspension. As a matter of fact, Umpire Owens should have gotten about 30 days from Ban Johnson.

Manager Mack continues to try out college players and to investigate reports of his scouts who have been touring the South and the New England states. Connie has picked up some likely looking lads this year, but they need more seasoning. Where they have failed to shine particularly is at bat. The lads stand up well to the plate and hit fairly good [sic], but they have not been getting the ball in safe territory. The reason is they have been looking at a far better brand of pitching than they have been accustomed to. It will take considerable time for them to pick up in this department.

Owing to injuries and illness of players, Connie has been sending in the youngsters and it begins to look as though he had some fine prospects in [Otis] Lawry, a second baseman, and [Lee] King and [Ralph] Mitterling, outfielders. [Whitey] Witt is improving fast at shortstop and will be up to the major league standard next spring, if not before the present season is over.

[Charlie] Pick was badly spiked by a St. Louis runner last week and he will probably be out of the game for four weeks. [Stuffy] McInnis was given permission last week to go to his home in Gloucester, MA as he was suffering from a charley horse. Stuffy will not report for several days.

There was no surprise when Rube Oldring consented to return to baseball after a retirement of less than three weeks. Rube is now the world's champion retirer. He retired last winter, got a change of heart, and came back last spring. He resigned late in June, and the fifteenth of the month of July found him on the payroll of the New York Yankees. With a chance to get into the World Series money, Oldring will probably put more heart into his playing than he did last year or this season. That World Series check is a wonderful lure. Mack's players from 1910 to 1914 inclusive got so many such checks that they thought no one else ever had a right to aspire to one, much less get one in his possession.

On Wednesday, July 19, the Cleveland Indians were the next AL outfit to visit the reeling Athletics at Shibe Park. Indians manager Lee Fohl was aghast at the poorly kept playing field, especially the grass which had gone quite a spell since a groundskeeper last mowed it. "The Indians arrived in Philadelphia to find the grass in the infield grown to a length of three or four inches, thus slowing the diamond considerably," wrote Henry P. Edwards, Cleveland's correspondent for *The Sporting News*, in the July 27 edition. Fohl was so miffed by Shibe Park's lack of upkeep that he sent a telegram to AL president Ban Johnson to complain about it. When the grass still wasn't mowed by the third game of the series, Indians first baseman Chick Gandil took matters into his own hands. During the Indians' pregame warmup, he hid a ball in the long infield grass about six feet in front of first base. At an opportune moment in the home half of *the seventh inning*, Gandil asked for time, dramatically searched through the high grass, retrieved the ball, and tossed it with a grin to surprised base umpire Billy Evans. "It was such a rich joke," declared Edwards, "that Connie Mack had the first good laugh he has had in two years." Shibe Park's greensward was neatly mowed before the next day's game.

To no one's surprise, the Indians, contenders for the AL pennant, romped to an easy 12–5 win in the first game, powered by an even dozen hits. Although Cleveland did not require any extra assistance from the home team, the A's helped their guest by committing four errors. Three of them were blunders by shortstop Whitey Witt, who now had 41 on the season. Witt attempted to make good on his defensive miscues by hitting two triples. (Typical of the inability of the Athletics to muster much meaningful offense, Witt was stranded at third base twice.) George Hesselbacher picked up his fourth loss of the year for the A's. In going the full nine innings, eight of the 12 runs that Hesselbacher surrendered were earned. It was Hesselbacher's MLB swansong; he never again appeared in a big league box score. By now Connie Mack was of the mind that his starters should go the full nine innings in lopsided games regardless of the severity of the beating they were taking. After all, the hurlers who had emerged from the A's bullpen had rarely shone in 1916. Jim Bagby went the distance for the victors from Cleveland. Jack Graney homered for the winners, who were behind 3–1 after two innings.

The first of two games between Cleveland and Philadelphia on Thursday, July 20, was much more competitive than the previous day's encounter. This time Cleveland managed only eight hits, all of them singles, but a three-run second inning was decisive in the Tribe's 4–2 win over the Mackmen. Tom Sheehan lasted eight innings before being yanked for a pinch-hitter. All four runs were charged to Sheehan as Elmer Myers recorded a perfect ninth inning for the home team. Stuffy McInnis, recently back in the lineup after being sidelined with a debilitating charley horse, and newcomer Lee McElwee both got two hits for the home team in a losing effort. Altogether Philadelphia managed just six safeties, all singles, off Cleveland right-hander Fred Beebe, who was in the final year of an MLB career that began in 1906. In what was becoming almost a daily occurrence, shortstop Whitey Witt made his 42nd error of the season. The loss was the 60th of 1916 for the woebegone Athletics.

The second game of the doubleheader provided a rare July bright spot for the Athletics—a 2–0 victory over Cleveland. Philadelphia got both of their runs in the bottom of the sixth inning. Amos Strunk's double was the key blow for the White Elephants. Joe Bush was terrific on the mound for the A's, allowing just four hits and a solitary base on balls in the complete game. The much-needed win was Bush's ninth against 14 losses. Grover Lowdermilk went seven innings in the loss for the visitors. Despite the triumph, Philadelphia was now 19–60. They were 27.5 games out of first place and, more embarrassingly, 15 games behind seventh-place St. Louis.

Normalcy returned to Shibe Park on Friday, July 21, as Cleveland won handily, 7–2. Jack Nabors did not have much on his pitches to puzzle the Indians' hitters. Cleveland recorded 12 hits, all singles, but also benefitted from three errors, three walks, a hit batsman, and a wild pitch. Cleveland opened up a 6–1 lead after the top of the third inning and cruised home from that point. Philadelphia got seven hits, but their rallies were routinely squelched by three Cleveland double plays, all of them beginning with a ground ball to pitcher Fritz Coumbe, then a throw to shortstop Bill Wambsganss, then a relay toss to first baseman Chick Gandil. Coumbe was 6–4 on the season. Nabors dropped to 1–11. He had lost ten consecutive decisions since after starting the season 1–1. Ralph Mitterling, one of Mack's collegians, was released after the game after going 0 for 3 with a strikeout. He would never play another MLB game. The A's were now 19–61.

Rain and travel meant the A's got a few days off to lick their wounds, but the rest seemingly did no good when they resumed AL play in St. Louis on Tuesday, July 25. The Browns cruised to an 8–3 win, scoring six times in the second inning. All six runs were added to the ledger of Red Lanning, who lasted just 1⅓ innings, allowing five hits, three walks and a hit batsman, before manager Mack had seen enough and gave him the hook. Tom Sheehan came in for a very long relief stint—6⅔ innings—and allowed just two more St. Louis runs. Six Browns had multiple-hit games. Ward Miller had a double, a triple, and three RBI. Veteran Nap Lajoie stroked three singles for the vanquished A's, who did muster ten hits but could not overcome a daunting eight-run deficit after five innings. The Athletics were suddenly without the services of catcher Billy Meyer, who had proven to be a competent presence behind the plate. He had taken ill while riding on the team's train and required an appendectomy upon the A's arrival in St. Louis. Abdominal surgery being what it was in 1916, Meyer was lost for the rest of the season. Since catchers were in short supply with Wally Schang and Meyer both sidelined, another new face entered the Athletics' lineup late in the game, almost out of necessity. Nineteen-year-old Val Picinich replaced collegian Doc Carroll as catcher and recorded an assist and a putout in his abbreviated MLB debut. Picinich was a native New Yorker who was attending school in Maine. He would prove to be the most enduring of Mack's collegiate bunch. Picinich would play in the majors until 1933, although only in 1916 and 1917 as a member of Connie Mack's squad. Nevertheless, he would catch the game that was easily the highlight of the 1916 A's season.

In the July 27 edition of *The Sporting News*, William G. Weart apportioned little space in his column disseminating the new run of disheartening losses by the Athletics. Instead he focused on the regress and progress of Mack's collegiate prospect Lee McElwee, the serious and frightening injury suffered by reliable Wally Schang on July 18, and the unusually long Shibe Park grass that irked Cleveland's manager Lee Fohl to no end. Weart also managed to get in a subtle shot at Rube Oldring, although the departed Rube was not specifically mentioned.

The long home stay of the White Elephants was a disastrous one in the matter of games won, the Mackmen only being able to beat two teams. These were St. Louis and Cleveland and each time Joe Bush shut out the opposing combination. Manager Fielder Jones of the Browns protested the game in which his team was beaten, but nothing has been heard from that protest.

There was not the progress made in the development of the Athletics that had been hoped for during the month the team was at home. Manager Mack kept shifting the players around, no matter how good or how poor they looked in any position. This policy bore fruit in one instance. This was the case of [Lee] McElwee, a big left-handed hitter from Bowdoin College. McElwee did not look good at third base when first tried there. Then he was sent to first base where he looked worse.

Next McElwee was given a chance to watch a few games from the bench. Last week the lad was again sent to third base. He immediately began to make a decided impression. He has been hitting the ball hard and fielding in good style. During the week McElwee looked like the best third baseman Connie Mack has had since Frank Baker. Connie has tried out more than a dozen players there and the problem will be solved if McElwee's recent showing is not a flash.

McInnis returned to the game last week after a long layoff caused by a charley horse. The rest did McInnis a lot of good and certainly improved his batting eye. He has been hitting around the .500 mark since his return, and his slugging has improved the team in a department in which it has been very weak all season.

Before Stuffy got back, however, Wally Schang met with another serious injury. Schang was out of the game for a long time in the spring and he is again lost to the team. At that Wally is lucky that he is living. The accident occurred in a [July 18] game with the Chicago White Sox. In going after a foul fly off [Shoeless Joe] Jackson's bat, Schang ran close to the cement wall in front of the left field pavilion. Just as he clutched the ball he stumbled and plunged against the cement wall. He struck his head and shoulder and was rendered unconscious. Schang was carried off the field by players of the two teams and he did not regain consciousness for fully 20 minutes. He escaped with a broken jaw, a sore head, and a bruised shoulder.

Wally will not be able to return to the game until the Athletics return from their western trip. As he was one of the most dependable hitters on the team, his loss has been severely felt. Schang is one of the few members of Mack's old champions who gave the club the best that was in him every day of the week. He played just as hard for the team when it was last as when it was first and the thought that there was no

World Series check in sight never made him slow up or threaten to retire from the game.

One of the most unique protests on record occurred and was sent to president Ban Johnson of the American League by manager [Lee] Fohl of Cleveland when the Indians were here. Fohl complained that the grass at Shibe Park was too long and he wired Ban asking that he have the grass cut. The grass was probably longer than ever seen at a major league park, but manager Mack said he could not have it cut until the team went away, because he wanted his young players and not his groundskeepers on the playing field every minute possible while the team was at home.

On Wednesday, July 26, in the first game of a doubleheader, the A's mounted a ten-hit assault against St. Louis' Carl Weilman but were still shut out, 5–0. Elmer Myers gave up five runs on six hits in going the distance for the loss. (His 8–12 record, though not great, still qualified him as an ace on the A's staff in this season of few successes.) Browns catcher Hank Severeid got three of the home team's hits. Myers allowed six walks. Two of them were to veteran Browns third baseman Jimmy Austin, who scored two runs without getting a hit. Athletics catcher Val Picinich, in his second MLB game, got two hits. He also was the pivot man in a nifty 3–2–3 double play he turned with first baseman Stuffy McInnis. Weilman, who raised his record to 12–11, generated many ground-ball outs as first baseman George Sisler had 12 putouts.

The second game of the twin bill was a 5–1 win for the hometown Browns. St. Louis carried a five-run lead into the seventh inning before the A's scored their first run of the day. It was scored by relief pitcher Red Lanning, who was called upon by Connie Mack for an extra long outing. Joe Bush was pulled after facing five batters in one inning, allowing two walks, a hit and a wild pitch and falling behind, 2–0. Meanwhile Browns starter Dave Davenport went the distance and permitted just six Athletics hits. A's catcher Doc Carroll, who committed two passed balls, went 1-for-3 before being lifted for a pinch-hitter in the ninth inning. It was Carroll's last game in the majors as afterward he informed Connie Mack that professional baseball was not to his liking. The staggering Athletics, losers of four straight games, were 45 games under .500 at 19–64. They had scored 228 runs thus far while their opponents had scored 430 times. Both figures were MLB worsts by a considerable margin.

The A's battled well in the Thursday, July 27, game at St. Louis's Sportsman's Park but still came up a run short in a 3–2 loss. Jack Nabors continued to be the A's hard-luck loser. This time the Browns waited until the bottom of the eighth inning to score twice and edge into the lead after Philadelphia had taken a 2–1 lead in the top of the eighth. On paper, the A's deserved to win, having outhit the home club, 11–6. Every Athletic in the starting lineup excluding rookie catcher Val Picinich and pitcher Nabors got at least one hit. In contrast, St. Louis managed just six base hits, although they certainly benefitted from the five bases on balls Nabors presented to them. Earl Hamilton lingered around long enough to get credit for the St. Louis win. Bob Groom retired the Athletics on three strikeouts in the ninth inning, but he also allowed two hits to make things interesting.

The following game, played on Friday, July 28, was only in doubt in the last inning. Until the final frame, Connie Mack's crew looked like a thoroughly beaten outfit. St. Louis won, 8–6, with the A's scoring four times in the ninth to give the appearance of respectability. Bob Groom struggled to hold onto the win. Groom held the AL record of losing 19 straight decisions, compiled in 1909 when he was a Washington Senator. With his lead eroding to the point of danger, Groom gave way to Ernie Koob, who faced three A's before getting the final out. Tom Sheehan was permitted by Mack to go the distance to lose his tenth game of 1916 despite falling behind 6–0 after two innings. Five Athletics' errors hurt the visitors' cause. Two came at the hands of shortstop Whitey Witt, who now had an unsightly 48 for the season. The A's once again outhit their hosts, but it mattered little. St. Louis frolicked on the base paths, stealing five bags off Mack's Sheehan-Picinich battery. Burt Shotton was the offensive star for the winners, stealing two bases, getting two hits, and scoring three runs. Philadelphia, now burdened with a sixth consecutive loss, was 19–66.

To make up for their washed-out series earlier in the season, Saturday, July 29, brought an A's-White Sox doubleheader at Comiskey Park. The White Sox added more distress to the A's dismal July with a fairly easy sweep. Game one went 6–1 to the home team. Five White Sox runs in the first three innings broke things open early. Elmer Myers went the distance, but only one of the six runs he allowed was earned. Five more Athletics' errors plagued the team. In contrast, Chicago's Red Faber allowed the same number of hits as Myers but had solid defense behind him. The White Sox committed no errors. Jimmy Walsh and Amos Strunk each contributed two hits to the A's losing effort.

The second game, a 6–4 White Sox triumph, was closer thanks to a late A's rally that fell short. Again the White Sox got off to a quick start and held a 6–1 lead going into the top of the ninth. Triples by Joe Jackson and Happy Felsch powered the Chicago offense. Jackson scored three of the six White Sox runs. Joe Bush could not blame the A's defense for letting him down. The Athletics committed no errors—a rarity this season. Bush pitched the full eight innings and was replaced in the ninth by an unusual pinch-hitter: coach Harry Davis! He came off the bench for a cameo appearance, and drew a base on balls. It was his only appearance of 1916 as a player. Catcher Ray Haley, on loan from Boston to help the A's fill their prominent catching void, got a hit and scored a run. Chicago starter Joe Benz seemingly had things in command until faltering in the top of the ninth inning. With one out, reliever Ewell (Reb) Russell made the situation worse for the home team by issuing three walks to the four batters he faced in one-third of an inning. Eddie Cicotte needed to be summoned to quell the upstart Athletics. He retired the final A's batter, Jimmy Walsh, with a strikeout to preserve the White Sox victory. Philadelphia had now lost eight straight games and had a 19–68 record for a miserable winning percentage of .218. Averaging just 2.7 runs scored per game, the Athletics were 22.5 games in arrears of the seventh-place St. Louis Browns.

Sunday baseball was perfectly legal in the Windy City, so the White Sox and A's contested another doubleheader on July 30 to help make up for the early-season rainouts. Chicago won both games handily. In the first game the A's scored a run in the first inning and proceeded to lose, 10–1. With manager Mack showing little inclination to employ a reliever, Red Lanning was forced to endure a 19-hit barrage for the full eight innings. One of the hits was a two-run homer smacked by Happy Felsch in the third inning that increased the White Sox advantage to 7–1. Stuffy McInnis got three of the A's seven hits off Eddie Cicotte. The White Sox also discouraged the Athletics by turning three double plays. The game marked the major league debut of Charlie Grimm, who played left field for the Athletics and went 0 for 3 at the plate with a walk and a strikeout. It was the beginning of a solid 20-year playing career for a man who would go on to greater fame as a very capable MLB manager.

The second game was competitive for a while. The White Sox held onto a 1–0 lead until the bottom of the sixth, when they added six runs to assume an insurmountable 7–0 lead, which is how the game ended. Joe Jackson belted a three-run homer in the fateful frame. Marsh Williams, one of Connie Mack's touted collegians, went the distance for the loss. Mellie Wolfgang, a diminutive right-hander, picked up the shutout, harmlessly scattering seven A's hits and two walks along the way. Stuffy McInnis was the busiest of the Athletics, getting two hits and making 14 putouts at first base. Philadelphia failed to score in the final 17 innings of the doubleheader. Their losing streak was now at ten and their season's record was an appalling 19–70. They were 32 games behind the front-running Boston Red Sox.

July mercifully came to an end for Connie Mack's club with a single game at Comiskey Park on Monday, July 31. It was an extra-inning battle in which the White Sox eventually prevailed, 4–3, thanks to an unearned run off reliever Joe Bush in the decisive 11th inning. Tom Sheehan pitched decently for the Mackmen for the first seven innings, although he served up a home run ball to Happy Felsch in the fourth inning with a runner on base. Chicago took a 3–0 lead into the top of the eighth inning, meaning that the visitors had failed to score a run in 24 consecutive frames. The A's finally showed some offensive spark by leveling the score 3–3, but succumbed three innings later. Pinch-hitter Jack Fournier's single drove in pinch-runner Ray Schalk with the game-winning run with two outs in the home half of the 11th inning. Starter Lefty Williams went 7⅓ innings for Chicago before giving way to reliever Red Faber. The latter was credited with the win, his tenth of the season. Joe Bush, somewhat unluckily, was now 9–17. Nap Lajoie hit his first triple of 1916, but he also made an error. Shortstop Whitey Witt's seasonal error total was now at an even and ugly 50.

The Philadelphia Athletics had experienced a horribly bad July—quite possibly the worst month ever endured by an MLB team. Of the 30 games they played in July, they won just two of them while dropping 28. Even the awful 1899 Cleveland Spiders lost only 27 games in their worst calendar month. The end of the month saw the Mackmen locked in the midst of an awful 11-game losing streak. They were mired in the AL cellar with a 19–71 record with even the seventh-place St. Louis Browns, who were hovering close to the .500 mark, opening up a huge gap between the two teams. Entering August, the Athletics' winning percentage was an abysmal .211. Three pitchers on the club (Myers, Sheehan and Nabors) had the second-, third-, and fourth-worst ERAs in the AL. Bush and Myers were one-two in the AL in losses. Nap Lajoie was suddenly showing this his advancing age did matter. His .266 on-base percentage was the second-worst in the league. Inexperience, injuries, ineptitude, and just plain bad baseball had turned the A's 1916 season into an utter catastrophe. Connie Mack could only hope for better things for his lackluster White Elephants as they resolutely played out the string in the remaining two months of the nightmarish season, even though they really had nothing to play for but pride.

August: The "Little Tonic Team of Baseball" Rises from Its Nadir

With the Athletics entering August deep in the throes of another horrendous losing streak, even the optimistic baseball weekly, *The Sporting News*, in its August 3 edition, was forced to concede the obvious: Manager Connie Mack's much heralded, youth-oriented focus on raw collegiate players had been a spectacular bust. For the final two months of the season, as correspondent William G. Weart declared, the A's would rely on minor league professionals to fill the team's needs. "Connie Falls Back on Minor Leaguers" shouted a headline in *The Sporting News*, with the accompanying subheading "Amateurs and Collegians Fail to Aid in His Plans." Weart also delved into the Athletics' dearth of experienced catchers and openly pitied them for the glut of doubleheaders they had to play in Chicago to make up for June's rainouts.

> Manager Mack of the Athletics is now getting ready to experiment with his third class of recruits for 1916. The first two classes did not yield much, considering the many vacancies that Connie has to fill, but in an ordinary year that crop would be fairly satisfactory. Practically all of the scores of boys from amateur and semi-pro teams who had tryouts at Shibe Park failed to make good. Then came the second class, the collegians, who had been highly touted. Few of these were promising enough to keep on the list and some went back home of their own free will, confident that the major league was too classy for them.
>
> Now manager Mack, Harry Davis, Ira Thomas, and Pat Flaherty, the former southpaw pitcher, are combing the small leagues in search of new material. What they have been finding is not known and probably the secrets will be well guarded until time for Connie to pull the strings and bring youngsters into the White Elephant fold.
>
> One player who has been added to the list, though, is Ray Haley, a catcher of the Buffalo team in the International League. Connie has been in sore straits for a backstop for several days. Following the injury to Wally Schang, there came the illness of Billy Meyer, who had been doing the bulk of the catching this year. Meyer was taken sick on the way to St. Louis and he was operated upon there for appendicitis. He will be lost to the club for several weeks.
>
> This left Mack with only [Doc] Carroll and [Val] Picinich to work behind the

bat, neither with any sort of real experience. To cap it all, Carroll concluded that he didn't want any more of professional ball and decided to retire. Haley had been sent to Buffalo by the Red Sox. [Boston owner Joe Lannin], sympathetic to Connie's predicament, offered to recall him and let the Athletics have him in their emergency.

The Athletics started their western tip with five losses at St. Louis, although they gave the Browns a scare in two of those contests. In nearly every game they outhit the Browns, but the same old story was in evidence. The players could not make safeties with runners on the bases.

The White Elephants are now in Chicago where they are trying to make up for the long rest of four days there in June by playing a bunch of doubleheaders, though it would seem that one game a day is all a charitable world should ask of them.

August started out the same way July had ended: two more losses in a doubleheader for the struggling Athletics at Comiskey Park on Tuesday, August 1. In the first game, the White Sox prevailed, 3–0. Jack Nabors continued to get little help offensively or defensively. He went the distance, allowing nine hits, walking just one Chicago batter, and surrendering only one earned run. Yet he still was tagged with his 12th straight loss and now possessed a miserable 1–13 record. The A's could muster only six hits, all singles, off Chicago's Reb Russell. Two middle-infield errors from Nap Lajoie and Whitey Witt extended White Sox rallies and ultimately hurt the anemic A's chances of winning.

In the second game, it was the White Sox who blundered frequently, committing four errors. Still the home team prevailed, 3–2, in a squeaker. Athletics hurler Elmer Myers tried to help his own cause with a 2-for-4 day at the plate, but it was not enough. Six walks augmented the seven singles the White Sox produced. A two-run Chicago fifth inning and a single run in the sixth were enough for the win. Dave Danforth got the win in relief of Jim Scott, who would later become a National League umpire. The pitiful Athletics had now lost 13 straight games—a skein that surpassed their earlier 11-game winless streak—and were 19–73. By comparison, the last-place team in the NL, the Cincinnati Reds, had won twice as many games as the A's.

Philadelphia left Chicago winless in eight attempts at Comiskey Park after dropping an 8–2 decision to the White Sox on Wednesday, August 2. The A's actually led 2–0 before falling apart. Jing Johnson took the two-run edge into the fourth inning before getting roughed up for the tying tallies. Marsh Williams entered the game in the fifth inning and was rudely battered about by the home team. In two innings of work, Williams faced 12 White Sox batters and gave up five runs, six hits and a walk. Red Lanning mopped up the last two innings and gave up one more run. All told, the White Sox connected for 13 hits to the A's seven. Chicago's sound defense turned three double plays to help Joe Benz get the win in relief of Eddie Cicotte. It was the 14th consecutive loss for the lowly Athletics. Eight of those losses had occurred in the doubleheader festival at Comiskey Park. The winless drought in one series was believed to be a dubious

MLB record. George S. Robbins, Chicago's correspondent for *The Sporting News*, took pity on the A's widely beloved manager in the August 10 edition, blaming the Athletics' obvious woes on the team's inability to pick up quality players from other MLB clubs or sign any of those who had returned from the defunct Federal League.

> Connie Mack has benefitted from none of these sources. Mack has helped build up several of his competitors and is out to compete with teams he strengthened. That his team is outclassed is no cause for hurling invectives at this wonderful developer of diamond talent. Give him time. Had the Federal League remained in business and had some of the deals not been put over that were consummated in the last year or so, Connie Mack might probably be leading the league in which he is now managing a trailer.
>
> The White Sox cleaned up the entire series of eight games on the Philadelphia Athletics and the poor showing of the Mackmen gave certain critics occasion to lambast Mack and his team. They declare that Mack should be panned brown for foisting such a club on the baseball public. The writer can't see his way clear to agree with those critics. In all the fields of sport there isn't a leader for whom the writer has more respect or admiration than for Mack. Those who assail Mack for the lack of class of his ball club are simply ignorant of conditions in baseball. They indict themselves.

Thursday, August 3, was the beginning of an Athletics-Indians series at Cleveland's tiny Dunn Park. The change in location and the hitter-friendly ballpark did nothing to spur the visitors to thoughts of victory. The sluggish offense sputtered again in Cleveland's 3–1 victory. Both teams got seven hits, but the Indians made better use of theirs. Even pitcher Jim Bagby contributed offensively with a third-inning triple. Philadelphia did not score their lone run until the top of the ninth, when Nap Lajoie tripled and eventually crossed the plate. Joe Bush pitched well, but still lost his 18th game for the Mackmen. It was now 15 straight losses for Connie Mack's squad.

Friday, August 4, brought nothing new in the way of good fortune to the struggling A's. Cleveland took the second contest in the series by a 5–2 score. Four second-inning runs provided most of the damage the home team inflicted upon the bedraggled Athletics. Starter Tom Sheehan got the hook after allowing five hits and a walk in the two innings. He was pulled in favor of a pinch-hitter, 22-year-old Edward George (Moxie) Divis, who was making his MLB debut. He failed to get a hit. Marsh Williams made up somewhat for his shabby recent performance by going the remaining six innings on the mound and allowing only one Cleveland run. The A's got nine hits off Fred Beebe. Whitey Witt and Amos Strunk got two hits apiece and each scored a run. The loss, the 16th consecutive for Mack's troops, dropped the Athletics to 19–76 and gave them a winning percentage of just .200. Every other AL team had at least a .500 record.

The Saturday, August 5, game was not competitive in the least. The Indians scored at least one run in each of the first seven innings as they romped, 12–3. Starter Jing Johnson gave up four runs in three innings and took the loss. His replacement, Red Lanning, was worse: He gave up four runs in one inning. Lanning was released by the team following the game. Tom Sheehan, the third Athletics hurler of the dreary afternoon, was the most competent of the bunch—but not by much. He gave up four runs in four innings. Whitey Witt socked his first career home run, a two-run shot, in the fifth inning off winner Stan Coveleski. Witt also stole a base and committed his 52nd error of 1916. Cleveland knocked out 16 hits in the barrage and was up 8–0 before Philadelphia got on the scoreboard. Philadelphia's 17th straight loss dropped them to 19–77. Their winning percentage dipped below .200.

Sunday, August 6, was not a day of rest as the A's and Indians met once again at Dunn Field with the same result as the previous two days. The Indians won, 5–2. Connie Mack got creative with his pitchers, using three of them and yanking his starter 12 batters into the game for no apparent reason. Starter Jack Nabors gave up no runs in his three innings of work. Elmer Myers relieved Nabors in the fourth, gave up three runs and was tagged with the loss. Joe Bush finished things off by allowing two Cleveland runs in two innings. Guy Morton got the win for the Tribe by going seven strong innings before giving way to Ed Klepfer. Philadelphia managed nine hits, none for extra bases. Moxie Divis, who had played left field in Saturday's game, pinch-hit for Bush in the top of the ninth inning, struck out—and was promptly cut loose by Mack. Divis apparently did not make much of an impression on anyone. His official record does not indicate which way he threw or batted. The 18th consecutive loss by the Athletics put them 30 full games behind the seventh-place St. Louis Browns in the AL standings.

Detroit was the next stop on the Athletics' ongoing futility tour. While there, Mack was interviewed by H. G. Salsinger, Detroit's correspondent for *The Sporting News*. The Athletics' cheerful manager humorously pointed out to Salsinger in this monologue how helpful his club was being to the rest of the AL.

> You'll have to give the Athletics credit for one thing. We are making it a good race. When we went into St. Louis to start our western trip, I told them in St. Louis they had a great ball club. They looked incredulous. Then the Browns beat us five straight and everybody perked up. And you know what the Browns have done since trimming us those five.
>
> We swung over to Chicago for eight games. The Sox did not expect to take them all, of course. But they did. They gained the league lead, and Chicago is now convinced the White Sox will surely cop the flag this year.
>
> Cleveland was about resigned to drop into the second division when we reached that city. They took all of the games we played and that gave them a fresh start and new hope. Now they are going pretty well again.

We are the race makers, although this is not doing us any particular good. But we are the little tonic team of baseball. We come along when any other club is sick and get it back to health.[1]

In the first game of the Tigers-A's series on Monday, August 7, the home team eked out a 4–2 win. In this game, the Athletics jumped out to the best possible start. Whitey Witt led off the proceedings with a home run off Harry Coveleski, the brother of Stan, who had beaten the A's two days before in Cleveland. The home side managed only five hits to the Athletics' nine but still triumphed. Elmer Myers pitched admirably in defeat. He struck out five Tigers, but also walked five of Hughie Jennings' crew. Two errors by catcher Ray Haley proved extremely costly to the visitors as they accounted for two unearned Tigers runs—the difference in the game. Myers' loss was his 16th of the season against eight wins. The A's streak of consecutive defeats was at 19, just one shy of the AL record.

On Tuesday, August 8, the once proud Philadelphia Athletics attained the embarrassing plateau of 20 consecutive defeats, suffering a 9–0 shellacking at the hands of the Tigers at Navin Field. It was also the A's 19th consecutive road loss. Jack Nabors was forced to endure a complete-game pummeling. The loss equaled the woeful AL record of the Boston Red Sox who, a decade earlier, had dropped a score of games without recording a win from May 1 to May 24, 1906. (Like the 1916 A's, the 1906 Red Sox had been pennant winners just two years before.) The league record would be matched by another of Connie Mack's squads from August 7 to 24, 1943, during that wartime season, but it would not be surpassed until the 1988 Baltimore Orioles set a new standard for lousiness with 21 straight losses. (The O's added a little extra panache to their mark by losing those 21 games to start the season.) Detroit pounded out 16 hits in securing the victory, although 14 of them were singles. It was loss number 14 for Nabors against just one victory. Winning pitcher Bernie Boland got in on the Tigers' offensive fun by getting two hits and scoring two runs. There were few offensive highlights for the downtrodden visitors from Philadelphia; one was Amos Strunk's 21st double of the season. The Athletics also stole four bases, but Detroit mercilessly stole five. Philadelphia was 19–80–1 after 100 official games. They had reached their nadir. "I had a haunting feeling we'd never win another,"[2] recalled Tom Sheehan years later.

In response to the ceaseless gloom and defeats emanating from the Athletics games, William G. Weart ignored the lowly American League club in his city—at least as much as he could—and instead focused much of his Philadelphia report in the August 10 edition of *The Sporting News* discussing the fortunes of the Phillies. However, Weart did briefly mention the A's awful, record-setting, and futile stopover in Chicago and the unending line of hopefuls who continued to be assessed by Connie Mack.

It looks now as though the Athletics will pass the century mark in the matter of defeats this season, and unless the team makes a big race, the chances are that the century mark will be passed in the middle of September. Day after day the reports have come in of one or more defeats for the White Elephants and a record was made for the club when it dropped eight games in one series to the Chicago White Sox.

Manager Mack continues to pick up young players and he has already given trials in the West to a couple of outfielders who enjoyed local fame in St. Louis and Cleveland. Reports are being received of more players who are going to come [to Shibe Park] for tryouts when the Athletics get back from their western trip.

The Athletics may make a record for losing games this season, but they will also establish a record for giving trials to more players than any club in the history of the sport. It would probably be impossible even for manager Mack to tell how many players have been wished on him this season and who have been looked over at Shibe Park this year. All came with big reputations from enthusiastic admirers of Connie Mack, but unfortunately it is rare for them to show the signs of baseball genius after they strike Shibe Park.

Wednesday, August 9, was a red-letter day in the Philadelphia Athletics' 1916 campaign: They ended their horrendous 20-game losing streak with a solid 7–1 win over the Detroit Tigers at Navin Field. It was a rare comfortable triumph for the Mackman. Joe Bush was in excellent form, striking out nine Tigers and allowing four hits. Ty Cobb got two of them. (Bush did issue six walks, though.) The A's got only seven hits, but for the first time in weeks they effectively bunched them together to produce runs. The first five Athletics in the lineup all scored at least one run. It was 5–0 for the visitors after three innings and 7–0 heading into the bottom of the ninth. Bush looked to be on his way to an emphatic shutout, but Jimmy Walsh misplayed Ed McKee's fly ball into what was deemed a triple by the official scorer. McKee later scored the home team's only run. Jean Dubuc was the Tigers starter. He lasted just three innings and picked up the loss, which probably had a certain degree of shame attached to it. For Bush, it was win number ten. It was only the third Philadelphia victory in their last 42 games. Bush had won all three of them.

The *Philadelphia Record*, a daily newspaper that had gotten a lot of mileage from the A's losing streak for the past week, had been jokingly rooting for the team to eclipse the record 20-game losing mark set by the terrible 1906 Red Sox. The next day's *Record* featured a cartoon that portrayed Bush locked in a stockade. Denounced as the "Benedict Arnold of Baseball," a sign around his neck said, "For Sale: Joe Bush." Apparently the sentiment to see the A's set a new AL record for futility was common. Some sportswriters seriously criticized Mack for pitching the capable Bush instead of sending one of his dreadful collegians to the mound. The win was the Athletics' 20th of the year. They were now 29 games behind the seventh-place Washington Senators, the only other team in the AL that was out of the pennant race.

On Thursday, August 10, it was back to the usual routine for the Athletics. Detroit, likely embarrassed by the previous day's loss to the lowly A's, rebounded with a fairly easy 10–4 win. Philadelphia led 2–0 after the top of the third inning, but Detroit tied the score in the home half of the third, scored five runs in the fifth and three more in the eighth. The final three runs were courtesy of Ty Cobb's third home run of the season. Marsh Williams went the distance for the Mackmen and gave up 16 hits. Willie Mitchell picked up the victory for the home team.

H. G. Salsinger, Detroit's correspondent for *The Sporting News*, had very few kind words to say about the Athletics in the August 17 edition, even though Connie Mack's club did manage to win once against the Tigers in the four-game series. He pointed out that the A's players often did not have their heads totally focused on the game.

> Outside of Strunk, Lajoie, McInnis and Bush, Mack certainly has a sorry looking outfit. Elmer Myers might be included on the list, for Elmer is one first-class pitcher. However, the only way Elmer can win is to keep the batsmen from reaching first. That is what his fellow hurler, Mr. Bush, must do when he wants to land one.
>
> In two different games here, the Athletics continued playing after the third Tiger was retired, until umpire [Billy] Evans called their attention to the fact that there were three out. They are even too bored to keep track of the number of outs.

Bolstered by their memorable win in Detroit, the A's spent Friday traveling to New York, where they promptly swept both games of a Saturday doubleheader from the Yankees on August 12 by scores of 9–3 and 2–0. In the opener, the A's managed 16 hits before a stunned gathering at the Polo Grounds. Every player in the Athletics lineup got at least one safety. Winning pitcher Elmer Myers got three. George Mogridge was roughed up for the loss and didn't make it through the seventh inning. The A's made three errors, one of them shortstop Whitey Witt's 55th of 1916, but they proved to be harmless.

Joe Bush pitched his second straight masterpiece in the second game. He scattered nine Yankees hits but never conceded a run. He struck out five New Yorkers and walked none. Meanwhile, the A's were held to just three hits but scored twice, once in the second inning and once in the ninth. Twenty-five-year-old rookie Urban Shocker was the tough-luck loser. The high-flying A's, winners of three of their last four games, were now 22–81.

There was no game on Sunday. When action resumed on Monday, August 14, the A's very nearly made it three consecutive wins, a feat they had not managed all season. Jack Nabors fell behind 4–0 in the first inning. Only two of the Yankees' runs were earned as Whitey Witt and Charlie Pick were back to their usual low standard of defense. That was all the offense the home team could muster for the game, but it was enough for a tight 4–3 win. The visitors got nine hits but could score only single runs in the second, fifth, and sixth innings.

Nick Cullop got the win for New York and raised his record to an outstanding 11–1. The luckless Nabors dropped to 1–15. His lone win, versus the Red Sox in April, seemed eons ago.

The Yankees got another win versus the A's on Tuesday, August 15, to split the four-game series. It was a 6–2 verdict decided by two key home runs. Wally Pipp hit a three-run shot in the third inning, while Roger Peckinpaugh notched a two-run blow. Both home runs, part of a 12-hit Yankees attack, came off losing pitcher Marsh Williams, who was now 0–4. Philadelphia could manage only four hits off Bob Shawkey, who won his 15th game of 1916. The loss dropped the Athletics to 22–83.

In the August 24 edition of *The Sporting News*, William G. Weart succinctly summarized the Athletics' recent spell of good results.

> The Athletics succeeded in winning one game during their western trip. Although their pitching and hitting was good enough to have given an ordinary team something like an even break. In many games the Mackmen got more hits than their opponents, but nearly every day they could not drive runners over the plate, while costly errors kept cropping up.
>
> It was at Detroit that Joe Bush turned in a victory over the Tigers. It was the third victory for the Mackmen in 42 consecutive games, and Bush stopped the losing streak each time, while he also figured in the double victory over the Yankees on Saturday.
>
> The Athletics' latest losing streak equaled that of the [1906] Boston Red Sox, 20 straight. History repeated itself, for the Red Sox checked their streak by beating Detroit just as the Athletics did by beating the Tigers. Last Saturday the Athletics sprung one of the biggest surprises of the season by twice defeating New York, and it may be significant of an upturn of their fortunes.

The suddenly hot St. Louis Browns were the next AL crew to arrive in Philadelphia, and they got a far tougher battle from Mack's crew than they figured. They played a doubleheader against the Athletics on Thursday, August 17, to make up for a rainout on Wednesday. Eddie Plank, Mack's former favorite hurler from yesteryear, went past the ninth inning in an attempt to get a win for the Browns. The Athletics, however, prevailed 4–3 on a bases-loaded walk in the tenth inning. Plank had been relieved by Dave Davenport once the bases were filled. He faced one batter, Wally Schang, who was back on the field for the first time in a month, issued the free pass, and the A's added another one to the win column. Plank dropped to 12–11. Joe Bush, easily the most successful pitcher on Mack's 1916 staff, got credit for the victory, although it was not one of his best efforts of the year. In the ten-inning complete game, Bush allowed eight hits and four walks, but he struck out six Browns. He also threw a wild pitch and hit a batter. Wally Schang hit his third home run of the season. Amos Strunk had a double. In this game, it was the Browns who looked like the A's, making five errors.

Davenport redeemed himself in the second game. He tossed a complete-

Wally Schang was supposed to be the A's regular catcher in 1916, but an injury on Opening Day scuttled those plans. He spent most of the season as an outfielder and performed admirably there. Schang batted .266 and hit seven homers in 1916 (National Baseball Hall of Fame Library, Cooperstown, N.Y.).

game eight-hitter as St. Louis won, 3–2. Elmer Myers was the losing pitcher. He allowed five St. Louis hits, but three of them were for extra bases. One was a home run hit by Del Pratt in the sixth inning to break a 2–2 tie. Whitey Witt made his 57th error of the season, although it did not end up hurting Myers. Newcomer Lee McElwee had two hits, including a double, for the Mackmen in a losing effort. The doubleheader split put the Athletics' record at 23–84. They were 40 games behind the first-place Boston Red Sox, who had opened a 3.5-game lead over both the Indians and the White Sox. The A's had allowed 556 runs thus far in 1916—102 more than the next most porous AL team.

Friday, August 18, brought a tough 11-inning loss for the home team. The Athletics used three pitchers in their failed attempt to thwart the Browns. Jack Nabors went six innings and permitted the visitors only three runs on two hits and actually had a no-hitter through five innings before crumbling. Tom Sheehan came in next for two adventurous innings in which he surrendered three walks but no runs. Joe Bush pitched the final three frames. In the top of the 11th inning, Bush cracked. He allowed the winning run to trot home on a wild pitch, and St. Louis claimed a hard-fought 4–3 triumph. St. Louis starter Bob Groom went nine strong innings before leaving for an unsuccessful pinch-hitter in the top of the tenth. Carl Weilman pitched the final two harrowing innings for the Browns, which featured three A's hits and two walks. Weilman somehow escaped the danger unscathed and got credit for the win, his 15th. None of Philadelphia's hits was for extra bases. The key play of the game occurred in the bottom of the tenth inning. With the score tied 3–3, the Athletics had the bases loaded with two out and Amos Strunk batting. With the faithful patrons of Shibe Park greatly excited, Strunk worked Weilman to a full count. Then, with the drama at its highest point ... Whitey Witt was carelessly picked off second base, suddenly ending the threat and the inning! It was a psychologically crushing blow to the Mackmen, who lost the game the following inning and fell to 23–85.

The Detroit Tigers made another appearance At Shibe Park on Saturday, August 19. In one of the stranger games of the year, the Athletics and Tigers were deadlocked 1–1 after nine innings. Both Jing Johnson and Harry Coveleski went the distance for their respective clubs. Johnson suddenly was touched for five Tigers runs in the top of the tenth, yet wasn't relieved. In the bottom of the tenth, the A's got one run back but still lost, 6–2. The only Philadelphia substitutions occurred in the bottom of the tenth inning, and both were successful. Otis Lawry pinch-ran for Ray Haley, who had singled, and scored the Athletics' second run. Val Picinich pinch-hit for Johnson and got a base hit. The A's made five errors on the day. Whitey Witt characteristically contributed his 58th of the season. Coveleski got the win for the Tigers, his 16th. Johnson fell to 0–3 for the vanquished Mackmen. Philadelphia was 23–86 and 41 games behind the league-leading Boston Red Sox.

Sunday was an off-day, allowing the Tigers time to rest, reload and pummel the Athletics, 7–1, on Monday, August 21. Bobby Veach was the key offensive figure for Detroit, collecting three of his team's 11 hits plus a walk. The Athletics could only scrape together five hits. Their lone run came in the bottom of eighth inning when they were hopelessly behind by seven runs. Elmer Myers did not have an especially good day on the mound for the Mackmen, giving up 11 hits, but he did go the distance in defeat, which was slowly becoming an admirable trademark of this bad team. Detroit's Hooks Dauss was considerably better and deserved his 14th victory of 1916. Myers dropped to 9–18. Whitey Witt made error number 59.

In one of their better performances of the summer, the A's beat the Tigers, 1–0, on Tuesday, August 22. The lone run scored on Amos Strunk's double in the seventh inning that scored Jimmy Walsh, who had walked. Bill James of Detroit surrendered seven hits to Philadelphia, while Joe Bush permitted just five Tigers hits in tossing a complete-game shutout. Bush did make things interesting with six walks, but James was nearly as generous, allowing five passes to the Mackmen. The Athletics' defense played solidly for a change, with only one error in the ledger. On this day Whitey Witt was conspicuously error-free; the blunder was charged to second baseman Nap Lajoie. The win gave the Athletics a 24–87 record. The run was the 299th they had scored on the season. None of the other seven AL teams had scored fewer than 371 runs. The lowest-scoring NL team had 353.

Fleet-footed and sure-handed outfielder Amos Strunk was the subject of a flattering feature story in the August issue of *Baseball Magazine*. Plaudits were heaped upon Strunk by giddy author J. C. Kofoed in flowery and unabashed fashion.

> There's a Quaker down in Quakertown whose pedals are the fastest in the Big Top. No one can step down to first in any quicker time than he, and for all-around worth, there are few who can gallop in the same heats. Some call him the Mercury of the American League, but they all know Amos Strunk, no matter what the handle they plaster on him.

As for Strunk's defensive prowess, the writer's compliments (and obvious hyperbole) continued unabated:

> He had apparently taken lessons in fancy diving and lofty tumbling, for he could catch a fly ball after turning a dozen somersaults. For five years now, Amos has demonstrated to his fellow townsmen that, barring a few immortals like Cobb and Speaker, he need doff his chapeau to no one.
>
> Among the green recruits with whom Mack has surrounded himself in these dreary days, Strunk stands out like a monolith. He is at the zenith of his career, and should be making impossible catches when Mack grabs another pennant, which he claims is not so far into the future.

We all like Amos for his ball playing ability and himself personally. He's pretty near at the top of the heap now. Let's hope he stays there until the Czar of Russia joins the International Workers of the World.

The following day's game, on Wednesday, August 23, was no contest. Detroit romped to a 10–3 win and held a 10–0 lead at one point. Four Tiger runners scored in the top of the first inning off Marsh Williams, who retired only one Detroit batter of the four he faced before getting the hook from manager Mack. Tom Sheehan was hastily summoned for an extra long relief session. He pitched the remaining 8⅔ innings and gave up six further Detroit runs, five of them in the top of the eighth to put the game out of the Athletics' reach. Detroit accumulated 14 hits off the two A's hurlers. Three of them came from the bat of George Burns, who hit a solo home run in the Tigers' big eighth inning. Meanwhile, Tigers pitcher George Cunningham held the Mackmen off the scoreboard until they scored three runs in the bottom of the eighth to avoid the shutout. Whitey Witt committed his 60th error of the year as Philadelphia fell to 24–88. The loss, combined with first-place Boston defeating Cleveland at Fenway Park, 7–3, officially meant the A's were mathematically eliminated from winning the American League pennant in 1916.

"Macks Lose On but They Play 'Em Hard" was the headline atop William G. Weart's Philadelphia report in the August 24 edition of *The Sporting News*. The subheading further declared, "Browns Were Lucky to Escape with Two Games." Weart wrote glowingly of the A's fighting spirit while hopelessly out of the AL pennant race, Connie Mack's act of sportsmanship toward the St. Louis Browns' pilot, the imminent departure of coach Ira Thomas, and the recent arrival of five new youthful prospects—three of whom would never see action in an MLB game.

> Victories are few and they are coming hard for the Athletics, but there has certainly been a decided and satisfactory improvement in the work of the team during the past few weeks. The White Elephants are now engaged with the western teams and they sent one team out of the city [Philadelphia] mighty glad to escape with the series by two games to one. This team was the St. Louis Browns, who came here on the crest of a great winning streak.
>
> Every one of the contests with St. Louis was decided by a one-run margin. One game went to ten innings and was won by the home team when [Dave] Davenport gave [Wally] Schang a base on balls with the bases loaded. The final contest went 11 innings and was won by St. Louis on a wild pitch by Joe Bush. Following the Browns came the Tigers, and just to prove that they mean business against all comers, the Athletics fought [Detroit manager Hughie] Jennings' crew to a standstill for ten innings.
>
> [St. Louis manager] Fielder Jones' combination never looked for such a reception here and the Browns were extremely fortunate to get away with the series. In the last game the Mackmen had a great chance to win in the tenth inning. Then the bases were filled with two out and [Amos] Strunk at bat. Amos worked [Carl] Weilman

for a count of three balls and two strikes. The fans had visions of the game being decided—as was one the day before—with a pass, when Whitey Witt went asleep off second base and was put out by Weilman's throw to [Del] Pratt.

In that game the Browns got only two hits in nine innings. [Jack] Nabors, who has a peculiar habit of having one or two bad innings per game, did not allow a hit for five innings. In the sixth he gave two passes and these were followed by two singles and a sacrifice fly and the Browns put three runners over the plate.

While the Browns did not do much hitting here, they gave a great exhibition of fielding. In one contest, [Armando] Marsans and [Burt] Shotton robbed Strunk and Schang of respective home run drives. [Doc] Lavan, Pratt and [Jimmy] Austin also gave a grand display of their ability to stop and throw, while [George] Sisler, despite a bad foot, managed to keep up the reputation which he has made for himself as a star batsman and fielder.

During the present inter-sectional series, as well as when he meets the eastern teams, manager Mack does not intend to have anyone say that he played favorites. So far as Mack is concerned, it is an open race and he is going to have his team do all it can to beat every contender. On the record of number of games won and lost this season, this should not scare any team, but the Mackmen have a habit of making their opponents play for every game.

The day the Browns came here it was cloudy until half an hour before the game was to start. It started to sprinkle when the Browns were taking their fielding workout and it kept up when the Athletics took their fielding practice. It was up to Mack to decide whether or not the game should start.

"Jones will probably be disappointed," said Mack, "if the game is called off. His team is going fine and he has a chance for the pennant. He undoubtedly doesn't want his men to lay idle. I'll put it up to Jones."

So Connie sent a messenger to Jones and asked him to come to the Athletics' dugout. Connie told the Browns' manager that he would give him the choice whether or not to play. Jones decided in the affirmative, but the shower continued and there was no chance to start the game.

When the other clubs come here and the weather is threatening, Connie intends to give them the same privilege that he gave Jones—that is, let the visiting manager decide whether or not there shall be a game. If this isn't giving every team a square deal, I cannot think of anything that would approach that distinction.

Five new players made their appearance here when the Mackmen returned from their long trip. These players are Charley [sic] Grimm, an outfielder who was picked off the lots of St. Louis; Pat Haley, the catcher who was secured from Buffalo when Billy Meyer was taken ill with appendicitis; George Poindexter, a big first baseman from the Virginia League; Chester Bemis, a pitcher from the town of Fitchburg, MA, which turned out Pat Moran and Jimmy Callahan; and Ed Brounder, a southpaw from the University of Kentucky.

Manager Mack has confirmed the report that Ira Thomas has signed a contract to coach the Williams College baseball team for the next five years. Thomas, it is expected, will not sever his connection with the Athletics entirely, but will do some scouting in New England for manager Mack. Thomas has lately been scouting on the [west] Coast, and one of the players he landed out there is none other than Ping Bodie, who will join the Mackmen next spring.

Who will be Ira's successor as coach of the Athletics' pitchers is not known. Ira has had a number of likely looking pitchers under him. Several of the lads looked as though they would develop into stars, but they lacked ambition and were finally sent to other clubs. Only one of them, Bob Shawkey, has even done anything notable with a major league team since turned adrift from the Mack School. There was a report that Art Fromme of the Vernon Coast League team, who formerly pitched for Cincinnati and the New York Giants, would coach Mack's pitchers in the future, but nothing is known of this here.

The Cleveland Indians ventured into Shibe Park on Thursday, August 24, to begin what would turn out to be a memorable five-game series with the Athletics. They were hoping the A's porous defense and less-than-stellar pitching would help them end an awful seven-game losing streak that had severely hurt their pennant aspirations. To their chagrin, they found the hosts not quite as gracious as in previous engagements. Philadelphia won the opener, 6–5. Jack Nabors got the starting assignment for the home team. After displaying too much wildness for Connie Mack's liking, Nabors was yanked from the mound during the third inning after allowing six walks and two hits. Yet, Nabors held a 4–2 lead at the time of his departure because of a four-run outburst by the Athletics in the bottom of the second inning. Elmer Myers pitched the remainder of the game for the home team and picked up his tenth win of the season for his long-relief efforts. Cleveland tied the score in the top of the fifth inning only to see the Athletics take a 5–4 lead in the bottom half. The Tribe eventually used 16 players over the course of the game but never managed to assume the lead. Tris Speaker was spiked during the game. He had to leave the contest and did not take part in the second half of the doubleheader. Speaker was replaced in the Tribe's lineup by Braggo Roth, a strategic move which turned out to be a short-term windfall. Ed Klepfer, the second of four Cleveland pitchers, picked up the loss. Nap Lajoie and Stuffy McInnis both had great afternoons at the plate for the Mackmen, each recording three hits. The A's 25th victory of the season was devastating to Cleveland, as their eighth straight loss dropped them 8.5 games behind Boston in the AL pennant race. Cleveland now was sitting in sixth place as the front-running Red Sox were starting to open up a lead on the rest of the field.

The second game of the Thursday doubleheader was the Braggo Roth show. Batting third and patrolling Tris Speaker's center field, Roth smashed two home runs (doubling his season's output in that department) and stole home in Cleveland's 4–2 victory. The first circuit clout was a two-run shot off Jing Johnson in the fifth inning that vaulted the visitors into a 3–2 lead. The second Roth homer was a solo shot that put the icing on the cake in the top of the eighth. With his steal of home in the fourth inning, Roth, in one way or another, accounted for all the Tribe's scoring. Cleveland needed every smidgen of Roth's contribution. The A's outhit the visitors, 12–6, and probably deserved to win. Charlie Pick had four hits for the vanquished home team. Rookie Cleveland right-hander Al Gould gave up no walks, though, and Roth's bat and swift feet gave the hurler enough support for the win that ended Cleveland's damaging losing streak. Athletics hurler Jing Johnson was his own worst enemy. He committed Philadelphia's only error, a blunder that lead to an unearned Cleveland run. The split of the doubleheader put the A's record at 25–89.

Cleveland created a winning streak on Friday, August 25. They captured both halves of another doubleheader, scoring 23 runs in the two games. The Tribe scored runs in 14 of the 18 innings, including a run of 12 straight innings in which they put at least one tally on the scoreboard. Philadelphia committed 11 errors to provide extra assistance to the visitors. The first game was a 13–9 shootout in which the Athletics actually outhit the victors, 12–11. Jack Nabors did not get out of the second inning before being relieved by Marsh Williams. Nabors was responsible for only two runs and left the game with the score tied, 2–2. Thus Williams, who was made to suffer through eight innings of unceasing Cleveland hits, was tagged with the loss, the A's 90th of the season. The collegian was now 0–6—and he had played his final MLB game. Tris Speaker, who was on his way to ending the stranglehold that Ty Cobb had on the AL batting championship since 1907, was back in the Cleveland lineup and got three hits for the winners. Charlie Pick, another player who had recovered from a debilitating spike wound, made two errors at third base for the A's. His error total was an awful 35, though it paled before shortstop Whitey Witt's jaw-dropping total, which rose to 62 in the same game.

The second game lacked the competitiveness of the first tilt. Cleveland cruised to an easy 10–2 win. The usually reliable Bullet Joe Bush failed to dazzle very many Indians batters and was gone after three innings with his team already trailing, 5–0. Tom Sheehan, in another long relief stint, also gave up five runs in the rout, but it was Bush who got the loss and attained an unflattering milestone: It was his 20th defeat of the season. In contrast, Fred Beebe of Cleveland had an easy time of it, going the full nine innings while allowing only six A's hits. The Athletics matched their hit total with errors. Against all odds, none of the six was committed by either Witt or Pick. Henry P. Edwards, Cleveland's beat writer for *The Sporting News*, declared the second game of the twin bill to be "the first game on their road trip in which the Indians really played good ball in every department of the game, base-running and fielding as well as batting and pitching." With two more losses added to the ledger, Philadelphia was now 25–91. They had allowed 615 runs—a full 200 more than the seventh-place Washington Senators. In the August 25 doubleheader they had never looked more deservedly like the cellar-dwellers they were. The team's pitching was in utter disarray.

Bush was so disgusted with his subpar showing that he approached Connie Mack afterward and asked—nearly begged—for permission to start the following day's game versus the Tribe. Mack agreed. Why not? With his team 66 games under .500, on a three-game losing skein, and his so-called pitching rotation changing by the day, what did Mack have to lose?

August 26: The Masterpiece Among the Rubbish

"Any minute, any day, some players may break a longstanding record. That's one of the fascinations about the game—the unexpected surprises."—Connie Mack, *Baseball's Greatest Quotations*

"If virtue is its own reward and the good get joy out of knowing they are spotless, then Joe Bush of the Athletics should be happy and sleep well, whatever happens. While other players of Connie Mack's golden days have sulked or 'retired' because of the passing of World Series prospects, Bush has remained loyal to the core, giving Mack always his best, whatever the backing behind him and without regard to discouraging incidents."—*TSN*, August 3, 1916

Saturday, August 26, 1916, was undoubtedly the high point of the season for the bedraggled and woebegone Philadelphia Athletics, the laughingstocks of MLB. They were already mathematically eliminated form the AL pennant race with more than a month to go in the season. They had a winning percentage of .216. *Baseball Magazine* had justifiably taken to calling them the "Pathetics." Throughout the season, the Mackmen had shown a tremendous capacity not to be able to win tight games. Rarely were good pitching performances rewarded. In games where the A's did score more than one or two runs, the defense and pitching seemed to let them down. There was no reason whatsoever to expect something special at Shibe Park that afternoon, especially from a team that had been badly spanked in a doubleheader, 13–9 and 10–2, just the day before.

Nevertheless, some 5,000 souls paid their way into the ballpark to watch their much-maligned team vie against the pennant-contending Cleveland Indians, led by Tris Speaker, who was leading the AL batting race with a terrific .392 average. The pitching matchup that day seemed to favor the visitors. Spitballer Stan Coveleski, a right-hander with a 14–10 record, got the nod for Cleveland. Joe Bush, who had suffered through three rough innings in picking up his 20th loss just the day before, was back on the hill for the A's. It was not an unprecedented pitching move for the time: if a pitcher was knocked out of a game early, it was not unusual for Mack or any other manager of that era to send him back out to do battle the very next day. After all, according to prevailing wisdom, he should not be tired. Mack had already done the same thing with Bush and other A's hurlers several times in this hopelessly lost season. The Indians entered the Saturday matinee on a three-game winning streak, after losing their previous eight.

In the top of the first inning, Jack Graney, Cleveland's left fielder, drew a leadoff walk. Third baseman Terry Turner laid down a sacrifice bunt, fielded by Bush, who had no play at second base, so he fired to Stuffy McInnis at first base for the first out of the ball game. It was the only fielding play Bush would have to make all game. The sacrifice moved Graney to second base. Center fielder Tris Speaker struck out, as did right fielder Braggo Roth. Cleveland's threat ended with Graney stranded at second base. The A's went three up, three down, in the home half of the first.

Bush had little trouble with the Indians in the second inning. Bill Wambsganss grounded out to fellow shortstop Whitey Witt. First baseman Chick Gandil flied out to Wally Schang in left field. Second baseman Ray Chapman flied out to Jimmy Walsh in right field. The A's took a 1–0 lead in the bottom of the second when Schang tripled and scored as Wambsganss committed an error on Stuffy McInnis' ground ball.

Cleveland could muster nothing off Bush in the third inning. Catcher Steve O'Neill grounded out to Charlie Pick at third base. Pitcher Coveleski flied out to Walsh. Graney harmlessly popped up to Pick for the third out. Philadelphia also was retired in short order but still led 1–0 after three innings.

Turner was called out on strikes to start the fourth inning. Speaker grounded out to Witt. Roth grounded out to Pick. Philadelphia upped its lead to 2–0 when McInnis laid down a lovely squeeze bunt along the first-base line with the bases loaded.

Bush began the fifth inning strongly, whiffing Wambsganss on three pitches. The third strike was called by plate umpire Tommy Connolly. Gandil attempted to bunt his way onto base, but Pick, in the toughest fielding chance of the game by an A's defender, fired the ball to McInnis at first base. The ball beat Gandil to the bag and he was emphatically called out on a close play by base umpire Ollie Chill. Next, Chapman was punched out on strikes. Bush had retired the side on just ten pitches. After Graney's first-inning walk, Bush had retired 15 straight Indians batters.

Philadelphia gave Bush a comfortable five-run advantage by adding three more runs in a display of power hitting. Young Val Picinich led off the frame with a double and moved to third base on a passed ball. Joe Bush helped his own cause with a double, scoring Picinich. Whitey Witt tripled, scoring Bush. Jimmy Walsh drove in Witt with a sacrifice fly for the third run of the inning. It was 5–0 for the home team after five innings.

The sixth inning began with O'Neill grounding out to Nap Lajoie at second base. (No one knew it at the time, but it was the last chance accepted and final assist recorded in Lajoie's terrific MLB career.) Coveleski was lifted for pinch-hitter Danny Moeller, who promptly flied out to Walsh. Graney grounded out to shortstop Witt. Bush was two-thirds of the way to a no-hitter. The A's did not score in the bottom of the sixth, but did turn in a typical head-shaking play. Lajoie led off the inning with a triple. After McInnis lined out, Pick singled past second base—and Lajoie was thrown out at home by the strong and accurate arm of the Indians' shallow-playing Tris Speaker! Only the 1916 A's could have a runner at third base be thrown out at the plate on a base hit to center field. The triple was Lajoie's 3242nd and final MLB hit, although he had one more unsuccessful at-bat in the game.

In the top of the seventh inning, Turner worked Bush to a full count before flying out to Schang. Speaker flied out to Strunk. Roth did the same. Bush had retired 21 Indians consecutively.

The eighth inning opened similarly to the seventh as Wambsganss took Bush to a full count before flying out to Schang. Gandil popped out to Witt at shortstop. On the first pitch that Chapman saw, he hit a foul popup that was safely corralled by third baseman Pick. It was 5–0 after the eighth inning. More importantly, Cleveland had no hits and Bush had retired the last 24 batters he had faced.

With all the Shibe Park patrons' eyes glued on Bush's every move, Steve O'Neill led off the top of the ninth inning. The first two pitches from Bush were balls. Umpire Connolly called the next toss a strike. O'Neill fouled off three consecutive pitches to heighten the rising drama ... and then struck out. Bob Coleman was next up. He was pinch-hitting for Fritz Coumbe, who had ably replaced Coveleski on the mound in the sixth inning and allowed no further scoring by the Mackmen. Bush worked his way to a favorable 1–2 count but threw two consecutive balls to make it a full count. On the sixth pitch, Coleman struck out. Two Indians were out. Bush was just one out away from a remarkable no-hitter.

Jack Graney, the only Cleveland batter to have reached first base, was the last obstacle Bush had to overcome. He fouled off Bush's first offering. The next two pitches were balls. On the fourth pitch, Graney took a mighty cut and sent a high popup to first baseman Stuffy McInnis. He coolly made the routine catch for the 27th putout of the game. Ninety-nine minutes after the game had begun, Bush had completed a gem: a spectacular and wholly unexpected 5–0 no-hitter in which he had faced just 28 opposing batters, one above the minimum.

The A's fans, who had had precious little to cheer about throughout 1916, let loose with their emotions the moment the no-hitter was safely in the books. The *Washington Post* reported in its sports section the following day, "When

Bullet Joe Bush was the most reliable pitcher on Connie Mack's 1916 staff—although his 15 wins were offset by a league-leading 24 losses. Bush's unexpected no-hitter versus Cleveland was the highlight of the Athletics' season (National Baseball Hall of Fame Library, Cooperstown, N.Y.).

Graney ended the game by putting up a fly to McInnis, after O'Neill and Coleman had fanned, the crowd broke onto the field to congratulate Bush, and the latter was so excited that he pulled off his cap and joined the cheering."

Bush recorded seven strikeouts to go along with the lone walk issued to Graney. He liberally mixed outfield outs (8) with infield outs (12). No Athletic made an error, a rarity for the A's maligned "$10 infield" of 1916. As an added bonus, Bush augmented his own team's 12-hit offense with an RBI double. It was the second no-hitter pitched in the AL to that point in the 1916 season. (Boston's Rube Foster had thrown one versus New York on June 21. Dutch Leonard, another Red Sox hurler, would pitch one just four days after Bush's. His victims were the St. Louis Browns.) It was the third no-hitter in Athletics history and the first one since May 12, 1910, when Connie Mack's all-time favorite hurler, Albert (Chief) Bender, tossed a 4–0 masterpiece also at Shibe Park—and also versus the Cleveland Indians. In a truly strange coincidence, both Bush and Bender hailed from the same small town of Brainerd, MN.

Years later, Mack told his biographer Fred Lieb, "Considering the team I had that season, it was the greatest no-hit game ever pitched! It really was a wonderful achievement."[1] He also said that Bush's fastball, in terms of sheer speed, ranked behind only Amos Rusie's and Walter Johnson's. High praise indeed.

William G. Weart, whose August 31 Philadelphia report in *The Sporting News* surprisingly relegated Bush's thrilling feat to second billing behind the Phillies' recent losses to the Pittsburgh Pirates, succinctly summed up the unlikely goings-on at Shibe Park that afternoon. He also unknowingly referred to a hallowed baseball institution that was still two decades in the future.

> There have been games played here during the home stand of the Athletics in which Connie Mack and the team's followers have felt greatly encouraged, and there have been others which have caused a decided feeling of depression. As a rule, the hitting and the fielding have been satisfactory, but the work of the pitching department has been of an in-and-out character. Occasionally a young pitcher looks as though he has come through at last, but on the next turn on the rubber he would do very poor work. Recently wildness has been a drawback to the work of the pitchers and passes have been handed out in a reckless manner.
>
> Joe Bush is now in the Hall of Fame [sic!]. After doing such poor work in three innings last Friday that he was taken off the rubber, Joe went back at the Indians on Saturday and shut them out without a hit. He allowed only one batsman to get to first base. This was [Jack] Graney who opened the game with a base on balls, and taking second on [Terry] Turner's sacrifice, and from there Graney watched [Tris] Speaker and [Braggo] Roth strike out.
>
> After that it was a procession of putouts with only one hard chance, this being when [Chick] Gandil bunted and [third baseman Charlie] Pick got him at first base by very fast work.
>
> Bush and Bender are the only Athletic pitchers to get [no-hit] shutout games

against the Cleveland team. Oddly enough, both of these twirlers hail from Brainerd, MN. Brainerd probably is the only place on the entire map of the United States to have two no-hit pitchers in the major leagues.

Bush's no-hit game coincidentally also turned out to be Napoleon Lajoie's MLB swansong, although it was not intended that way. Before the A's next game, he hurt his back during pre-game batting practice. With a month to go in a depressingly bad season, at age 42 Lajoie saw no use in putting off the inevitable. He used the injury as a way to ease himself quietly into retirement. Although Lajoie wasn't among the first five members elected to the National Baseball Hall of Fame, he was in the first group inducted when the Hall opened its doors in 1939, an honor richly deserved for such an important person in baseball history. (Remember the Phillies' vindictive legal action that proscribed Lajoie from playing professional baseball in Pennsylvania during the AL-NL player war in 1902.) Lajoie, well liked by the fans and hugely respected by his peers, was a truly wonderful offensive and defensive player and one of the sport's all-time greats.

Nineteen-year-old Val Picinich, the catcher who was not too far removed from prep school when he caught Bush's masterpiece, would stay in the majors for 18 seasons, mostly as an expendable backup backstop. He would catch two other MLB no-hitters before hanging up his mitt for good, but not for the Athletics. As a Washington Senator, Picinich caught Walter Johnson's only career no-hitter on July 1, 1920, against Boston. Then, as a member of the Red Sox, Picinich caught Howard Ehmke's on September 7, 1923. The latter no-hitter occurred back at his old place of employment—Shibe Park—versus Connie Mack's Philadelphia Athletics. Only Jason Varitek, with four, has caught more MLB no-hitters.

August 26, 1916, was indeed a great day to be a fan of the Philadelphia Athletics. Bullet Joe Bush's spectacular pitching achievement, at least for a little while, could make the A's rooters forget that their team had, by a considerable margin, the most dismal won-lost record in either major league: 26–91.

August 28 to Season's End: Playing out the String

With no game scheduled for Sunday, the Athletics could savor Bush's no-hitter for a little longer than usual before returning to the fray of AL competition. The Chicago White Sox came to Shibe Park for the first game of a four-game series on Monday, August 28. They escaped with a narrow 1–0 victory in which neither team got an extra-base hit. Elmer Myers allowed only five Chicago hits, struck out six and walked two. He deserved a better fate than his 19th loss of the season. Chicago got its only run in the sixth inning. It was scored by Buck Weaver, who reached base on a fielder's choice. Right-hander Joe Benz was terrific for the White Sox. He allowed only three hits to the Athletics. Two of them were by Amos Strunk. The other was collected by his mound opponent, Myers. Benz struck out only three A's, but he allowed no walks. Whitey Witt made his 63rd error of the season, but it did not figure in the White Sox scoring. The A's were 26–92.

The A's hardly looked the part of a bottom-feeding team on Tuesday, August 29. They pounded the White Sox, 9–2, in one of their best efforts of 1916. In a ten-hit assault on three Chicago pitchers, the Athletics rapped out four extra-base clouts. Three were doubles by Amos Strunk, Wally Schang, and Stuffy McInnis. The most spectacular was a two-run homer by pitcher Jing Johnson in the five-run bottom of the seventh inning that blew the game open. In winning his first game of the season, Johnson allowed nine White Sox hits, but scattered them to minimize the damage. Although most of the A's scoring was off Lefty Williams, Eddie Cicotte got the loss for giving up three runs in five innings of work.

On Wednesday, August 30, the Athletics looked more like their old selves, committing four errors and losing to Chicago, 7–3. Starter Tom Sheehan allowed four runs, but only one earned run, in his eight innings. Nevertheless he took his 12th loss of 1916. Elmer Myers was totally ineffective in his one inning of relief, allowing three White Sox runs in the ninth to give the visitors some insurance. Red Faber allowed just four A's hits in picking up his 13th win of the season. A seemingly rejuvenated Stuffy McInnis had a good game for Philadelphia with a triple, an RBI, and a sacrifice bunt, but it mattered little: The A's were 27–93. The August 30 game was the last one Jimmy Walsh would play for the A's. He was traded on September 2 to the Red Sox for catcher Raymond Haley, making the loan of Haley to the Athletics a permanent move. The genial Walsh had failed to live up to his potential. His gift of footspeed was never fully realized.

August ended with Bullet Joe Bush's first appearance on the mound since his no-hitter. There was no drama this time. He surrendered four White Sox runs and eight hits in six innings before being removed for a pinch-hitter with his club trailing, 4–0. Jack Nabors pitched the last three innings for the Mackmen and gave up three more runs. Joe Benz pitched his second excellent game of the series for Chicago, allowing only four Philadelphia hits. One was a seventh-inning triple by Wally Schang, who scored on Stuffy McInnis' single. Joe Jackson provided a considerable amount of offensive punch for the visitors with a home run, a triple, and three RBI. The homer, a two-run blast, came in the sixth inning and was just his third of the season. White Sox shortstop Buck Weaver was tossed from the game by base umpire Ollie Chill. It was Weaver's second ejection of the season and the last of his career. Both in 1916 had come via Chill's thumb. Excluding New York manager Bill Donovan, Weaver was the only player whom Chill had tossed out the whole season.

Apart from his comments on Bush's no-hitter, William G. Weart's column in the August 31 issue of *The Sporting News* briefly talked about Connie Mack's minor league talent hunt and wondered if Mack would ever again repeat his mistake of relying too much on untested young players.

> Manager Mack's announcement last week that he had invaded the big minor leagues and grabbed several players, including two hard hitters like [Ping] Bodie of San Francisco and [Buck] Thrasher of Atlanta caused a lot of surprise. As a rule, almost the only Class AA [the highest classification a minor league could have in 1916] players who have joined the Athletics have graduated from Baltimore or else from clubs on the Coast, where Connie got some outfielders, some pitchers, and Billy Orr, an infielder, who did not come up to expectations.
>
> It is not believed that the landing of players from high-class minor leagues means that manager Mack will turn from his policy of developing youngsters. This plan will doubtless still be pursued, but it is doubtful if Connie will ever again try to fill so many positions at the same time with collegians and youngsters from small teams as he did this year.

Friday, September 1, saw the Athletics start a road trip in Washington where they faced off against the Senators in a doubleheader at Griffith Stadium. Walter Johnson was the first pitcher they would encounter. He already had 22 victories for the only other AL team besides the White Elephants that had given up any real hope of winning the pennant. Johnson's opponent was luckless Jack Nabors, who had one win, achieved in the first month of the season. The game turned out as one might have expected, but it was only a 3–1 win for the home team. The Senators managed 11 hits off Nabors, but just got single runs in the first, fifth and eighth innings. Johnson kept the Athletics off the scoreboard until the ninth inning, giving up just five hits. Whitey Witt got two of them. Otis Lawry, who had replaced the retired Nap Lajoie at second base in the A's lineup, also got two. Witt and Charlie Pick also made an error apiece that accounted for two unearned runs. The loss was Nabors' 16th of the season. Winning pitcher Johnson also had 16 losses, but now had 23 wins.

The second game featured a two-hit pitching gem (made complicated by eight walks and a hit batsman) turned in by Philadelphia's Elmer Myers. He turned in a terrific two-hitter that should have been a shutout. The only Senators' run was unearned. Joe Leonard and George McBride were the only Washington hitters to get a hit. Each was a single. On the other side of the ledger, the Athletics exploded for 12 hits in the 4–1 win off rookie pitcher Maurice (Molly) Craft, a 6'2" right-hander who was starting his first MLB game. He went the distance for the vanquished home team. Despite the great number of hits, an Athletics victory was not assured until the Mackmen scored twice in the top of the eighth inning. Whitey Witt had three hits for the winners. Even pitcher Myers got two. With the deserved win, the A's record was now 28–95. They were 42.5 games out of first place. By means of comparison, the last-place NL team on September 1 was the Cincinnati Reds, who had accrued 19 more wins than the Mackmen. They had also allowed 122 fewer runs than the A's had.

The Athletics and Senators got together on Saturday, September 2 for a single game at Griffith Stadium. It turned out to be an 11-inning thriller with lots of scoring and plenty of chances. At the end of one inning, the Senators had opened up a 4–1 lead, with A's starter Tom Sheehan looking quite shaky. The A's, who would collect 14 hits in the game, scored twice in the top of the second to narrow the Senators' lead to 4–3, as Washington left-hander Harry Harper appeared vulnerable himself. The Senators got nine hits on the day and had a 6–3 lead entering the eighth inning. The Mackmen rallied for three runs in that frame to level the score at 6–6. Bert Gallia replaced Harper in the ninth and threw two-hit ball through the eleventh inning. Sheehan, who gave up only three earned runs, coughed up the fatal seventh Senators run with two outs in the home half of the 11th to give Gallia his 12th win. Sheehan fell to 1–13. Stuffy McInnis got three hits for Philadelphia. Whitey Witt stole his 15th base of the season, but he also made his 65th error. The Athletics were 28–96, 33.5 games behind the seventh-place Senators.

On Labor Day Monday, September 4, most of the interest in the baseball world was focused on a specially arranged last-hurrah pitching matchup between Christy Mathewson, who had been traded to the Cincinnati Reds on June 20, and Mordecai Brown of the Chicago Cubs. The game was heavily promoted in Chicago in hopes of drawing a good-sized, nostalgia-oriented crowd to Weeghman Park to watch two struggling teams contest a doubleheader. It worked: the largest crowd of the season turned out to see the old rivals square off for the first time since 1912. Before the game, both hurlers were presented with bouquets of roses. Mathewson and Brown both went the distance in a 10–8 Reds win in the second game. The once-great pitchers had only their names now and were clearly on the wane: They combined to allow 34 hits. For both, it was their last MLB appearance. For Matty, it was career win number 373.

Meanwhile, after the mandatory off-day on Sunday, the Senators and Athletics clashed in an equally meaningless AL doubleheader at Griffith Stadium. The Senators prevailed in two pitching duels, 2–0 and 3–1.

In the opening game, Jack Nabors allowed just two Senators runs, both coming in the sixth inning, and six hits. Washington batters also drew four walks. The Athletics also got six hits, all singles, off Jim Shaw, but were unable to put anything other than zeroes on the scoreboard. Senators second baseman Eddie Foster had the game's only extra-base hit, a double. Nabors was now 1–17. It was Shaw's first win of 1916 against four losses.

In the second game, a two-run double in the bottom of the first inning off the bat of Washington cleanup hitter Elmer Smith was the key blow of the game. Washington scored all three of their runs in the first frame. Philadelphia got an unearned run back in the third inning but nothing more off Yancey (Doc) Ayers, who surrendered seven hits, the same as A's pitcher Bullet Joe Bush allowed to Washington. In absorbing their 97th and 98th losses of 1916, the Athletics fell 44.5 games behind the front-running Boston Red Sox. The A's generally anemic offense, which managed one lone run in 18 innings on this day, had scored 70 fewer runs than any other AL team.

The league-leading Boston Red Sox, who were being hotly pursued by both Detroit and Chicago in the AL standings, arrived in Philadelphia on Tuesday, September 5, hoping two wins in a Shibe Park doubleheader would give the Athletics 100 losses on the season. As it turned out, the teams split the twin bill, so the A's loss total only reached 99 instead of the embarrassment of triple figures. Amos Strunk was the man of honor for the A's in the first game. He blasted a home run in the first inning to start the Mackmen rolling in their convincing 5–2 win. Ernie Shore gave up the round-tripper to Strunk, his second of the year, and lasted just four innings. Shore trailed 3–1 when he was relieved by Babe Ruth. The Babe did not fare a whole lot better than Shore. He gave up two runs on seven hits. Meanwhile Jing Johnson had a solid game on the mound for Philadelphia. He gave up two runs on just eight hits in firing a complete game against the AL front-runners. Only one Boston run was earned. Whitey Witt's 68th error of the year, one of three he committed in the game, was responsible for one of the visitors' tallies. Witt did make amends with two hits. In all, four A's had multiple-hit games, including three by swift-footed Otis Lawry. Johnson now had a personal two-game winning streak, a feat not many A's pitchers could boast of achieving in 1916.

Things returned to the expected norm in the second game as Boston won handily, 7–1. The visitors' seven scores came on just six hits. Boston got three runs in the third inning and three more in the eighth inning to seal the win. Right fielder Jim Brown, making his 1916 debut with the Athletics (he had played in one MLB game for the St. Louis Cardinals in 1915), got a hit and scored the A's only run of the game in the home half of the fourth inning. Carl Mays allowed eight hits for the victors and got his 15th win of the year. Philadelphia's Elmer Myers, who recorded a complete-game defeat, reached the unfortunate milestone of 20 losses on the season. Charlie Pick had two errors at third base to raise his total to 39. He was on his way to recording an unflattering sub-.900 fielding average.

Boston took the Wednesday, September 6, game too, 5–2, without much difficulty. Wally Schang's fourth home run of the year in the second inning gave the home team a brief 1–0 lead. Boston replied quickly, scoring three times and never relinquishing the lead from that point onward. Tom Sheehan picked up another loss for the A's, his 14th of 1916 versus just one win, in a complete-game effort. Sheehan tried to help himself at bat; he hit a triple and scored Philadelphia's other run in the eighth inning. The loss was the dreaded "century" for the A's, whose record was now 29–100. Dutch Leonard was the winner for Boston, picking up his 15th triumph of the season. Larry Gardner and Hal Janvrin got two hits each for the victors, who maintained their tenuous one-game lead over the Detroit Tigers in the pennant chase. Boston was 75–55. Detroit also notched a win, a ten-inning triumph at home over the St. Louis Browns.

The following day, Thursday, September 7, was a terrific pitchers' duel at Shibe Park. Jack Nabors, still in quest of his second win of 1916, lost 2–0 to Boston's Rube Foster. The two runs the Red Sox scored in the top of the fourth inning were unearned, courtesy of an error by A's catcher Val Picinich. Boston only got four hits off Nabors, but it was enough. Nabors, who again got little offensive support from his teammates but must have been used to it, dropped to 1–18. Leonard scattered six Athletics singles and five walks in such a manner that nobody crossed the plate. Only Amos Strunk managed two hits for the White Elephants, who fell to 46.5 games behind the Red Sox. The A's and their hideous 29–101 record were the only team in the AL that was under .500.

Despite the ever-increasing loss total that mired the club deep in the AL basement, William G. Weart's unshakable faith and optimism in the Philadelphia Athletics and their revered manager were never more apparent than in his cheery report on the club in the September 7 edition of *The Sporting News*. According to Weart, not only had the A's nadir been reached, the team had resolutely rebounded, and great things were surely in store for the Athletics and their fans in 1917.

It can be safely said that the turn in the tide of the Athletics has been bridged. The team has been steadily doing better work and there is noticeable improvement in various departments. There is, too, a gratifying increase in the number of victories.

After their spring spurt, the Athletics seldom won a game for many weeks. They lost every game of one series after another, and it was a surprise whenever a victory was turned in. That streak of 20 straight defeats, however, was apparently the finish. Since then, the Mackmen have won one or more games in each of their last seven series. They defeated Detroit once at Detroit, broke even at four games in New York, won one game each form Chicago, St. Louis and Detroit here [in Philadelphia], defeated Cleveland twice at Shibe Park, and got a victory at Washington last Friday. The Mackmen some time ago stopped being easy picking for other clubs.

Connie Mack has picked up three fine catchers in Meyer, Picinich and Haley. He has shown the fans two splendid young pitchers in Elmer Myers and Jingling Johnson, in addition to Joe Bush, who is about the best pitcher in the American League.

In addition, Connie has developed Witt into a fair shortstop, and one who is improving steadily, and he believes he has got a trim quartet of outfielders for 1917 who will do wonderful work in both hitting and fielding. Connie now banks on Strunk, [Ping] Bodie, the star slugger of the Pacific Coast League, and [Buck] Thrasher, who is battling for the lead in hitting in the Southern Association, for his outfield. This will leave Schang for emergency duty behind the bat and in the outfield as well as for pinch hitting.

Connie's big problems now are to get a southpaw pitcher and to whip his infield into shape.

It would probably sound like a very far-fetched statement for one to state that the Athletics have the best pair of right-handed pitchers in the American League. A look at the standings of the pitchers shows that Bush has a record of 14 victories to 20 defeats and that Myers has won 11 games and lost 20. Search of the pitching statistics, however, shows what really wonderful work Bush and Myers have done when twirling for a tail-end team. These two men lead the American League in star twirling feats and no other pair of twirlers with any club can show so many performances of this class. In 11 games in which Bush has pitched, he has held his opponents to five hits or fewer. Myers has nine such marks to his credit.

With such stars as Bush and Myers as the backbone of his twirling department, and Jing Johnson showing that he has major league class, the prospects certainly look good for Mack's pitching staff for 1917.

The New York Yankees, sitting in fifth place but still hopeful of challenging the front-running Red Sox for the AL flag, were the next visiting team to drop into Shibe Park in the last month of the season. The Athletics continued their modest streak of winning at least one game per series by thumping New York, 8–2, on Friday, September 8. It was a game that almost nobody saw. Heavy thunderstorms blasted through Philadelphia most of the day, and very few people figured the Yankees-A's clash would go on as scheduled. In fact, only one reporter ventured to Shibe Park to cover the game, so certain were most of the men of the press corps that a rainout would be declared. Most fans felt that way too. Fewer than 100 spectators—and perhaps not even 50—paid their way inside the stadium. However, Connie Mack went out of his way to present the Yankees a chance to stick with the schedule and play the single game on Friday and a twin bill the next day, despite horrible field conditions resulting from the day's earlier downpours. New York manager Wild Bill Donovan accepted Mack's offer because it was the Yankees' last series in Philadelphia in 1916, and they had a lucrative exhibition game scheduled for Monday they did not want to cancel to make up for a rainout. (Playing on Sunday, of course, was out of the question due to Philadelphia's strict "blue laws.") The handful of people who did stick around for the game were rewarded for their loyalty as they saw something no MLB spectators had ever seen before.

Wally Schang was the batting hero for the Mackmen, hitting two home runs and creating a little baseball history at the same time: One of his homers was hit from the left side of the plate, the other from the right side. No MLB batter had ever before socked home runs in a game from each side of the plate. Schang, batting left-handed, rocked a grand slam off Yankees right-handed starter Allen (Rubber Arm) Russell to give the home team a 4–0 lead. Another home run, this one from the bat of newcomer Jim Brown in the bottom of the second inning, spelled the end for Russell as the A's roared out to a 7–1 lead. Schang's second homer, this time from the right-handed hitter's box, was a solo shot and was also part of the second-inning assault. This one came courtesy of reliever Slim Love, a 6'7" lefty from Mississippi. Altogether, Schang connected for three hits in the game, amassed nine total bases, and collected five RBI in front of a great many empty seats. Every Athletics player in the starting nine got at least one hit except pitcher Elmer Myers, who was quite content to cruise home with a rare laugher. Myers allowed ten hits, but surrendered no walks and struck out eight New Yorkers. It was Myers' 12th win of the season. Somewhere in the A's clubhouse, Sheehan and Nabors must have enviously wondered why they never seemed to get 14 hits and eight runs from their teammates as Myers did on this day. The lone negative of the game from the Athletics' standpoint was the two errors Charlie Pick committed at third base. He now had 41 on the season, an unacceptably high number for a third baseman. The win was the 30th for the A's against 101 losses.

The Yankees must have taken offense at Friday's soggy shellacking because they convincingly swept a Saturday doubleheader from the Mackmen on September 9. This time the A's scored but one run in 18 innings—and that score, an unearned tally, came in the bottom of the first inning of the first game. New York won the opener, 4–1, handing Jing Johnson the loss to end his modest personal winning streak. Bob Shawkey was the winner and allowed only four Philadelphia hits. The victory was Shawkey's 20th. The A's were exceedingly generous on defense, committing four errors. Two were by Charlie Pick and one came at the iron hands of Whitey Witt. The Yankees got just eight hits of Johnson, but they were enough. Frank (Home Run) Baker did not hit any homers for the New Yorkers, but he was the only visiting player to manage more than one hit.

Bullet Joe Bush put forth a decent effort in the second game but nevertheless was on the hook for a 4–0 loss. Home Run Baker lived up to his nickname this time. His ninth round-tripper of the season opened up the scoring in the top of the fourth inning. Three more runs in the seventh—the key blow being a two-run single by first baseman Wally Pipp—secured the win for the Yankees. The Athletics could muster only five hits in the game off promising rookie Urban Shocker. Two were belted by Stuffy McInnis, who connected for a double. Shocker was now 2–2 after the complete-game win. The Athletics were now 30–103. The Yankees' win propped them up into fourth place in the AL standings. They still possessed at least a mathematical chance to win the pennant.

In a delightful bit of irony, the Yankees released turncoat Rube Oldring at the end of the day. He had played in the first game of the doubleheader and had gotten a hit and an RBI in three times at bat. Since signing with the Yankees on July 13, Oldring had batted just .234 in 43 games with New York, 13 points below what he had batted for the A's in 40 games in 1916 before abandoning the Athletics' floundering ship in late June. Connie Mack was a forgiving soul, though. Oldring was inactive in 1917, but he would re-surface with the Athletics for about a third of a season in 1918 before retiring for the umpteenth time—and this time meaning it.

William G. Weart's Philadelphia report in the September 14 edition of *The Sporting News* was largely about the Phillies and their ongoing tight battle for the NL flag with the Brooklyn Robins, but he did pen a few paragraphs about the surprising non-rainout on September 8 that had more than a few critical tongues wagging in the New York City dailies.

> The Athletics have kept up their record of winning one or more games from every opponent. They did this last week when Boston came here and again against the Yankees.
>
> It is claimed that the White Elephants and the Yankees played to a record crowd for smallness in the number of paid admissions here last Friday. In order to get in three games in two days, the teams played on Friday after a terrific thunderstorm had passed over the city and on a field covered with water and mud. All accounts agree that the conditions were frightful for playing.
>
> The New York newspapers are blaming Connie Mack for the affair. As a matter of fact, [Yankees manager Bill] Donovan was responsible. As has been written before in this column, when manager Mack returned from his last trip, he decided to give

every club that came here a chance to say whether or not there should be a game if the weather was bad or the grounds in bad condition. This privilege was taken advantage of by [St. Louis manager] Fielder Jones and also by [Boston manager] Bill Carrigan. The Yankees wanted to pay because they believed they could win the game and also because they did not want to call off an exhibition game on Monday [to play a makeup game for a rainout].

To make matters worse for the Yankees, the Athletics handed them a severe defeat. Wally Schang made two home runs, one with the bases filled, and Don [sic] Brown, a newcomer, made one four-bagger.

Another record made that day was that only one reporter, George N. Young, saw the game. All the other [scribes] took it for granted that the teams couldn't play and remained downtown.

On page three of that same issue of *TSN*, an editorial about ex–Athletic Jimmy Walsh commented on his good fortune on being shipped to the Red Sox.

> Though Connie Mack still wallows in the *Slough of Despond*, the luck of the players he made famous continues. The latest instance is the case of outfielder Jimmy Walsh who has been transferred to the Boston Red Sox in payment for catcher Pat Haley and thus gets in line for a chance at more World Series riches and glory. Mack had Walsh under his wing for several years, and though he did not always play good ball, Connie never despaired of him. Connie farmed him out a couple of times and then sent him to the New York Yankees at a time when the Yankees needed help. When the Yankees became more independent, they shipped him back. Now he goes to Boston where he hopes to be in [the World Series] again. Some players are born lucky; others have their luck developed for them by Connie Mack.

After the series at Shibe Park versus the Yankees, the Athletics were inactive until Wednesday, September 13, when they began their next-to-last road trip of the season in Cleveland. The reeling Indians, who had lost nine of their previous ten games and had summarily dropped from the ranks of the AL pennant contenders, responded with an 8–4 win. The contest was not decided until the home half of the seventh inning when Cleveland expanded their 5–4 lead with three more runs. Tris Speaker showed why he was about to be crowned the batting champion. He got three hits in three at-bats. They were part of a nine-hit attack off ineffective A's pitcher Elmer Myers, who went the distance. Milo Allison had a big game for the Tribe, too, scoring three runs from the leadoff spot. Myers was constantly in trouble as he walked seven Indians. The Athletics had more success at the plate than Cleveland, garnering 12 hits off starting pitcher Fred Beebe and reliever Otis Lambeth. The first four Athletics in the batting order accounted for eight hits. One of them was a newcomer: a 24-year-old second baseman from the west coast named Roy Grover. With Nap Lajoie's sudden retirement, Grover was thrust into the role of the Athletics' second sacker for the remainder of the season. He would hold down the position for the 1917 season, too. In his debut game he got two hits (including a double), and handled four chances in the field flawlessly. Grover's efforts were not enough as Myers picked up his 21st loss of the season. Lambeth got the win in relief for the home team. The Athletics dropped to 30–104.

The A's-Indians game on Thursday, September 14, was no contest. The home team scored six runs in the second inning and romped to an easy 9–1 victory. The Indians got 11 hits, all of them singles. Every Cleveland player but catcher Hank DeBerry got at least one hit. (DeBerry was playing in just his third MLB game. His career would last until 1930.) Winning pitcher Al Gould, a right-handed rookie, scored two runs. Losing pitcher Jack Nabors did not get stellar defensive help (the A's committed three errors), but he did give up eight runs, of which five were earned. He picked up his 19th loss of the season. His losing soulmate, Tom Sheehan, gave up a run in one inning of relief work. Whitey Witt hit two triples for the Athletics, but he scored zero runs. The only Philadelphian to score was Raymond Haley, who pinch-hit for Nabors in the eighth inning. He drew a walk. The A's fell to 30–105. They had allowed 691 runs to their opponents in their 136 games. No other team in MLB had allowed more than 566 runs.

The Friday, September 15, battle at Cleveland's Dunn Field also went to the home team. This time it was a much closer affair; the Indians scored a run in the ninth inning to win, 3–2. Tom Sheehan, who had barely exerted himself in a short relief stint the previous day, got the start for the Mackmen. He went the distance—8⅓ innings—but got tagged with the loss. He was now 1–15. Ken Penner, a right-hander from Booneville, IN, making just his third MLB appearance and his first as a starting pitcher, went seven strong innings for Cleveland. He gave up two runs on six hits while striking out three A's and walking none. With Cleveland trailing 2–1 in the bottom of the seventh, Penner was removed for pinch-hitter Braggo Roth, who failed to get a hit. However, Cleveland did tie the score in that frame and won it with a run in the ninth. By that time, Clarence (Pop-boy) Smith was on the hill for the home team. The Athletics got eight hits off the two Tribe pitchers. Three players (Whitey Witt, Amos Strunk and Charlie Pick) got two hits apiece. Jack Graney got three hits for the winners. The A's produced the most spectacular defensive play of the afternoon: a seldom seen 5-3-4-2 double play, in which the ball started in third baseman Pick's hands, then went to Stuffy McInnis at first base, over to Roy Grover at second base, and finally to Raymond Boley at home. Good defensive play aside, the loss dropped Philadelphia to 30–106. Despite looking very capable on the mound, Penner would pitch just four games for Cleveland in 1916 and not resurface in the majors for another 13 years, when he pitched five games for the pennant-winning 1929 Chicago Cubs.

The A's began their final visit to Detroit's Navin Field in 1916 with a Saturday game on September 16, a 4–3 loss. Detroit's Howard Ehmke and Philadelphia's Jing Johnson each had a rough beginning to the game. The score was tied 2–2 after the first inning. The A's outhit the Tigers, 8–6, but it was Detroit which capitalized better on opportunities. Johnson walked six Tigers, and Whitey Witt's 70th error of the season hurt the visitors by creating an unearned Tigers run. Ehmke walked five Athletics, but he struck out seven. Ty Cobb got two hits for the winners (including a triple), as did Bobby Veach. Witt got two hits for the A's. So did Amos Strunk and Wally Schang. The 107th loss of the season was pretty much meaningless to the visitors, but the win put Detroit alone in first place in the AL standings after Boston lost to the White Sox in Chicago before more than 40,000 people. The White Sox actually moved into second place, half a game in arrears of Detroit and half a game ahead of Boston. Although five teams were still mathematically in the chase, it was basically down to a three-team race in the AL with only two weeks left on the schedule. The Tigers' sudden late-season surge had taken most everyone by surprise. Detroit correspondent H. G. Salsinger wrote in the September 21 issue of *The Sporting News*, "Had the Tigers been able to get together the same way during mid-season, the club could now be taking orders for World Series tickets." Salsinger would later edit the sports section of the *Detroit News*.

Sunday's game, at least on paper, should have been a victory for the A's. The hometown Tigers looked terrible on defense, making six errors. They were also outhit by a 12–7 margin, yet Detroit still prevailed in ten innings, 6–5. Both starting pitchers, Joe Bush for the Athletics and Harry Coveleski for Detroit, went the distance. Only one of the five Philadelphia runs was earned. Amos Strunk had three hits in the losing effort. Detroit's win kept them ahead of Boston by one game as the Red Sox beat Chicago, 6–2. In a game between two also-rans that same day at St. Louis' Sportsman Park, George Sisler of the Browns outdueled Washington's Walter Johnson, 1–0, in a terrific pitchers' battle. Sisler batted third for the Browns that day.

Philadelphia put an end to its latest losing streak with a well-pitched 2–0 win over the Tigers on Monday, September 18. Elmer Myers got the shutout, allowing only three Detroit hits. Myers hit two Tigers and walked four, but none came around to score. Detroit's Willie Mitchell allowed only four hits to Philadelphia, two of them by Stuffy McInnis. Whitey Witt made his 71st error of the season, but he also got the game's only RBI. The win was Myers 13th of the year against 21 losses. Detroit's loss was critical, as Boston's win in Chicago put the Red Sox into a first-place tie with the Tigers, with the White Sox 1.5 games back in third place. Philadelphia was now 31–108.

Comiskey Park was where the A's next stopped on Tuesday, September 19, as their season wound down with another head-shaking defeat. Connie Mack's two most luckless hurlers combined for a devastating loss. Jack Nabors, looking for his first victory since April 22, did extremely well and looked poised for an overdue win. He held a 4–2 lead through the top of the eighth inning. In the top of the eighth, Mack opted to replace Nabors with pinch-hitter Lee McElwee, who responded with a single. Bullet Joe Bush pinch-ran for McElwee and came around to score. Nabors' roommate, Tom Sheehan, got the nod from manager Mack to wrap things up on the mound. Sheehan got through the home half of the eighth unscathed, but he gave up three runs in the bottom of the ninth to lose, 5–4. Two White Sox pinch-hitters got base hits and another drew a walk. All three eventually scored. Dave Danforth fortuitously picked up the win with 1⅔ innings of solid work in relief of starter Joe Benz. The collapse meant an excellent three-RBI output by Amos Strunk went for naught. History has no record of what Nabors and Sheehan spoke about in their Chicago hotel room that night—or if they spoke at all. The loss put Sheehan at 1–16. It was his last appearance of the 1916 season, and he would not pitch in another game in the major leagues until he resurfaced with the New York Yankees in 1921. The A's record dropped to a miserable 31–109.

The following day, Wednesday, September 20, saw Connie Mack's crew lose another one-run game to the White Sox. This time the score was 8–7 and the A's never led. Jing Johnson was rocked for three runs and four hits in just one inning's work before being lifted for a pinch-hitter in the top of the second. Elmer Myers batted for Johnson, his eighth pinch-hitting appearance of 1916, and struck out. He did not stay in the game as a pitcher. The creative Mack instead called upon a Philadelphian named Harry (Socks) Seibold to relieve Johnson. Seibold had appeared as a center fielder in Detroit four days earlier. Seibold allowed four more White Sox runs in 4⅓ innings. Rube Parnham, a right-hander from the Philadelphia area as well, mopped up the final 2⅔ innings in his major league debut. Yet, for all the unorthodox maneuvers coming from Mack, the A's did play a competitive game. They managed 11 hits and scored two runs in an inning three times to keep the game within reach. The White Sox got 13 singles and a double and laid down five sacrifice bunts to win the game with "small ball." Reb Russell was the winning pitcher for Chicago. The win kept the White Sox 1.5 games back of Boston. The Red Sox edged Detroit, 4–3, that same day. The Tigers sat in third place, two games behind Boston in what was becoming a terrific battle for the AL flag. Meanwhile, at the bottom of the heap, the loss was the Athletics' 110th of the season.

There was not much to talk about as the Athletics wound down their dismal 1916 campaign to its inevitable last-place finish. Gloom and despair seemed to be pervasive in the September 21 issue of *The Sporting News*, in which the St. Louis correspondent predicted a "dreary" 1917 for that city's two MLB clubs. There was even bad news to report from the defunct Federal League, as its Pittsburgh club filed for bankruptcy, listing more than $173,000 in outstanding debts and only $50,000 in assets.

Meanwhile, Philadelphia correspondent William G. Weart wrote in that same issue about an attractive A's "championship reunion" barnstorming tour scheduled to begin once the season ended. Although frowned upon by club owners because they thought such tours somehow demeaned the World Series, MLB players not involved in post-season play could augment their bank accounts considerably by playing in exhibition games in towns small and large across North America. If the gate receipts and the weather proved to be especially good, some players could make nearly the equal of their MLB salaries by playing an extra month or so in the boondocks. Captivated rural and small-town baseball fans, hungry to see real major league players they had only read about, turned out in the hundreds and thousands to watch MLB players take on each other or local semipro or amateur outfits. The traveling pros, of course, got the lion's share of the money that ended up in the cash box. In this case, the lineup of star players—who were not too far removed from the Athletics' roster—would make the fans of the 1916 A's pine for the good old days of not so long ago. One of the players signed up for the tour was the enigmatic Rube Oldring, whose continuous retirements and un-retirements from baseball were becoming a predictable joke which correspondent Weart did not find particularly amusing.

> Rube Oldring is going to spring another comeback. To quote an old saying, "Wouldn't that jar you?" It is doubtful, though, if anything Oldring would do anymore would jar the fans. After resigning from the Athletics, Rube went back to his farm in New Jersey. Then he decided to play out the rest of the season with the New York Yankees. He again got a yearning for his farm, and when New York was here [in Philadelphia] a week ago, [Yankees manager Bill] Donovan gave him his release and paid him off the balance of the season. It was pretty soft for Oldring, and once more he was "going to quit for good." But once more Rube has heard the "recall." He is not going to sign a contract with a major league or minor league team. This time he is going to barnstorm and let his farm take care of itself again.
>
> As soon as the championship season is over, Harry Davis and Monte Cross are going to pilot a team of former world champions through the underbrush. They have secured promises from former stars of the Athletics that they will make a barnstorming tour through Pennsylvania, New Jersey and Delaware. All the men, except for Fritz Maisel [of the Yankees] who will play right field, helped to win at least two pennants and one world's championship for the Athletics.
>
> The lineup of the team will be Maisel, right field; [Rube] Oldring, left field; Eddie Collins, second base; [Frank] Baker, third base; [Stuffy] McInnis, first base; [Amos] Strunk, center field; [Jack] Barry, shortstop; [Wally] Schang and [Jack] Lapp, catchers; [Eddie] Plank, [Chief] Bender and [Jack] Coombs, pitchers. It will be the strongest team ever taken on a barnstorming tour and would give the winner of the next World Series a tough battle.
>
> The tour will start at Upland, PA where Frank Baker played after he quit the Athletics on October 7. Those players who are delayed in joining the team at the start

of the tour by the World Series or the Chicago City Series will join the barnstormers as soon as possible.

In his weekly report, Weart also praised the good offensive work of Whitey Witt, and accurately predicted that Witt would be better suited for a position other than shortstop.

> Of the infielders tried this year, only one has shown sufficient improvement to make the fans believe he is going to be a star. That is [Whitey] Witt. Lots of games were lost by the Athletics this season through Witt's greenness, but the boy has improved in the field, owing to the careful coaching of [Nap] Lajoie, and has also proved he is going to rank high as a slugger. It may be that manager Mack will shift Witt to some other position, but the chances are that the lad will continue to play regularly and be the leadoff batsman.

The Athletics finally made good on their opportunity to play spoiler in the AL pennant race on Thursday, September 21, by handing the White Sox a costly 8–0 shellacking in their final contest of the season at Comiskey Park. Bullet Joe Bush's shutout was not as impressive as his August no-hitter. He gave up five hits and six walks to the home team, but none of the baserunners came around to score. The White Sox stranded nine runners on base. It was Bush's 15th win of the season against 24 losses. The Athletics had a terrific day at the plate, rapping out 16 hits off two White Sox hurlers, Red Faber and Lefty Williams. Every Athletic had at least one hit, and six different A's had multi-hit games. In what was easily his best game of 1916, Jim Brown got three hits and scored two runs. A four-run ninth inning salted the game away for the Mackmen. Philadelphia's win undoubtedly pleased the Red Sox. In Detroit, Boston throttled the Tigers, 10–2, to move 2.5 games ahead of the White Sox and three ahead of the third-place Tigers. The New York Yankees were a distant fourth, nine games back of Boston. The New Yorkers were still mathematically alive in the pennant race, but just barely. The A's were 51.5 games in arrears of Boston with their 32–110 record. They did score their 400th run of the season, though. Washington had the next lowest total in the AL with 464.

On Friday, September 22, the A's began their last series of 1916 at Sportsman's Park in St. Louis, where a late Browns rally deprived them of their second straight win. The home team won, 6–3, by scoring four runs in the bottom of the eighth inning. Elmer Myers went the distance, allowing ten hits to the victors. Philadelphia's bats were still hot. The visitors collected 11 hits—all singles—off A's alumnus Eddie Plank. It was also a case of one player arriving and another one departing for the Mackmen. Bill Johnson, making his MLB debut, played center field for the A's. He got two hits and struck out twice in four at-bats. Meanwhile Jim Brown, the batting star of the A's win in Chicago, failed to get a hit in a pinch-hitting role in the top of the ninth and never appeared in another MLB game. Chicago, Boston and Detroit all won their contests to keep the race atop the standings interesting. The White Sox beat the Yankees, thus officially eliminating all other teams from the pennant chase. The Browns win gave them a 76–72 record. Mack's A's were 32–111.

St. Louis won Saturday's game as well, this time by a 4–2 count. The game featured two home runs, a rarity in 1916. Wally Schang hit his seventh of the season, a solo shot in the eighth inning off winning pitcher Bob Groom. Del Pratt of St. Louis hit his fifth of the year in the fourth inning off losing pitcher Jing Johnson. It too came with no runners aboard. Johnson had a complete-game loss that dropped his record to 2–8. There was also speed on display as each team stole three bases. The Browns had a more balanced attack than the Athletics, spreading their nine hits among seven players. In the more important AL games of the day, Boston won in Cleveland while Chicago and Detroit both lost. The Red Sox, with a timely hot streak, were starting to open up a gap on their two serious pursuers.

Socks Seibold was definitely the hero for the Athletics in the first game of their Sunday, September 24, doubleheader at Sportsman's Park. He threw a complete-game shutout and got two hits himself in the A's 2–0 triumph. The losing Browns pitcher was George Sisler, who batted third because of his offensive prowess. (It was not apparent on this day; Sisler went hitless in four at-bats.) Seibold allowed just three St. Louis hits, two of them by the Browns' Cuban-born center fielder, Armando Marsans. Philadelphia got six hits and scored single runs in the third and seventh innings. Stuffy McInnis hit a key triple and made 15 putouts at first base as ground balls to the A's infielders were plentiful. It was Sisler's third pitching appearance of 1916. His record was 1–2. He would not pitch again until 1918. Although Sisler pitched sporadically until 1928, he started only one more MLB game after this one. The loss to Seibold was the last MLB game in which Sisler pitched and figured in the decision.

The Browns earned a split in the doubleheader with a tightly contested 3–2 win. The A's outhit the Browns, eight to six, but the Browns held a 2–1 lead after the first inning. Burt Shotton and Ward Miller combined for four of St. Louis' hits. Each had a double as did Doc Lavan. Rube Parnham went the distance for the Athletics in the loss. Only two of the Browns' runs were earned. Parnham tried to help his own cause by smacking a double, his first. Whitey Witt also connected for a double, his 14th. Ernie Koob got credit for the win.

The second game of the doubleheader was the last appearance of the season for disappointing third baseman Charlie Pick. Pick had hit no home runs and just three triples while batting only .241. More glaringly, he made 42 errors and compiled an unacceptable .899 fielding percentage in his 108 games at the hot corner. In his eight games as an outfielder, Pick's fielding average was even worse: .882. No other regular MLB third baseman would have a fielding average below .900 for more than six decades until Butch Hobson posted an identical .899

mark in 133 games for the 1978 Boston Red Sox. In fairness, Hobson was playing that season with an injured elbow—exacerbated damage from his days as a backup wishbone quarterback at the University of Alabama. Most of his 43 errors that season were on bad throws. In Hobson's SABR biography, author Andrew Blume wrote, "A familiar sight in 1978 was Hobson making a play and then rearranging the bone chips in his elbow." Pick had no such physical ailment in 1916 to serve as an excuse. Philadelphia dropped to 33–113 with the second-game loss. The A's were fully 53 games behind the front-running Red Sox and 39.5 games behind the seventh-place Washington Senators.

On this day, the AL pennant race got tighter as Red Sox lost to Cleveland, while the Tigers and White Sox each won.

The September 28 edition of *The Sporting News* contained the usual optimism and praise for the Athletics courtesy of the typewriter of Philadelphia correspondent William G. Weart. Weart specifically mentioned how the A's intermittent shutout wins on the western road trip had affected the AL pennant race.

> The Athletics are finishing their third western trip a little better than they did their other trips to that section. The first trip west netted the Mackmen no victories. The second trip netted them one success at Detroit. On the trip which wound up Sunday, the Athletics helped to knock both Detroit and Chicago out of the [lead for the] pennant. Two well pitched games, one by Myers and one by Bush, helped the chances of the Boston Red Sox considerably. Myers shut out the Tigers and Bush blanked the White Sox, the former's victory knocking Detroit out of first place. Seibold blanked the Browns on Sunday, so oddly enough, all three victories were shutouts.
>
> Western critics have paid the Athletics a lot of compliments during their third invasion of that section. It has become apparent that manager Mack has caused a big improvement in his combination and that he is almost ready for the reappearance of his team in the class of pennant contenders.
>
> [Buck] Thrasher, the hard hitter from Atlanta, who is destined for a regular berth in the outfield, is waiting here [in Philadelphia] for the Athletics to return home, but [Ping] Bodie who will be in the outfield next year with [Amos] Strunk and Thrasher will not arrive until next spring.
>
> After getting home, Connie will have ten days to do some polishing up of his team for 1917, but whether or not he will have the Mack School kept open until late in the fall has not been announced.

That same issue of *The Sporting News* also addressed the increasingly popular idea of having the Chicago White Sox play the New York Giants in a special post-season series regardless of the outcomes of the two leagues' pennant races. According to the baseball weekly, the White Sox were considered by many to be the best club in the AL despite not being in first place. They also were thought to be the best box office draw in the AL when playing on the road. The Giants, who would finish fourth in NL despite starting the season as poorly as the A's, had reeled off a 17-game winning streak earlier in the season. In the middle of September they were in the midst of establishing an MLB record 26-game winning streak. John McGraw's outfit always attracted attention in good seasons and bad. His crew was the biggest gate attraction in the NL. However, the power brokers of MLB did not favor any sort of post-season encounter between the two clubs because of the very real chance it might overshadow and diminish the World Series. Such a series would cast "the big games in the shade," declared correspondent George S. Robbins. Furthermore, the White Sox and Cubs had a longstanding agreement to compete in an annual "Chicago City Series" if neither team won its respective league's pennant. Accordingly, Robbins declared that Charles Comiskey would not consider breaking his agreement with Cubs owner Charlie Weeghman.

Meanwhile the Boston Red Sox were busily denying rumors that if they were to win the AL pennant they would play their World Series home games at Braves Field instead of Fenway Park because of the greater seating capacity available in the NL ballpark. A bulletin in *The Sporting News* with a Boston dateline insisted, "The Red Sox will play at their own park. Though it may not seat as many spectators as Braves Field, still is expected to accommodate, with additional seating arrangements, fully 36,000 spectators." The Red Sox would make liars out of those folks who denied the rumor and the person who wrote the story.

The Athletics returned to Shibe Park on Wednesday, September 27, to face the Washington Senators, who were far in front of the Mackmen despite being in seventh place. As if to emphasize which team was in the AL cellar, the Senators pounded the Athletics, 13–3. Washington pounded out 17 hits, including a ninth-inning, two-run home run by Elmer Smith. Ray Morgan and Eddie Foster had four hits apiece for the winners. Philadelphia starter Elmer Myers was cruelly forced to endure the one-sided pasting for the full nine innings. Much-heralded southern slugger Buck Thrasher made his debut with the Athletics, getting one of the eight hits off Washington's Jim Shaw. Three Athletics got two hits apiece, but it far from offset the bludgeoning the Senators batters inflicted. The visitors led 6–0 after the top of the fourth inning and 11–2 after the top of the seventh. Washington also stole five bases in the onslaught, which may have smacked of rubbing it in. Harland Rowe made a pinch-hitting appearance for the Athletics in the ninth inning. He failed to get a hit and then vanished into oblivion with a career MLB batting average of .139. Rowe had connected for just one hit since July 1. The Athletics' record now stood at a pitiful 33–114.

In the only other AL game played that Wednesday—one that actually mattered—Boston beat the Yankees, 3–2, at Fenway Park. The win mathematically eliminated the Detroit Tigers from the AL pennant race. Only the White Sox, down by 2.5 games, could catch the Red Sox.

Jack Nabors reached the dreaded milestone of 20 losses on Thursday, September 28, in a 4–1 loss to the Senators. Typical of most of Nabors' outings, he did not pitch badly. With the A's trailing only 2–1 in the bottom of the eighth, Nabors was removed for pinch-hitter Lee McElwee, who reached base on a fielder's choice. The Athletics failed to score in the inning. Reliever Rube Bressler gave up two runs in one inning of work. Nabors did not walk a batter. He allowed seven hits and struck out four Senators. It would be the last decision he ever figured in as an MLB pitcher. It was also the swansong for McElwee, who never again played in the big leagues. Bert Gallia picked up his 16th win for the victors. A's third baseman Thomas Healy, making his first MLB appearance of 1916, got two hits and scored the Athletics' only run of the game. Amos Strunk got two hits. Whitey Witt got the only other hit for the home team, but fluffed two plays at shortstop to give him 74 errors on the season. With the win, Washington moved into a sixth-place tie with Cleveland. Both the Indians and Senators were 42 games ahead of the sputtering 33–115 A's.

Elsewhere, the Red Sox were beaten by New York, 4–2, at Fenway Park. With the other AL teams idle, Boston missed a huge chance to put the pennant just about on ice. The following day, when the Athletics did not play, Babe Ruth tossed a five-hit, 3–0 shutout to move the Red Sox three games ahead of the White Sox. It was Ruth's 23rd win of the year. The White Sox and Red Sox both had four games left to play. The Red Sox would end their schedule with a doubleheader versus the Athletics at Fenway.

On Saturday, September 30, few baseball observers concerned themselves with the Senators-A's doubleheader at Shibe Park. Quite properly, the interest of most American League fans was split. Action between Boston's Fenway Park, where the Red Sox were hosting the Yankees, and Dunn Field in Cleveland, where the Indians and White Sox were set to play a doubleheader, took precedence. Chicago did their best to keep their faint pennant aspirations alive by taking the two games by scores of 7–2 and 7–3. The second game saw Cleveland level the score at 3–3 in the ninth inning. Chicago scored four runs in the top of the 12th to secure the win. However, in Boston, the Red Sox managed to eke out a ten-inning, 1–0 win over New York to clinch no worse than a tie for the AL flag. The winning run was scored by pinch-runner Mike McNally, who scored on a daring squeeze bunt by Harry Hooper.

Meanwhile, the Senators and A's split their two games. In the opener, Washington scored four runs in the top of the ninth off Socks Seibold to turn an apparent 6–4 loss into an 8–6 win. Jack Nabors was called upon to retire the last two Senators after the Athletics' lead had been blown. Newcomer Buck Thrasher got three hits for the A's. One was a double; one was a triple. For Washington, Sam Rice and John Henry each had three hits. Rice replicated Thrasher's feat of hitting a double and a triple. Bert Gallia picked up his second win in as many games in relief.

The A's got their 34th victory of the season in the second contest of the day, keeping alive a modest streak of winning at least one game per series, with a ridiculous 10–9 win. The ten runs equaled the highest output the A's had managed in 1916 for a single game. (It had earlier happened on May 22 versus Cleveland.) The Senators scored three runs in the top of the ninth to take a 9–6 lead only to have the Mackmen score four times in the home half. Rube Parnham got his first win despite giving up nine runs and 13 hits and being behind 5–0 after the top of the second inning. Shortstop Whitey Witt made two more errors to raise his miscue count to 76 for 1916. But Philadelphia also got 13 hits, including a three-run homer by Amos Strunk in a big four-run seventh inning. Although all three Senators pitchers who saw action in the game were culpable for the ninth-inning collapse, Jim Shaw was tagged with the loss for allowing the winning run to score after failing to retire any of the three batters he faced. It was the final game of the year at Shibe Park. The wild finish and improbable victory gave the patient home fans something positive to remember. Be that as it may, the Athletics were still 34–116.

Boston was the last stop on the schedule for the bedraggled Athletics. Beantown was where the A's had opened the 1916 campaign with trepidation, and the Hub would be the finishing line. By the time the teams took the field for the first game on Monday, October 2, the AL pennant had been decided. The White Sox got only a split in their Sunday doubleheader in Cleveland. The 2–0 loss in the first game, in which Chicago managed only two hits, eliminated any hope they had of catching the Red Sox. Boston would be returning to the World Series to defend the crown they had won the previous year over the Philadelphia Phillies. The Red Sox's opponents had yet to be determined. The Phillies were in an exciting battle with the

Amos Strunk was probably the MVP of the 1916 A's. The steady outfielder played in 150 games and batted .316 (National Baseball Hall of Fame Library, Cooperstown, N.Y.).

Brooklyn Robins to see who would take the NL laurels. According to Boston's correspondent for *The Sporting News*, the identity of the Red Sox's World Series opponent mattered little. Either the Robins or the Phillies would receive "a good beating" from the Crimson Hose.

With no pressure upon their shoulders, the Red Sox played cavalierly and used 16 players in their October 2 game versus Philadelphia. The home side still won the contest 4–2. The Red Sox began the game with most of their starters in the lineup, but yanked them upon taking a 4–0 lead, including starting pitcher Ernie Shore, who left after pitching five hitless innings. Philadelphia made it close with two runs in the top of the seventh frame, but could get no closer. It was the White Elephants' 117th loss of the season. It would also turn out to be their last defeat. Jing Johnson did not get much offensive help as the A's managed just four hits to the Red Sox's nine. It was Johnson's ninth loss of the campaign versus two wins. A doubleheader the next day would end the nightmarish 1916 season for the Mackmen.

The season-ending twin bill versus the Red Sox was taken far more seriously by the visitors than by the reigning AL champions. The Athletics were rewarded with a doubleheader sweep—only their second of the dreary season. The scores were 5–3 and 7–5. The Red Sox employed 17 players in the first game to the Athletics' ten. The only Philadelphia substitute was pitcher Axel Lindstrom, a 21-year-old, Swedish-born right-hander, who pitched the last four innings of the game that Rube Parnham started. Lindstrom even managed a hit in two at-bats. His pitching line showed two earned runs, two hits allowed, a hit batter, and a strikeout. It would be his only MLB game. Offensively, the A's got five triples amongst their 12 hits. Roy Grover got two of the three-baggers. In the seesaw game, the Athletics scored twice in the fifth inning to assume a 3–1 lead. Boston got close, but would not manage to equal the score.

The second game of the day was even more of a free-for-all for the Boston club. Eighteen different Red Sox entered the game at some point. Again, Connie Mack just employed one substitute from his bench. Babe Ruth was the losing pitcher, but probably did not care too much. Philadelphia outhit Boston, 15 to 12, and led 7–2 going into home half of the ninth inning. Starting pitcher Elmer Myers had departed after five innings and got credit for the win, his 14th against 23 losses. The Red Sox made it close with three scores off Jack Nabors, the man who was the A's starter on Opening Day in Boston when a degree of hope and optimism was in the air. Mack probably put Nabors into the game as a goodwill gesture to see if he could deservedly end the season on a winning note despite having a 1–20 record. He did, although Myers got credit for the victory. Whitey Witt made two more errors to give him the appalling total of 78 for the year, but he did contribute three hits, including a double. Thomas Healy, the A's third baseman, smacked a triple in what would be his last MLB game. Weldon Wyckoff, who had been a member of the A's pitching staff until June, was the final hurler the Athletics had to face in 1916. He gave up three runs in four innings and did not look overly threatening. The Red Sox could now look forward to the upcoming World Series. The A's could only look individually and collectively toward the off-season and an uncertain 1917.

How did Philadelphia correspondent William G. Weart describe the A's doubleheader sweep in the pages of *The Sporting News*? He surprisingly did not! Weart's column in the October 5 edition focused completely on the Phillies and their battle with the Brooklyn Robins for the NL pennant. The Mackmen's positive finish to the dismal campaign did not merit a single sentence from the scribe who had been the Athletics' most conspicuous cheerleader all season long.

The debacle that was the 1916 Philadelphia Athletics was finally over for the players, manager Connie Mack, and the team's fans. Interestingly, the Athletics did not finish last in AL attendance; they were seventh. A total of 184,471 people made their way through the turnstiles at Shibe Park, an average of 2,427 per home game, a stat that does not recognize that many doubleheaders played there had single admission prices. It was also a 26 percent improvement on the 146,223 fans who had attended A's home games in 1915 even though the Athletics performed worse in 1916 than they had the previous year. Despite being hopelessly out of the pennant race almost from the middle of May, the lowly A's somehow managed to outdraw the Washington Senators, who drew just 177,265 paying customers in 1916 even with the likable superstar pitcher Walter Johnson on their roster.

Those resolute supporters of Mack's 1916 team did not see many victorious afternoons for their beloved White Elephants at Shibe Park—or any other AL ball yard. In 154 official American League games the A's won 36, lost 117 and tied one. They were 81 games under .500. Their winning percentage was .235, shattering the popular baseball adage that even the worst MLB team will win one-third of its games over the course of a season. Philadelphia missed achieving that mark by 15 wins. The A's were 54.5 games behind Boston and 40 games in arrears of the seventh-place Washington Senators. The Mackmen scored 447 runs and generously allowed 776 runs to their grateful opponents. The Athletics were 11–32 in one-run games. In games decided by five or more runs, the A's were 7–39. Their longest winning streak had been a mere two games.

The A's were treated equally shabbily by the entire league. In the balanced 1916 schedule, in which they faced the seven other clubs 22 times each, the Athletics won no fewer than four games and no more than seven games versus each opponent. By being so universally hapless, Mack's lousy bunch did not dramatically affect how the AL pennant race unfolded in 1916. The pennant-winning Red Sox won 16 of their 22 encounters with the Mackmen. The Tigers and the White Sox, who were furiously chasing Boston during the final week of the season, beat the Athletics 18 times apiece.

The Athletics tied the Washington Senators for the worst team batting average in the AL with a .242 mark. They hit the fewest doubles (169). Interestingly, the A's hit the second-most home runs in the league (19) and the fourth-most triples (65). They were sixth in slugging percentage (.313). There were some surprising individual bright spots on such a poor team. Whitey Witt's 15 triples tied him for third best in the AL. Amos Strunk batted .316, a figure that was fourth best in the league. Wally Schang's seven home runs were good enough for third-best in the league in an era when round-trippers were clearly a rarity. (Wally Pipp of the Yankees led the circuit with just a dozen. His teammate, Home Run Baker, was second with a mere ten.)

Fielding, though, was a glaring problem for Connie Mack's bunch. The White Elephants' 314 errors—an average of more than two miscues per game—was the most in the AL in 1916 by far. The next closest team to the A's was St. Louis with 248 errors. Their overall team fielding percentage of .951 was the league's worst, a full 12 points behind the Browns.

The Athletics' pitching statistics clearly demonstrate that it was an area of severe weakness, too. Mack's hurlers allowed 715 bases on balls, an average of 4.64 per game. Six AL teams issued fewer than 500 passes. The A's team ERA was 3.92. Every other AL club had an ERA below 3.00. Although it was an unknown stat in 1916, the A's compiled just three saves all year—and two of them came in the meaningless doubleheader that concluded the season at Fenway Park on October 3. Conversely, the A's led the AL in complete games with 94, ten more than the two next-closest clubs, the Yankees and the Senators. The explanation for this quirky accomplishment seems obvious once the games' box scores are thoroughly examined: Mack would routinely leave his starter in a game long after other managers would have relieved him simply because sticking with the starter was a better proposition than deferring to the unreliable A's bullpen. Such was the lack of depth among the relievers that, in numerous cases, a Philadelphia starter had to muddle his way through a game that was hopelessly out of reach. Given the circumstances surrounding the team and the atypical burdens put on the starting pitchers, it is remarkable that the Athletics did not lose more horribly one-sided contests than they did in 1916. A couple of A's hurlers actually appeared among the AL leaders in positive pitching categories. Bullet Joe Bush was third in complete games (25), second in shutouts (8), fourth in strikeouts (157), and fourth in fewest hits per nine innings pitched (6.97). Elmer Myers trailed only the great Walter Johnson in strikeouts (182). Myers was also fourth in innings pitched (315).

But baseball is a team game, and individual statistics count for little outside the collective goal of all team sports: achieving wins. Despite the good performances of a select few players, the end result was that the 1916 Philadelphia Athletics were a cellar-dwelling outfit, a team that was unable to rise above fifth place at its apex of mediocrity in May. The 1916 version of the White Elephants were hopelessly outclassed by every other team in the AL, and their record clearly showed it. Those doubters, who had brashly predicted in spring training that Mack's combination of youthful newcomers and raw collegians mixed in with a few veterans here and there would not produce a competitive major league squad, had been absolutely correct in their disheartening forecasts. The 1916 A's really had been what *Baseball Magazine* had dubbed them: the Pathetics. Mack himself took a more pragmatic view of the dismal season that had just concluded for him and his bedraggled White Elephants. "You can't win them all," he told a reporter, undoubtedly following the comment with a wry, engaging smile.[1]

Heroes and Pleasant Surprises, Villains, Disappointments and Busts

No recap of any MLB team's season can be complete without a thorough post-mortem to see which members of the roster fared well, which ones flopped, which ones displayed heroics, and which ones were negative influences. Even a team as undeniably bad as the 1916 Athletics ought to be examined in such a manner.

Heroes/Pleasant Surprises

Amos Strunk—Speedy and durable Amos Strunk was Connie Mack's most reliable and impactful player over the course of the long, disappointing season. He played in 150 games, mostly in center field, and batted a very respectable .316, an average good enough for fourth place in the AL. He made only seven errors while accruing 20 assists, a terrific total in any era. Strunk would be an obvious choice for the team's MVP if such a thing had existed in 1916.

Wally Schang—The A's starting catcher on Opening Day, Schang injured himself in the first game of the season in Boston. He played mostly left field after May and fielded his position surprisingly well despite having little experience there. Schang was the A's best power hitter all season and practically their only home run threat. Schang batted a respectable .266 with seven home runs. He even recovered nicely from a scary concussion he sustained on July 18 when he collided solidly with Shibe Park's imposing concrete wall while recklessly chasing a Joe Jackson fly ball into foul territory.

Bullet Joe Bush—Bush was the A's most reliable pitcher when reliable pitching was a sorely needed commodity—which was constantly. His spectacular no-hitter versus Cleveland on August 26 was a well deserved and fitting reward for a man who pitched his heart out in a joyless season, one in which Bush performed not too badly at all. He was 15–24 with a 2.57 ERA and completed 25 of the 33 games he started.

Elmer Myers—Elmer Myers' pitching record was almost as good as Bush's (14–23 with 31 complete games out of the 35 he started). Like Bush, Myers put up respectable pitching stats (182 strikeouts, for example) under very trying and disheartening circumstances.

Stuffy McInnis—McInnis played solidly at first base, fielding at a .992 rate and making just 12 errors in 1,214⅔ innings—very noteworthy considering the wildness of fellow infielders Whitey Witt and Charlie Pick. He was temporarily laid low with a mid-season charley horse but still turned in decent stats at bat (.295, and led the team with 60 RBI) and in the field (96 assists and 1,404 putouts). The stalwart McInnis finished all 140 games he started—quite remarkable considering how Mack liked to tinker and experiment with his lineup once the season became a write-off.

Whitey Witt—A green rookie, Whitey Witt's 78 errors clearly made him a liability at shortstop. His batting average was .245, but he nevertheless hit consistently, never going into a prolonged slump throughout the season. Witt also had surprising pop in his bat, rapping out 15 triples. Witt got on base frequently, scored 64 runs (second best on the team) and was fleet of foot enough to make him a capable leadoff hitter. After Sam Crane quickly proved he woefully lacked enough hitting skill to be a big-leaguer, Witt became the team's unquestioned shortstop. Filled with enthusiasm, among the raw recruits Witt was Connie Mack's prize find of 1916.

Billy Meyer—Meyer proved to be Connie Mack's best catcher in 1916. He was not especially threatening in the batter's box (he batted .232), but he was the most reliable replacement for Schang behind the plate. An emergency appendectomy suddenly and sadly brought Meyer's season to an end in late July. The fact that Mack experimented with so many backstops after Meyer was disabled—most of the time with very little success—testified to Meyer's competence and capability. His absence for the second half of the schedule was a significant blow to the team. It probably was a factor in the A's horrendous losing streak from July 21 to August 10.

Napoleon Lajoie—Nap Lajoie really had no reason to still be playing professional baseball in 1916, especially for a sorry squad stocked with a revolving door of college-bred hopefuls and having no hope whatsoever of being anywhere near the top of the AL standings. But Lajoie did play in 1916 as he did in 1915, partly as a favor for his old boss Connie Mack, and partly for one last hurrah in the city where his MLB career had gloriously begun late in the 19th century. For his age, 41, Lajoie did not fare too badly at all. His .246 batting average was nowhere near what he once was able to accomplish in his fearsome heyday, but how many of MLB's everyday second basemen are over the age of 40? He had a .973 fielding percentage, and, like Stuffy McInnis at first base, the veteran second sacker provided more than a degree of leadership and experience. He performed even better defensively at first base and in the outfield on the occasions when he was called upon to do so. A back injury forced his sudden retirement in late August a week before his 42nd birthday, but Lajoie's future place in the Hall of Fame was already assured even if he had not played an inning in 1916. He gets full marks for his efforts.

Villains

Rube Oldring—The man who was voted the most popular professional baseball player in Philadelphia in 1913 basically quit on the struggling 1916 A's in the middle of the season. Even before 1916, the fickle Oldring made a habit of retiring and unretiring more often than Brett Favre. His short-lived retirement abruptly ended, to no one's great surprise, when the New York Yankees picked him up about a month later in an attempt to bolster their chances to win the AL flag. Baseball suddenly became more fun for the petulant Oldring if he could play for a pennant contender. Oldring's stats for New York were worse than what they were for the A's and he was dropped by the Yankees three weeks before the 1916 season concluded. Ironically, Oldring's last game was in Shibe Park— so he finished his season in Philadelphia despite his best intentions to do otherwise!

Mother Nature—The Athletics had an entire series rained out in Chicago early in June. It was a two-pronged disaster: The postponements netted the team a big zero for their share of the gate receipts while they still incurred the usual travel and hotel costs associated with any road trip. The June rainouts also forced the A's to make up the lost games with a cruelly draining number of doubleheaders at Comiskey Park when they retuned there in late July. The White Elephants lost eight games in five days during their worst stretch of the season. Later in the season a heavy downpour and the mistaken assumption of a rainout also kept fans and most of the baseball writers away from Shibe Park on Friday, September 8. That was a shame because on that date Wally Schang became the first player in MLB history to homer from each side of the plate in the same game. It seems completely unfair that Schang's noteworthy feat, a rare highlight for the downtrodden team in 1916, was performed in a nearly empty ballpark.

Disappointments & Busts

Shag Thompson—What can you say about a player who was lauded for his supposed hitting prowess in spring training, who was projected to be a mainstay in the Athletics' outfield for years to come, and then went a dismal 0 for 17 at the plate? Connie Mack likely said, "Good riddance!" No player on the 1916 A's was more disappointing than Shag Thompson—and that is saying something! Thompson does hold the distinction of being the last of the 1916 A's; he died at age 96 in 1990.

Sam Crane—Sam Crane was quite competent with the glove, so Connie Mack penciled him in as the team's shortstop on Opening Day in Boston. His minor league defensive prowess was well known, but Crane could not hit a baseball to save his life. He was 2-for-29 in the handful of games he played for the A's in 1914 and 1915. Even minor league pitching vexed him. Weak hitting shortstops can sometimes eke out a career in MLB. Non-hitting shortstops have a much tougher time of it. He played all of two games for Mack in 1916 (getting one hit in four tries) before getting the hook. Error-prone Whitey Witt was more acceptable at shortstop to Mack because the enthusiastic rookie frequently made contact with the ball while batting. In contrast, Crane was totally out of his element swinging a bat and was virtually an automatic out. Crane was a utility player for three MLB teams afterward, but he did not attract much attention on a national level again until he shot up a barroom in a jealous rage one fateful night in August 1929.

Cap Crowell—Cap Crowell was arguably the most disappointing of Connie Mack's pitchers. The big right-hander had pitched decently in 1915, going 2–5 for a bad team. Mack had high hopes for Crowell to mature and become a regular in the A's shaky pitching rotation, but he failed to pass muster. He continuously had poor outings for a team that absolutely required a solid pitching effort if they had any chance of winning. It seldom happened. In nine games as a starter and reliever, Crowell went 0–5. In one horrible outing in New York in May he walked 11 Yankees. Crowell was cut loose by Mack by the second week of June.

Jimmy Walsh—Connie Mack patiently waited for his Irish-born, fun-loving outfielder to blossom into the feared slugger and speedster he had been in the minor leagues. It never happened. Walsh batted .233 before being dealt to the Boston Red Sox in early September in a trade for Raymond Haley. It was a typical anemic year at the plate for Walsh, who did not do anything spectacular all year except get himself ejected by umpire Brick Owens on two consecutive days.

Jack Nabors—One can defend Jack Nabors' 1–20 pitching record by saying he should have won five or six more games in 1916 if he had gotten any reasonable amount of offensive and defensive support from his teammates. If he is conceded those fictitious victories, the numbers would still make Nabors no better than a pitcher who lost three-quarters of his starts. The lanky right-hander had that rotten record for a reason: He could not seem to win. That is not a good quality in a big league pitcher.

Tom Sheehan—See above section on Jack Nabors. Sheehan, another tall right-hander, was 1–16 in 1916 after compiling a somewhat passable 4–9 record the previous season for the A's. In 1916 Sheehan had even fewer could-have-been wins and should-have-been wins than his downtrodden road-trip roommate. Sheehan vanished from the majors after the 1916 campaign and did not return for another five years. Anyway you slice it, he was a bust.

Charlie Pick—Third baseman Charlie Pick turned out to be a major disappointment in all departments. His 42 errors, sub-.900 fielding percentage, and disappointing offensive stats made him truly expendable. He batted .241 and had only 13 extra-base hits, none of which were home runs. Connie Mack ended up sending Pick to San Francisco of the Pacific Coast League as a "player to be named later" to complete the deal that brought Ping Bodie to Philadelphia in 1917.

Marsh Williams—Williams was arguably the most disappointing of Connie Mack's collegians. Mack gave him ample opportunity to prove his mettle on the mound, but nothing came of it. In ten games, the right-handed hurler went 0–6 and compiled an awful 7.89 ERA. With a WHIP of 1.987, Williams was asking for trouble, and he routinely got it. He walked nearly twice as many batters as he struck out.

Connie Mack—Despite his revered stature in Philadelphia and throughout Organized Baseball in general as the Tall Tactician and the game's courtly gentleman, Mack did not do very much to help his own cause in 1916. He entered the season having made zero off-season moves to improve his stunningly bad 1915 squad. Instead, Mack heavily relied on his pet theory that college campuses were an unrecognized and untapped resource of MLB talent. (He had struck gold with Eddie Collins in the past and truly believed that exception was the rule.) The Athletics' practice of having ongoing open tryouts at Shibe Park throughout much of the year was an indication of Mack's desperation and a source of amusement to the other seven AL clubs. Mack's college-boy theory was proved wrong time and time again when his charges showed they could not handle MLB competition. By the time Mack realized the best MLB prospects were already playing in the minor leagues, the season was a write-off. Mack's policy of leaving his pitchers in games long after they should have been yanked probably did not do wonders for team morale—especially the morale of the pitchers. (Bob Shawkey, a fine pitcher who became a mainstay on the New York Yankees' roster for nearly a decade, basically demanded to be dealt from the Athletics in 1915 because of the unrelenting punishment Mack forced him to endure as a starter.) Overall, Mack's failures as both a manager and general manager in 1916 far outnumbered his successes. Something to ponder: Had Mack not been a part owner of the A's, would he have lasted the season as manager? Not likely.

The Aftermath and Beyond

"I shall never forget Connie Mack's gentleness and gentility."—*Ty Cobb, in a September, 19, 1948,* New York Times *interview*

When the final out was made in their 1916 season, the A's could at least accurately note that they had beaten the soon-to-be World Series champs twice in their own ballpark in the same afternoon to end the utterly dreary campaign. In fact, the Athletics' two surprise triumphs were the last MLB games played at Fenway Park in 1916.

Despite losing the season-ending doubleheader to the lowly Athletics, the AL champion Boston Red Sox rebounded and knocked off the Brooklyn Robins in five games to win the 1916 World Series. The triumph proved the team's management to be correct: The controversial trade that sent outfielder Tris Speaker to Cleveland at the end of spring training was not overly detrimental to the Red Sox's prospects of repeating as World Series champs.

The seemingly carved-in-stone pronouncement that had appeared in the September 28 edition of *The Sporting News*, categorically stating that the Red Sox would play their World Series games at Fenway Park, turned out to be a whopper of a fib. The allure of potentially greater box office receipts at the more spacious Braves Field proved too much for the club's bean-counters to ignore. All three of Boston's home games were shifted across town to the more cavernous NL ballpark. The Red Sox won all three games played there, including the opener on Saturday, October 7, and the eventual clincher on Thursday, October 12. The American League champion had now won every World Series but one since 1910. The lone NL victory was the Boston Braves' surprise win over Connie Mack's powerhouse 1914 Athletics—the thoroughly shocking upset that prompted an angry Mack to dismantle his pennant-winning team prior to the 1915 season.

Twenty-one-year-old left-hander Babe Ruth was the pitching star for the Red Sox in the World Series, going the distance in a 2–1, 14-inning win in the second game at Braves Field on Monday, October 9. No other World Series game in history has ever gone more innings, and only one has equaled it. After a first-inning run on a fortuitous inside-the-park homer by Brooklyn's Hy Myers when two Red Sox outfielders collided, Ruth shut the door on the NL champs. He was well in the process of establishing a streak of 29⅔ consecutive innings of shutout World Series pitching that would remain unchallenged until the heyday of Whitey Ford more than four decades later. Ruth also helped his cause by driving in the tying run from third base in the third inning on a ground out. It was the only game in the 1916 World Series in which Ruth appeared. He was hitless in his five at-bats in the marathon game. Brooklyn's only victory came in the third game. The winning pitcher was Jack Coombs, a refugee from Connie Mack's pennant champs of 1914.

The Sporting News reported on October 26 that AL president Ban Johnson was more than a little bit displeased with the group of MLB players who took part in the lucrative circuit of exhibition games in Pennsylvania, Delaware and Maryland as part of a barnstorming tour once the regular season concluded. The majority of the players were either A's or ex-members of Connie Mack's squad. Rumor had it that Johnson was preparing to levy suspensions and fines on them for disobeying his order not to engage in post-season tours that might take the luster and the fans' attention off the World Series. William G. Weart blamed the situation on a misunderstanding, because the tour had Connie Mack's blessings, and, of course, the esteemed Mr. Mack would never deliberately disobey an edict from the president of the AL. Meanwhile, the annual Chicago City Series between the White Sox and the Cubs, which had the blessings of MLB, drew very sparse crowds in the Windy City. It seemed that the MLB cities had had their fill of quality professional baseball in 1916, but there was an insatiable appetite for it and its star players in the smaller communities across America.

Figuring it could not hurt his team—and always trying to bring out the gentlemanly qualities in his charges—Mack's created a Code of Conduct for his Athletics following the 1916 season:

- I will always play the game to the best of my ability.
- I will always play to win, but if I lose, I will not look for an excuse to detract from my opponent's victory.
- I will never take an unfair advantage in order to win.
- I will always abide by the rules of the game—on the diamond as well as in my daily life.
- I will always conduct myself as a true sportsman—on and off the playing field.
- I will always strive for the good of the entire team rather than for my own glory.
- I will never gloat in victory or pity myself in defeat.
- I will do my utmost to keep myself clean—physically, mentally, and morally.
- I will always judge a teammate or an opponent as an individual and never on the basis of race or religion [Kashatus, *Connie Mack's '29 Triumph*, 35].

By late October a rumor was circulating in the baseball world that Connie Mack would sell his 50 percent ownership of the Athletics and take the managerial job in Boston—a position that had only recently been vacated by Bill Carrigan shortly after his Red Sox won the World Series. In the November 2 issue of *The Sporting News*, William G. Weart said the story was a fiction; Mack was happily remaining in Philadelphia where he was indefatigably occupying his hours with the difficult task of rebuilding his A's into a pennant contender.

> When the Athletics reported at Jacksonville last spring and had a chance to thaw out, Connie realized he had not made the progress that he anticipated. He then declared that it would take him longer than he planned to get his team going right. He had hoped to start his drive at about midseason of 1916. Because certain players did not come up to anticipation, and two pitchers and an outfielder who were counted on fell down on the job, the going was mighty rough. But before the campaign was over, rival managers and critics began to see a lot of good in the Athletics. With his task just half over, no one who knew Connie Mack intimately would have taken that story about his going to Boston seriously. It scarcely needed Connie's denial to spike the yarn. The same reports had the Shibes selling their holdings, either all or in part, to a Mr. George Johnson of Binghamton, NY. The Shibes were also emphatic in their statement that they had no intention of selling their interests in the Athletics. Therefore, there is not even a remote possibility of the Athletics changing ownership or management for the season of 1917, unless something that can not now be foreseen should occur.

Nothing unforeseen did occur. The Athletics were ready for business back at Shibe Park for 1917. To no one's great surprise, Connie Mack was back at his usual post, managing the White Elephants as they attempted to put a competitive product on the field for the first time in three seasons. The club's prospects of improving from 1916 were not significantly improved, though. With the baseball season about to open, the nasty European war became more and more of a world issue. Increased American shipping losses to German submarines swayed public opinion away from neutrality and the United States finally entered the Great War. Suddenly the national pastime was not quite as important in the grand scheme of things, at least for the moment. The Chicago White Sox took the AL pennant in 1917, as the promise they had displayed for much of 1916 came to fruition. They won the World Series, too, beating John McGraw's Giants in six games, continuing the AL's recent grip on the Fall Classic laurels. (The Pale Hose would not win another until 2005, though.) Mack's A's were not a factor in the pennant chase, finishing in the cellar for the third straight season, 44.5 games in arrears of the high-flying White Sox. Their 55–98 record was a marked improvement over their 1916 debacle, however.

The wartime version of MLB affected numerous teams as many big leaguers were forced by edicts of the federal government to do their shares for the war effort in one way or the other. Mack's team wasn't affected at all. They finished dead last again in 1918. Prior to the season Mack, suffering at the ledger, held another 1915-type fire sale of his capable players. Wally Schang, Joe Bush, and Amos Strunk were scooped up by the free-spending owner of the Boston Red Sox, Harry Frazee. In exchange, Mack got $60,000 in cash, a has-been pitcher, and a couple of forgettable prospects. Just before spring training began, Mack dealt the last of his old guard, faithful and reliable Stuffy McInnis, to Boston. McInnis had already reported to the A's camp in Jacksonville when he was informed of the move. In the March 21, 1918, edition of *The Sporting News*, correspondent Jimmy Isaminger angrily declared Mack to be a "team-wrecker" who now had nothing "but himself and home plate." In return for McInnis the A's eventually received Larry Gardner, Tillie Walker and Forrest Cady.

Peace and economic prosperity returned to America not long after the 1918 World Series concluded. (The Fall Classic was won by the Red Sox, who greatly benefitted from the off-season deal with Mack. The Red Sox, of course, would not win another title until 2004.) Prosperity on the diamond was still an elusive commodity for the White Elephants. They had a truly awful campaign in 1919, one sadly comparable to the shambles of 1916. In an abbreviated schedule in which each AL team played 14 fewer games than they did prior to the war, the Mackmen compiled a 36–104 record. They ended up a whopping 52 games behind the front-running White Sox. (Theoretically, if these A's had played another 14 games and lost them all—a realistic possibility considering the dearth of talent on the club—they could have eclipsed the much-maligned 1916 bunch to set a new AL record for losses in a single season!) The only positive note from the 1919 season was that the A's had no connection whatsoever to the infamous World Series fix perpetrated by the AL champion White Sox that October.

The 1920 and 1921 seasons saw the birth of the lively ball era and the emergence of the home run as a regular offensive weapon in MLB. Those seasons also witnessed the A's finish in the AL cellar both years. Philadelphia thus dismally achieved seven consecutive bottom-of-the-heap results from 1915 through 1921. Yet owner/general manager Connie Mack saw no reason to relieve field manager Connie Mack of his duties. The Tall Tactician continued to wear business suits in the dugout and wave his scorecard to position his fielders, all to no avail. But the Athletics' fortunes were going to change, but not immediately. A steady return to respectability—and then to glory—was on its way.

The 1922 version of the A's compiled a 65–89 record, good enough for seventh place, one notch ahead of the lowly Boston Red Sox, whose fortunes had dramatically tumbled since they dealt away Babe Ruth and a fair chunk of his supporting cast after the 1919 season. The Athletics were still far in arrears of the league-leading New York Yankees, but to a club that had endured seven consecutive campaigns in the AL basement, seventh place must have seemed like rarefied air. Ben Shibe, Mack's business partner for two decades, passed away in 1922. The club's financial operations were inherited by his two sons, Tom and John.

Sixty-nine wins in 1923 elevated the Mackmen to the gaudy heights of sixth place. The Athletics rose to fifth spot in 1924, second place in 1925, and third place in 1926. A renaissance of Athletics baseball was beckoning.

By 1927, Mack had rebuilt at least the foundation for another great club. Al Simmons, fiery Mickey Cochrane and Max Bishop were now the regular stalwarts. A young slugger named Jimmie Foxx was making the transition from a part-time catcher to a regular first baseman. Ty Cobb, approaching 41, was Mack's first-string right fielder. The talented but surly Lefty Grove, Rube Walberg, Ed Rommel, and the veteran Jack Quinn supplied the pitching talent. Philadelphia's 91 wins might have won the AL pennant in another season, but the famed 1927 Yankees cruised home with 110 wins. They were never out of first place the entire season. In 1928, a long-in-the-tooth Tris Speaker was added to the A's for veteran leadership and occasional outfield play. The Athletics and their combination of age and youth made a serious challenge for the AL flag, but finished 2.5 games behind New York.

The tables turned in 1929. Mack's A's cruised through the season with a 104–46 record, easily outdistancing the Ruth-Gehrig Yankees by 18 games to cop the AL flag for the first time since the turbulent 1914 season. The White Elephants topped the Chicago Cubs in five games to win their first World Series since 1913. In Game 4 the A's set a World Series record by scoring ten runs in a single inning to overcome an 8–0 deficit. (To date it is still the greatest single-game comeback in MLB post-season history.) In Game 5, at Shibe Park, the A's scored three runs in the bottom of the ninth inning to clinch the series with a win, 3–2. Mack, nearing 67, reputedly wept for joy when Al Simmons crossed the plate with the winning run. Mack tried to seek solitude in his office once the game ended, but he was besieged by well-wishers. One New York newspaper reported that Mack was kissed by an overjoyed office girl.

The 1930 season was only slightly less of a cakewalk for the A's than their 1929 breakthrough year. The Athletics went 102–52. Their closest pursuers were the Washington Senators, who were eight games in arrears. The St. Louis Cardinals were dispatched in six games in the World Series. The Mackmen were the toast of the baseball world once again.

The following season, 1931, was the pinnacle of the second A's dynasty. Mack's team romped to 107 wins, 13.5 games clear of the Yankees. The Cardinals repeated as NL pennant winners and beat the Athletics in an exciting seven-game World Series. The last game was a 4–2 St. Louis win, with the A's scoring twice in the top of the ninth to make things close. It was the last World Series game Mack would ever manage. The next time the A's played in the World Series would be 41 years later. By that time they were two relocations separated from Philadelphia.

The Great Depression hit Mack's club hard. Despite fielding one of baseball's all-time great lineups that accrued three consecutive AL pennants and two World Series titles, the A's struggled at the turnstiles, though not as much as other teams. In their pennant years from 1929 to 1931, the yearly attendance totals at Shibe Park were: 839,176; 721,663; and 627, 464. Those figures were third, second, and second in the AL. In 1932 the A's dropped to second place. In 1933 they dropped a notch lower to third place. With money tight, Mack was in a selling mode once again. Jimmie Foxx, Lefty Grove and Al Simmons were all dispatched elsewhere. The Philadelphia Athletics fell into a funk from which they never truly emerged. They Yankees reloaded and became the perennial, almost unstoppable, power in the AL for the next three decades. In comparison, after finishing fifth in 1934, the Athletics were doomed for the final two decades of their existence in Philadelphia to battle it out with the St. Louis Browns and Washington Senators just to stay out of the league basement. Apart from a fifth-place finish during the war year of 1944, the Athletics endured a catastrophic decade. They finished either seventh or eighth in the AL standings from 1935 through 1946.

By 1937, both of Ben Shibe's sons had died, which left Mack as the sole owner of the team. He was approaching 75 and the task was daunting. (That same year Mack was elected to the Hall of Fame as one of the sport's five "pioneers." By the time of the induction ceremony, he was the only one still living. Mack would attend the induction ceremony in Cooperstown in 1939 to stand alongside all the living Hall of Famers who had been elected starting in 1936.) Mack's advanced age was becoming a problem. A's players noticed occasional erratic behavior from Mack by the late 1940s. Once in a while he would call for a player who had not been on the team in decades. Other times he would signal plays that made no sense whatsoever. These were usually ignored by the players. "[Mack] wasn't senile, but there were lapses,"[1] recalled shortstop Eddie Joost years later. Quite frequently Mack slept through parts of games in the A's dugout. Nevertheless, the A's fared reasonably well in 1947. Their 78–76 record was the first time they had finished above .500 since 1933.

In both 1948 and 1949 the A's challenged for the pennant for at least part of the season, but finished fourth both times. By 1950, with Mack nearing his 88th birthday, his sons Roy and Earle, who had taken over the business operations of the team, persuaded the Grand Old Man of Baseball to step down at the end of the season. It was not easy to persuade the Tall Tactician that he was no longer suitable to be managing an MLB club. "I'm not quitting because I'm getting old, I'm quitting because I think people want me to,"[2] he gruffly told one reporter.

Still, 1950 was a season of celebration for the club. To mark Mack's 50th season at the helm of the White Elephants—a record that will surely never be broken—the team sported special uniforms trimmed in blue and gold. The A's were a bust on the field, though, ingloriously returning to the AL cellar with a dismal 52–102 record. Towards the end of another dismal campaign, the 87-year-old Mack, in an uncharacteristic display of temper, publicly squabbled with 26-year-old left-handed pitcher Lou Brissie, who was suffering through a disappointing season. It was an ill-advised spat; Brissie was a decorated Second World War veteran who had recovered from a devastating battle wound he suffered in December 1944. He was the lone survivor of his infantry unit. After the war ended, he won 25 minor league games in 1947 while pitching with a metal brace on his left leg. Brissie went 16–11 for the A's in 1949. When the season ended, Mack issued a public apology to Brissie, admitting he had been too hard on him and had expected too much.

On Sunday, October 1, 1950, the Athletics did manage a rare victory in the final game of the season, a 5–3 triumph over the Washington Senators at Shibe Park, to send Mack into retirement a winner. A 30-year-old rookie right-hander named Johnny Kucab picked up the win in front of a sparse gathering of 1,387 fans. It was Kucab's first MLB triumph as a pitcher. It was Mack's 3,731st win as an MLB manager. Three days earlier Mack had suffered his 3,948th and final loss, a ten-inning, 8–6 defeat to the New York Yankees. Both totals are records that are seemingly secure forever. Red Smith wrote, "Toward the end [Mack] was old and sick and saddened, a figure of forlorn dignity bewildered by the bickering around him as the baseball monument that he had built crumbled away."[3]

Coincidentally, 1950 marked the resurgence of the Philadelphia Phillies as a force in the National League. The team won its first pennant since 1915 and quickly became the favored club in the City of Brotherly Love, something utterly unthinkable just two decades before. After relinquishing the managerial duties of the club, Mack still attended many games as the team's figurehead president where he was revered as a living link to baseball's past. Over the next four years the A's struggled at the gate. In stark contrast, their co-tenants at Shibe Park since 1939, the Phillies, drew more than 1.2 million customers in 1950 as they won the NL pennant. (At one point Mack's sons were forced to mortgage the team to a life insurance company to stay afloat. Years later Red Smith quipped, "The last people who went broke in baseball were Roy and Earle Mack, Connie's sons. And I claim they did it on merit."[4]) Jimmy Dykes, a 22-year MLB veteran who had played on Mack's teams from 1918 through 1932, managed the club from 1951 to 1953. Gus Zernial was the field pilot for the Philadelphia A's last hurrah in 1954.

At Yankee Stadium on September 26, 1954, the Philadelphia A's won the final MLB game they ever played by a score of 8–6. In the bottom of the ninth inning, with Marion Fricano pitching for the White Elephants, New York's Bob

Cerv grounded to third baseman Joe DeMaestri, who threw to Lou Limmer at first base for the final putout ever made by a Philadelphia A's player. (Limmer never played in another MLB game.) Eddie Joost had gotten the team's final hit in the top of the ninth. Joe Astroth had scored the A's final run in the top of the seventh. Exactly one week earlier, in the team's swansong at Shibe Park, the Yankees had won, 4–2, in front of a mere 1,715 paying customers.

The A's had drawn only 304,666 spectators for the entire 1954 season, an average of fewer than 4,000 fans per home game, far and away the worst total in the AL. The Athletics were now an embarrassment to the entire AL both on the field and at the box office. Gate receipts at Shibe Park (which had been unofficially renamed Connie Mack Stadium in 1953) were so low that visiting clubs now loathed coming to Philadelphia because their cut of the cash was so pitiful.

The AL now had to address the ongoing "Philadelphia problem" seriously. The Mack brothers were verging on bankruptcy. Connie Mack was now merely the club's honorary president but it did not seem right to end the A's long tenure in Philadelphia without his say-so. While resting in his sick-bed, with great sadness Mack approved his sons' plans to sell the club at the AL's insistence. Although there were some interested buyers who wanted to keep the A's in Philadelphia, the AL thought the best interests of the league would be served by uprooting the once-proud franchise and re-establishing it elsewhere. It was not unprecedented; in fact relocation was becoming an MLB trend in the 1950s. The former Boston Braves were drawing fabulous crowds in their new Milwaukee home. Similarly, the lackluster St. Louis Browns were doing much better business in Baltimore as the newest incarnation of the Baltimore Orioles. On October 12, 1954, the Philadelphia Athletics were sold to Chicago businessman Arnold Johnson and would begin play as the Kansas City Athletics in 1955. Mack, nearing his 92nd birthday, was said to have turned ashen at the news. The team—an original AL club that he himself had built from scratch—would no longer operate in Philadelphia after a run of 54 seasons in which they won nine pennants and five of the eight World Series they contested. The Phillies became the sole MLB tenants of Shibe Park/Connie Mack Stadium. It remained their home until 1970.

Mack attended the 1954 World Series as a spectator—as he always did in the years his famous White Elephants were not involved in the Fall Classic. He even managed to get out to a handful of ballgames in 1955. However, Mack fractured a hip in a fall on October 1, 1955, and missed attending any World Series games for the first time ever. He was confined to a wheelchair for the final few months he had left to live. Incapacitated, Mack celebrated his 93rd birthday on December 22, 1955.

Mack, despite the confines of his wheelchair, seemed to be fine while at his daughter's house on Tuesday, February 7, 1956. Then he began noticeably to fade. At 3:20 p.m. on Wednesday, February 8, 1956, baseball's grand old gentleman took his last breath about three hours after a Catholic priest had been summoned to perform the sacrament of extreme unction. He was survived by his second wife of 45 years, Kathleen; three sons; four daughters; 19 grandchildren; and five great-grandchildren. Officially, it was announced to baseball fans that Mack had died of old age and complications from his hip surgery. Two days later Mack's funeral was held in his Philadelphia parish church, St. Bridge's. He was buried in Holy Sepulcher Cemetery, just outside Philadelphia, in a crypt bearing the name "McGillicuddy." Fittingly, MLB commissioner Ford Frick, both AL and NL presidents (Will Harridge and Warren Giles), and the owners of all 16 MLB clubs were on hand to serve as pallbearers. Thousands of nostalgic fans attended the funeral and burial.

Mack's lengthy obituary in the February 9, 1956, *New York Times*, which reverently referred to him as "Mr. Baseball," described him this way:

> Connie Mack was the master builder of baseball teams.
>
> No one manager in the history of the game ever handled more young players and brought more of them to stardom and on to fortune. But it is probable that he will be best remembered for his sensational scrapping of championship machines, the tearing apart of teams that other men would have been eager to lead.
>
> "My greatest thrill," he recalled on his 79th birthday, "was starting Howard Ehmke as the surprise pitcher against the Cubs in the first game of the 1929 World Series. My biggest disappointment was the 1914 team that lost four in a row to the Braves in the World Series."

Apart from noting that Mack's dismantling of his 1914 championship club had resulted in seven straight last-place finishes for his White Elephants, no specific mention was made in the obituary of Mack's notoriously pathetic 1916 A's. Perhaps it was just as well.

Although Connie Mack died more than half a century ago—longer than he managed the Philadelphia Athletics—his memory is kept very much alive in his birthplace of East Brookfield, MA. On September 14 and 15, 2012, the 150th anniversary of Mack's birth was grandly celebrated there (albeit three months early to take advantage of the late summer weather). Although the house where Mack grew up had burned down long ago and the field where he learned to play baseball is now occupied by a bank, a two-day celebration honoring the Grand Old Man of Baseball was held. The impetus for the event was provided by Dan Lambert, an East Brookfield town official. He happened to visit the Philadelphia A's Historical Society museum in Hatboro, PA, and discovered that Mack's milestone birthday was approaching.

"The young people here don't know [about] him," said Larry Gordon, whose house on North Brookfield Road stands on property the Mack family once owned. He told the *Philadelphia Inquirer*, "The old people probably know that he was an old-time baseball player but have no idea about the other things that made him famous. He just isn't as popular up here as he is in Philadelphia."[5]

That ignorance may have vanished. The old shoe-factory town 12 miles west of Worcester, MA, paid tribute to its most noteworthy native, and it was a spectacular success.

"We decided we really had to do something," said Gordon. "Dick Rosen, the president of the Philadelphia A's Historical Society, planned this whole event [a series of talks on various aspects of Mack's life]. The whole thing has grown so much bigger than we ever envisioned."[6]

The tribute included scholarly lectures on the Friday as well as an exhibit of Mack-related memorabilia. Saturday's agenda was filled with the kind of small-town events 19th-century Americans like Mack were familiar with—a Main Street parade, a carnival, a band concert, and a chicken barbecue. The grand finale of the old-time fun was a re-created 1883 baseball game at Connie Mack Field. One can almost picture Mack being present at such a game—a lanky, bare-handed catcher positioning his fielders and encouraging his pitcher in his piping voice to throw strikes. Perhaps the cagey Mack might even trick the umpire into calling a phantom foul-tip out at some point along the way. Fittingly, the celebrations did not extend into Sunday. In accordance with his mother's wishes, Mack liked to honor the Sabbath as a day of rest.

According to one news report, "The commemoration attracted an eclectic mix of family members, Philadelphia-linked Mack disciples, and locals who were curious to learn more about a fellow citizen who overcame a lack of formal education, a bad temper, and an alcoholic father to lead the A's to nine pennants and five World Series titles."[7]

Somewhere in the great beyond, the grand old gentleman of the nation's grand old game was undoubtedly pleased by the posthumous attention.

Mack, quite properly, is permanently honored in his adopted home of Philadelphia where he was the face of baseball for so many decades. A bronze statue of Mack prominently stands across the street from Citizens Bank Park, the newest home of the Phillies, who are now two stadiums removed from their days as the last MLB tenants of Shibe Park. A Connie Mack Memorial Committee, chaired by civic leader Arthur C. Kaufmann, was established shortly after Mack's death to oversee the project. Funded by $20,000 in public donations, the statue was sculpted by artist Harry Rosin. It was originally erected outside Shibe Park. The official unveiling and dedication took place before the Phillies' home opener on April 16, 1957. As the Phillies changed homes, so did Mack's statue. It traveled with the team from Reyburn Park (across Lehigh Avenue from Shibe Park) to the intersection of Broad Street and Pattison Avenue in front of Veterans Stadium. In 2004 the statue was restored and put in its present location on Citizens Bank Way in time for the first game at Philadelphia's new ballpark. The attractive sculpture immortalizes Mack—enlarged to a height of eight feet—as he will be always remembered by baseball fans: Mack is clad not in a uniform but in a conservative business suit. His left foot is positioned inside the dugout with his right foot on the top step. Eyes fixed on the field of play, he is familiarly waving a scorecard in his right hand.

Whatever Happened To...?

Connie Mack's post–1916 career is well known to most scholarly baseball fans. But what about the key players he managed that dreadful summer? Here's what fate had in store for a few of the noteworthy 1916 Athletics:

Bullet Joe Bush managed an 11–17 season for the 1917 A's—a team very nearly as bad as the 1916 version. At the end of 1917, Mack, always strapped for cash, dealt Bush to the Boston Red Sox, where he went 15–15 for the 1918 AL champions. He compiled a career-best 2.11 ERA that season. Bush hurt his arm in 1919 and faced retirement. However, he developed a forkball that rescued and resuscitated his career. He went 26–7 for the 1922 Yankees. The following year he compiled a 19–15 mark for the World Series winners from the Bronx. Thus Bush achieved the rare feat of playing for three different World Series-winning franchises. Bush eventually played for the Browns, Senators, Pirates, Giants and Athletics (again) before retiring at the end of the 1928 season. After baseball, Bush worked as a racetrack clerk well into his seventies. He died shortly before his 82nd birthday in 1974.

Sam Crane was supposed to be Mack's full-time shortstop in 1916, but a charley horse sidelined him after the first two games of the season. While brilliant with the glove, Crane was inept with the bat. Cut loose from the A's, Crane got into 32 games with Washington in 1917 but batted just .179. After bouncing around several minor league clubs where he won rave reviews for his defensive play, Crane resurfaced in the big leagues with the 1920 Cincinnati Reds. He lasted two seasons with the Reds, batting .215 and .233 respectively. (Oddly enough Crane was used as a pinch-hitter ten times in those two years. He went 0 for 10.) After a brief, three-game stint with Brooklyn in 1922, Crane never played again in the majors. Biographer Jack Kavanagh summed up Crane's career with this cutting quip: "Crane was a light-hitting shortstop who continually impressed with his brilliant play in the minors. He never won a permanent place until he was convicted of killing his girlfriend and her male companion in a hotel bar [in 1929]; he then secured a long-term position as the shortstop on the prison team." Crane was convicted of two counts of second-degree murder. Mack corresponded with Crane while he was serving his sentence at Graterford

Prison 30 miles outside of Philadelphia and offered him work at Shibe Park upon his release. Although described by the warden as an ideal inmate, Crane was not set free by a parole board until 1944, when he was 50 years old. He turned down Mack's longstanding employment offer to instead work in a war plant where the pay was higher. Crane died of cancer in 1955. He was 61.

Nap Lajoie never played another game after Joe Bush's spectacular no-hitter. Rated by some historians as the greatest second baseman in MLB history, Lajoie was the sixth player elected to the Hall of Fame, just missing being included among the famous first five of 1936. He died at age 74 in 1959.

Stuffy McInnis played one more season with the A's—his ninth for the White Elephants—before being dealt to the Red Sox in another one of Mack's desperate cash grabs at the end of 1917. He continued to be a superb defensive first baseman and a capable hitter throughout his career, which lasted until 1927. In 1921 McInnis committed just one error in 1,652 fielding chances, a spectacular achievement considering the small gloves and infield maintenance of the era. Only twice between 1913 and his retirement did McInnis' fielding percentage drop below .990. He managed one MLB season—his 1927 Phillies finished last—and then coached Harvard's baseball team for five seasons. McInnis died at age 69 in 1960.

Billy Meyer became Mack's favorite backup catcher in 1916 after Wally Schang injured his hand on Opening Day in Boston. By default, the 23-year-old rookie caught more games than any other member of the A's. Meyer later claimed that Connie Mack preferred to position valuable players, such as Schang, safely in the outfield when young, unproven pitchers were on the mound. Expendable players, such as Meyer, were left to handle the team's inexperienced and potentially wild pitchers. Given the pitiful state of the 1916 Athletics' staff, Meyer acquired plenty of experience. Schang had fully recovered by 1917, so Meyer became the A's backup catcher. After 1917, Meyer spent the rest of his playing days in the minor leagues. By 1926 Meyer was the manager of the Louisville Colonels (replacing Joe McCarthy). Meyer had successful managerial stints in Binghamton, Oakland, and Kansas City, but it is believed a heart condition cautiously kept MLB teams from promoting him while others with fewer qualifications were elevated to big-league posts. Meyer managed in the minors for 22 seasons before finally getting a job with the downtrodden Pittsburgh Pirates in 1948. Meyer held the position until resigning late in the 1952 season, but he failed to craft Pittsburgh into anything close to pennant-contender status. His 1952 Pirates were a truly terrible outfit. They lost 112 games and are always mentioned in the same discussion with the 1916 Athletics as one of MLB's worst teams ever. (Egad! Imagine being a member of both the 1916 A's and 1952 Pirates!) Meyer compiled an unimpressive 317–452 record in his five seasons as

Pirates skipper. He stayed with the organization as a scout. In May 1955, he suffered a debilitating stroke while having a telephone conversation with general manager Branch Rickey. Meyer died on March 31, 1957, of a heart attack at the age of 64. His obituary in the *Pittsburgh Press* noted that Meyer was "one of the best liked men ever to come into baseball. He was popular with everybody: players, managers, coaches, owners, umpires, writers and the fans."

Elmer Myers, who went 14–23 in 1916, had a halfway decent season for the lowly 1917 A's—at least by that team's dismal standards. He went 9–16 with a 4.42 ERA. He followed with a 4–8 record in 1918 before being dealt to Cleveland. Myers was unluckily dealt from the eventual pennant-winning 1920 Indians in a mid-season deal with the Red Sox, thus missing a chance to play on a World Series winner. By 1922 he was out of the majors. Myers died in 1976 at age 82.

Jack Nabors, the tough luck right-handed hurler, did not have much of a career or much of a life after the horrible 1–20 season he endured in 1916. He was back on the A's staff in 1917, but he was cut loose after appearing in just two games, having pitched a mere three innings. Nabors became ill during the 1919 Spanish influenza epidemic and never fully regained his health. He was a bedridden invalid for the last three years of his life. He died at age 35 in 1923 of heart and respiratory failure, becoming the first of the 1916 A's to pass on.

Rube Oldring, having basically quit on Mack partway through 1916, was signed by the Yankees and released before the end of the season. Oldring did return to the A's for part of the 1918 season when capable players—even those past their primes—were in short supply due to the war, thus Mack was in no position to hold a grudge. Oldring batted .233 in 49 games and then called it a career. He suffered a heart attack in 1960 and died of acute blockage of the arteries in 1961 at age 77.

Charlie Pick made 44 errors at third base for the 1916 A's, his lone season with the club. He did not resurface in the major leagues again until 1918 when, with good timing, he appeared in 28 regular-season games with the Chicago Cubs and got into the World Series. He collected seven hits in the six-game Series and batted .389. He played for the Cubs and Braves in 1919. In 1920, his last season in the majors, Pick set a single-game record on May 1 that still stands: In the famous 26-inning, 1–1 tie between Boston and Brooklyn, he got no hits in 11 at-bats—the worst single game any MLB player has ever endured at the plate. Pick died in 1954 at the age of 66.

Wally Schang batted .285 in 1917 before being dealt in one of Connie Mack's fire sales to Boston prior to the 1918 season. He played a large role in the Red Sox winning the 1918 World Series, batting .444 in the five games he played. By 1921 Schang had been acquired by the New York Yankees, and he played on their 1923 World Series–winning team (joining Joe Bush as one of the few players to win World Series titles with three different clubs). Schang eventually played for the Browns, returned to the A's in 1930, and finished his MLB career with the 1931 Tigers. Hit hard by the Great Depression, Schang continued as a minor leaguer for purely financial reasons long after he should have hung up his spikes. As a coach for the 1936 Cleveland Indians, he was the first roommate of Bob Feller. Late in life, Schang took up golf and often played 36 holes a day after his 70th birthday. Schang died at age 75 in 1965.

Tom Sheehan vanished from MLB until 1921 after his disastrous 1–16 season in 1916. He went 1–0 with the 1921 Yankees and then did not appear in another MLB game until the 1924 Reds acquired his services. After going 0–2 with the 1926 Pirates, Sheehan's playing career came to an end, but not his association with baseball. He became a coach and scout for the Giants and even managed them for part of the 1960 season, becoming a rookie field pilot at age 66. He returned to scouting after that season and stayed with that job until 1976. He died in 1982 at age 88. Many of the amusing anecdotes about the 1916 A's survive through Sheehan's newspaper interviews.

Amos Strunk was the standout player for Mack's 1916 club, and he had another solid performance for the lowly 1917 A's, batting .281 and scoring 83 runs. As was often the case with Mack's stars, Strunk was sold to the Red Sox in the same deal that sent Joe Bush and Wally Schang packing for Boston. He was traded back to the A's in 1919 and then was dealt to the Chicago White Sox during the 1920 campaign. In 1921 Strunk batted .332, the best mark of his career. He finished his MLB days with the A's as a part-time player in 1924. In 1925 Strunk was hired as the player-manager of the Shamokin Shammies of the New York-Penn League. He was batting a lofty .396 when a leg injury forced him into retirement. Strunk spent his post-baseball career as an insurance agent. In his later years he frequently bemoaned what he perceived as a lack of fire in modern ballplayers. He died in 1979 at age 90.

Jimmy Walsh, after being dealt in mid-season to the Red Sox, got into one World Series game in 1916 where he played the outfield and went 0 for 3. He played 57 games for Boston in 1917 to conclude his MLB career. He never came close to living up to Connie Mack's high expectations. Walsh died at age 74 in 1962.

William G. (Billy) Weart did not live very long to reminisce about the terrible team he thoroughly chronicled from spring training to its 154th game in 1916. The baseball scribe from the *Philadelphia Evening Telegraph*, whose unabashedly biased coverage of both the A's and Phillies for *The Sporting News* bordered on cheerleading, died in December 1917. He passed away at the young age of 45 after enduring years of ill health. Weart was one of the founding members of the Baseball Writers' Association of America and held the position of secretary-treasurer within that organization until his untimely and sudden death. Attesting to his popularity, *The Sporting News* noted in its December 13, 1917, edition, "Baseball fans, writers and players deplore the death of Billy Weart, baseball writer of the *Evening Telegraph*, who was a friend to everybody. Never robust, Mr. Weart had been making a brave fight of it for many years. Several times he had been seriously ill, but his indomitable grit [had] always carried him through the crises."

Whitey Witt was the last living regular from the 1916 A's roster. The "green as grass" rookie lived until 1988, passing away at the advanced age of 92. (The disappointing Shag Thompson lived to be 96, dying in 1990.) Despite Witt's record-setting 78 errors in 1916, Mack kept him at shortstop for most of 1917 where he made 38 errors in 112 games. By 1921 Witt had been converted to a full-time outfielder, where his speed was more useful and his errors far less frequent. After enduring year after year of demoralizing last-place finishes with the Athletics, Witt persuaded Connie Mack to deal him to the Yankees just prior to Opening Day in 1922. Witt figuratively went from the outhouse to the penthouse. That season, during a heated series of crucial games in St. Louis that would decide the AL pennant, Witt was knocked unconscious by a bottle thrown from the stands at Sportsman's Park. The culprit was never caught. Strangely, AL president Ban Johnson ridiculously tried to downplay the dangerous incident. He concocted the nonsensical fiction that Witt had accidentally stepped on a bottle which then catapulted high into the air and violently struck him on the head! In 1923, Witt had the honor of being the first member of the home team to bat in brand-new Yankee Stadium. He was also the last living member of the 1923 Yankees—that franchise's first World Series winners.

Were the 1916 A's Really the Worst MLB Team of the 20th Century?

It is somewhat fashionable for scholarly baseball fans to label Connie Mack's misfits from 1916 to be the most inept MLB club of the 20th century. But is it an accurate assessment? Certainly there were claimants to that dubious title from the first decade of that century to the last. In order to settle the question, the authors conducted a computer simulation, using *Out of the Park Baseball 13*, to run a fictitious "league" comprised of our picks for the eight worst teams of the last century. We bluntly dubbed the cyber circuit the ATL—an abbreviation for Awful Teams League. Each team would play a balanced 154-game schedule (22 games versus each of the seven other ATL clubs, 11 at home, 11 on the road).

In choosing which seven teams beside the 1916 A's had the honor of vying for the title of the worst of the worst in the ATL, a few stipulations were made. Firstly, no franchise could be represented more than once. (That particular restriction eliminated the embarrassing proposition of Connie Mack's 1916 Athletics squaring off against his inept 1919 club.) Secondly, we excluded teams from the Second World War era, as they were largely under the severe handicap of fielding MLB rosters composed of players who were deemed too old or otherwise unfit for military service. Thirdly, in order to encompass the entire 20th century, we tried to get teams that spanned a good chunk of those 100 years. As it turned out, our choices were spread over only 75 years, but they include some first-rate dead wood from the 1904 Washington Senators to the 1979 Toronto Blue Jays. (Although they played in the era of the designated hitter, in the interest of equality and fairness, the 1979 Jays' pitchers batted just like those on the other seven teams in the ATL.) Heavy consideration was also given to the 1988 Baltimore Orioles and the 1996 Detroit Tigers in the ATL, and we likely would have included both those teams had we chosen to expand the league to ten teams instead of the eight that existed in each major league in 1916.

Also, to account for the changes that have occurred in the game over the last century and to prevent teams like the 1904 Senators and our A's from being handicapped from playing in a less offensive era, we had *Out of the Park Baseball 13* normalize the statistics (and the player ratings based on those statistics) for all eight teams prior to beginning the simulation. Additionally, the simulator was calibrated to 1960 data as much as possible. Finally, each of the eight teams had their managerial decisions handled by *Out of the Park*'s artificial intelligence, using bullpen management and strategies from around 1960. As it turned out, the eight teams we chose consisted of four from the NL and four from the AL. Here they are in chronological order:

1904 Washington Senators—Here was a team that finished 38–113. Consider that pitcher Jack Chesbro of the second-place New York Highlanders (later renamed the Yankees) won 41 games individually that year! To state that pitching was a bit of an issue for the 1904 Senators is to understate the situation greatly. The team's ace, Casey Patten, was 14–23. Their second- and third-best pitchers were 5–23 and 5–26 respectively. Ouch!

1916 Philadelphia Athletics—If you've made it this far, you ought to now know their sad story very well.

1928 Philadelphia Phillies—The Robinson and Salzberg book, *On a Clear Day They Could See Seventh Place,* got its title from a pithy baseball scribe's quote about this lackluster ball club that went 43–109. Enough said.

1935 Boston Braves—This lowly lot managed to go 38–115, despite having two future Hall of Famers (Babe Ruth and Rabbit Maranville) on their roster. Granted, the 1935 version of Ruth was 40 years old, overweight, over the hill, and utterly uninspired. Declaring his brief stint on the 1935 Braves to be a "drudgery," he batted only .181 with six home runs before calling it quits after playing in just 28 games. Maranville was a 43-year-old utility second baseman. He played just 23 games and batted .149 before bailing out. These two players had been around long enough to recognize a bad team when they saw one.

1939 St. Louis Browns—When choosing a lousy St. Louis Browns season, just about any team after 1922 will do. The 1939 version was particularly inept, staggering home with a sorry 43–111 record. No pitcher won more than nine games. One starter, George Gill, complied a Jack Nabors-like 1–12 record with a 7.11 ERA. These Browns fit the bill nicely.

1952 Pittsburgh Pirates—During his broadcasting days, Joe Garagiola, a catcher on this pitiful squad, was quick to joke about this Pirates team's inept play. It was easier to laugh than cry over a team that finished 42–112 despite Ralph Kiner's 37 home runs. Their manager was Billy Meyer—the 1916 A's catcher!

1962 New York Mets—Casey Stengel's expansion misfits famously took advantage of the NL's newly instituted 162-game schedule to become the only

MLB team in the 20th century to lose 120 games in a single season. For the record, they were 40–120. Two rainouts that were not rescheduled probably saved them from finishing below .250.

1979 Toronto Blue Jays—In their third season of operation, this hapless team set a post-expansion record by losing 60 games away from their home park (Exhibition Stadium). Their porous pitching staff included notorious, eccentric, and world-class tantrum-thrower Mark Lemongello, who habitually *beat himself up* after games he lost. They finished at the bottom of the AL East at 53–109.

So how did this coterie of MLB misfits fare against each other over the course of our full 616-game schedule? Here are the ATL's final standings:

Team	*Won*	*Lost*	*GB*
1928 Phillies	88	66	—
1939 Browns	85	69	3
1916 A's	85	69	3
1962 Mets	78	76	10
1904 Senators	77	77	11
1979 Blue Jays	70	84	18
1952 Pirates	70	84	18
1935 Braves	63	91	25

There you have it: The 1916 Philadelphia Athletics finished tied for second place in the ATL with the 1939 Browns. According to modern computer analysis, they were not the worst team of the 20th century—the 1935 Boston Braves were! Of course, any computer simulation, despite the wonders of modern technology, cannot faultlessly replicate human activities or mimic what goes on in the minds of the players and manager of a professional baseball team. Thus any computer-generated results of this type must be taken with more than one proverbial grain of salt.

In battling it out over the course of the season, the eight ATL teams were quite evenly matched; in fact, only 12 games separated the first-place club from the eighth-place club as late as August 1. We found the overall results of the ATL to be surprising, considering how poor the real 1916 A's had been in comparison to the rest of the American League that year. Be that as it may, in looking at the ATL results closely, the A's pitching was hardly stellar. The team was sixth worst in runs allowed. Only the Phillies and the Pirates—both with notoriously bad staffs in real life themselves—had worse pitching stats in ATL play. The Athletics staff stayed true to its 1916 form in allowing more walks than any other team. Similarly, Whitey Witt and Charlie Pick were both in the top ten in the league in errors. However, there was a noticeable improvement in the A's offensive output; their batters enjoyed greater success against the awful pitching that characterized the cyber-circuit. Amos Strunk won the ATL's batting title with a solid .341 average. Wally Schang had a terrific MVP-caliber season, batting .302, smacking 31 homers, and driving in 100 runs. It is amazing what can happen when one does not suffer a debilitating injury on Opening Day!

A few other things need to be pointed out. First, the computer simulation used players quite differently on a daily basis than Mack did in 1916. Notably, Rube Oldring put in a full season in the simulation and was likely more enthusiastic about being on the ATL A's than he was about playing for Connie Mack's authentic 1916 squad. One suspects that competing for a pennant in the ATL was enough to keep the brooding outfielder from walking out on his team, unlike what actually occurred during the low point of the dismal summer of 1916. Additionally, the A's ATL team did not have Mack's revolving door of collegiate players taking significant playing time away from the core of regulars and obsessing the manager. Obviously it was more beneficial have Nap Lajoie (albeit the 41-year-old version) or even Roy Grover at second base for the Athletics than any number of untried college boys. Finally, as the case of Wally Schang dramatically proved, injuries played out differently within the confines of the simulation, both for the A's and the other seven ATL teams. One can only speculate how differently the real-life A's might have done with a full season of an uninjured Schang on their roster. Along those same lines, how much easier was it to defeat the already toothless 1952 Pirates after their best player, slugger Ralph Kiner, missed the second half of the ATL season with an injury?

What we can conclude, though, is that these eight teams, despite being evenly matched, were all pretty darned horrible. An injury to any team's star player, a twist of fate, or a lucky bounce or two, might make the difference between finishing second or finishing sixth in the ATL. Depth was not a characteristic of any of the eight ATL teams.

Perhaps most important was how Connie Mack handled his 1916 club compared to how the computer simulation performed the same task. The real Mack was focused on long-term goals for his club and did not particularly care whether his A's finished 35 games out of first place or 55 games in arrears on the frontrunners. The 1916 season was absolutely a write-off by the end of June when the A's were already 26 games below .500. Surely Mack must have realized by the end of April that his roster was not one of championship mettle. In all likelihood, he managed his team accordingly for the rest of the 1916 campaign. Mack, of course, spent the bulk of the season experimenting with an array of newcomers in an attempt to find his club's next big star—a search that ultimately proved fruitless. Meanwhile, the computer version of Connie Mack, in the midst of a tight ATL pennant race, saw fit to employ the best possible roster every day to contend for the league's championship. Predictably, the simulated team performed considerably better over 154 games than the real 1916 A's did. Let us suppose that Mack set aside future considerations and actually managed his 1916 team with the objective of accruing as many wins as possible to avoid being listed among MLB's worst teams in history. Further, let us be exceedingly generous and imagine they ended up increasing their victory total by 50 percent, winning 54 games. Make no mistake: The 1916 Philadelphia Athletics would still be a lousy ball club, but they would not be nearly as noteworthy or notorious as the genuine team that finished a staggering 54.5 games behind the Boston Red Sox (and 40 games out of seventh place) with their 36–117–1 record. Nor would they have inspired this book.

The 1916 Philadelphia Athletics Season

Game-By-Game Results

Game	Date	Opponent	Score	W/L	Record
1	04-12-1916	at Boston Red Sox	1-2	L	0-1
2	04-13-1916	at Boston Red Sox	2-8	L	0-2
3	04-15-1916	at Boston Red Sox	1-2	L	0-3
4	04-18-1916	at New York Yankees	2-4	L	0-4
5	04-19-1916	at New York Yankees	1-2	L	0-5
6	04-20-1916	vs Boston Red Sox	1-7	L	0-6
7	04-21-1916	vs Boston Red Sox	3-1	W	1-6
8	04-22-1916	vs Boston Red Sox	6-2	W	2-6
9	04-24-1916	vs Boston Red Sox	0-4	L	2-7
10	04-26-1916	at Washington Senators	3-2	W	3-7
11	04-27-1916	at Washington Senators	2-4	L	3-8
12	04-28-1916	at Washington Senators	6-7	L	3-9
13	04-29-1916	vs New York Yankees	2-4	L	3-10
14	05-01-1916	vs New York Yankees	4-2	W	4-10
15	05-02-1916	vs New York Yankees	4-9	L	4-11
16	05-03-1916	vs New York Yankees	3-2	W	5-11
17	05-04-1916	vs Washington Senators	1-5	L	5-12
18	05-06-1916	vs Washington Senators	4-1	W	6-12
19	05-08-1916	vs Washington Senators	4-2	W	7-12
20	05-09-1916	vs Detroit Tigers	2-16	L	7-13
21	05-10-1916	vs Detroit Tigers	3-9	L	7-14
22	05-11-1916	vs Detroit Tigers	3-2	W	8-14
23	05-12-1916	vs Detroit Tigers	6-8	L	8-15
24	05-13-1916	vs St. Louis Browns	4-3	W	9-15
25	05-15-1916	vs St. Louis Browns	5-4	W	10-15
26	05-17-1916	vs St. Louis Browns	4-7	L	10-16
27	05-18-1916	vs Chicago White Sox	5-1	W	11-16
28	05-19-1916	vs Chicago White Sox	1-0	W	12-16
29	05-20-1916	vs Chicago White Sox	0-11	L	12-17
30	05-22-1916	vs Cleveland Indians	10-8	W	13-17
31	05-24-1916	vs Cleveland Indians	4-5	L	13-18
32	05-26-1916	at Washington Senators	1-2	L	13-19

Game	Date	Opponent	Score	W/L	Record
33-I	05–27–1916	at Washington Senators	3–5	L	13–20
34-II	05–27–1916	at Washington Senators	1–3	L	13–21
35	05–29–1916	at Washington Senators	5–5	T	13–21–1
36-I	05–30–1916	at New York Yankees	2–7	L	13–22–1
37-II	05–30–1916	at New York Yankees	1–0	W	14–22–1
38-I	05–31–1916	at New York Yankees	7–8	L	14–23–1
39-II	05–31–1916	at New York Yankees	5–9	L	14–24–1
40	06–01–1916	at New York Yankees	5–0	W	15–24–1
41	06–03–1916	at St. Louis Browns	2–3	L	15–25–1
42	06–04–1916	at St. Louis Browns	3–4	L	15–26–1
43	06–10–1916	at Cleveland Indians	1–10	L	15–27–1
44	06–11–1916	at Cleveland Indians	2–7	L	15–28–1
45	06–12–1916	at Cleveland Indians	1–3	L	15–29–1
46	06–13–1916	at Cleveland Indians	2–11	L	15–30–1
47	06–15–1916	at Detroit Tigers	1–5	L	15–31–1
48	06–16–1916	at Detroit Tigers	3–4	L	15–32–1
49	06–17–1916	at Detroit Tigers	3–7	L	15–33–1
50	06–18–1916	at Detroit Tigers	2–8	L	15–34–1
51	06–20–1916	vs Washington Senators	1–2	L	15–35–1
52-I	06–22–1916	vs Washington Senators	4–2	W	16–35–1
53-II	06–22–1916	vs Washington Senators	1–6	L	16–36–1
54	06–23–1916	at Boston Red Sox	0–1	L	16–37–1
55-I	06–24–1916	at Boston Red Sox	2–3	L	16–38–1
56-II	06–24–1916	at Boston Red Sox	3–7	L	16–39–1
57	06–26–1916	at Boston Red Sox	8–5	W	17–39–1
58	06–27–1916	at Boston Red Sox	2–7	L	17–40–1
59	06–28–1916	vs New York Yankees	7–9	L	17–41–1
60	06–29–1916	vs New York Yankees	0–5	L	17–42–1
61	06–30–1916	vs New York Yankees	0–7	L	17–43–1
62	07–01–1916	vs New York Yankees	4–5	L	17–44–1
63	07–03–1916	vs Boston Red Sox	4–6	L	17–45–1
64-I	07–04–1916	vs Boston Red Sox	2–11	L	17–46–1
65-II	07–04–1916	vs Boston Red Sox	2–5	L	17–47–1
66	07–06–1916	vs Detroit Tigers	4–9	L	17–48–1
67	07–07–1916	vs Detroit Tigers	2–9	L	17–49–1
68	07–08–1916	vs Detroit Tigers	2–3	L	17–50–1
69-I	07–11–1916	vs St. Louis Browns	3–8	L	17–51–1
70-II	07–11–1916	vs St. Louis Browns	3–0	W	18–51–1
71-I	07–12–1916	vs St. Louis Browns	3–8	L	18–52–1
72-II	07–12–1916	vs St. Louis Browns	1–2	L	18–53–1
73	07–13–1916	vs St. Louis Browns	3–7	L	18–54–1
74-I	07–15–1916	vs Chicago White Sox	1–4	L	18–55–1
75-II	07–15–1916	vs Chicago White Sox	0–1	L	18–56–1
76-I	07–18–1916	vs Chicago White Sox	2–9	L	18–57–1
77-II	07–18–1916	vs Chicago White Sox	2–3	L	18–58–1
78	07–19–1916	vs Cleveland Indians	5–12	L	18–59–1

Game	Date	Opponent	Score	W/L	Record
79-I	07-20-1916	vs Cleveland Indians	2-4	L	18-60-1
80-II	07-20-1916	vs Cleveland Indians	2-0	W	19-60-1
81	07-21-1916	vs Cleveland Indians	2-7	L	19-61-1
82	07-25-1916	at St. Louis Browns	3-8	L	19-62-1
83-I	07-26-1916	at St. Louis Browns	0-5	L	19-63-1
84-II	07-26-1916	at St. Louis Browns	1-5	L	19-64-1
85	07-27-1916	at St. Louis Browns	2-3	L	19-65-1
86	07-28-1916	at St. Louis Browns	6-8	L	19-66-1
87-I	07-29-1916	at Chicago White Sox	1-6	L	19-67-1
88-II	07-29-1916	at Chicago White Sox	4-6	L	19-68-1
89-I	07-30-1916	at Chicago White Sox	1-10	L	19-69-1
90-II	07-30-1916	at Chicago White Sox	0-7	L	19-70-1
91	07-31-1916	at Chicago White Sox	3-4	L	19-71-1
92-I	08-01-1916	at Chicago White Sox	0-3	L	19-72-1
93-II	08-01-1916	at Chicago White Sox	2-3	L	19-73-1
94	08-02-1916	at Chicago White Sox	2-8	L	19-74-1
95	08-03-1916	at Cleveland Indians	1-3	L	19-75-1
96	08-04-1916	at Cleveland Indians	2-5	L	19-76-1
97	08-05-1916	at Cleveland Indians	3-12	L	19-77-1
98	08-06-1916	at Cleveland Indians	2-5	L	19-78-1
99	08-07-1916	at Detroit Tigers	2-4	L	19-79-1
100	08-08-1916	at Detroit Tigers	0-9	L	19-80-1
101	08-09-1916	at Detroit Tigers	7-1	W	20-80-1
102	08-10-1916	at Detroit Tigers	4-10	L	20-81-1
103-I	08-12-1916	at New York Yankees	9-3	W	21-81-1
104-II	08-12-1916	at New York Yankees	2-0	W	22-81-1
105	08-14-1916	at New York Yankees	3-4	L	22-82-1
106	08-15-1916	at New York Yankees	2-6	L	22-83-1
107-I	08-17-1916	vs St. Louis Browns	4-3	W	23-83-1
108-II	08-17-1916	vs St. Louis Browns	2-3	L	23-84-1
109	08-18-1916	vs St. Louis Browns	3-4	L	23-85-1
110	08-19-1916	vs Detroit Tigers	2-6	L	23-86-1
111	08-21-1916	vs Detroit Tigers	1-7	L	23-87-1
112	08-22-1916	vs Detroit Tigers	1-0	W	24-87-1
113	08-23-1916	vs Detroit Tigers	3-10	L	24-88-1
114-I	08-24-1916	vs Cleveland Indians	6-5	W	25-88-1
115-II	08-24-1916	vs Cleveland Indians	2-4	L	25-89-1
116-I	08-25-1916	vs Cleveland Indians	9-13	L	25-90-1
117-II	08-25-1916	vs Cleveland Indians	2-10	L	25-91-1
118	08-26-1916	vs Cleveland Indians	5-0	W	26-91-1
119	08-28-1916	vs Chicago White Sox	0-1	L	26-92-1
120	08-29-1916	vs Chicago White Sox	9-2	W	27-92-1
121	08-30-1916	vs Chicago White Sox	3-7	L	27-93-1
122	08-31-1916	vs Chicago White Sox	1-7	L	27-94-1
123-I	09-01-1916	at Washington Senators	1-3	L	27-95-1
124-II	09-01-1916	at Washington Senators	4-1	W	28-95-1

Game	Date	Opponent	Score	W/L	Record
125	09-02-1916	at Washington Senators	6-7	L	28-96-1
126-I	09-04-1916	at Washington Senators	0-2	L	28-97-1
127-II	09-04-1916	at Washington Senators	1-3	L	28-98-1
128-I	09-05-1916	vs Boston Red Sox	5-2	W	29-98-1
129-II	09-05-1916	vs Boston Red Sox	1-7	L	29-99-1
130	09-06-1916	vs Boston Red Sox	2-5	L	29-100-1
131	09-07-1916	vs Boston Red Sox	0-2	L	29-101-1
132	09-08-1916	vs New York Yankees	8-2	W	30-101-1
133-I	09-09-1916	vs New York Yankees	1-4	L	30-102-1
134-II	09-09-1916	vs New York Yankees	0-4	L	30-103-1
135	09-13-1916	at Cleveland Indians	4-8	L	30-104-1
136	09-14-1916	at Cleveland Indians	1-9	L	30-105-1
137	09-15-1916	at Cleveland Indians	2-3	L	30-106-1
138	09-16-1916	at Detroit Tigers	3-4	L	30-107-1
139	09-17-1916	at Detroit Tigers	5-6	L	30-108-1
140	09-18-1916	at Detroit Tigers	2-0	W	31-108-1
141	09-19-1916	at Chicago White Sox	4-5	L	31-109-1
142	09-20-1916	at Chicago White Sox	7-8	L	31-110-1
143	09-21-1916	at Chicago White Sox	8-0	W	32-110-1
144	09-22-1916	at St. Louis Browns	3-6	L	32-111-1
145	09-23-1916	at St. Louis Browns	2-4	L	32-112-1
146-I	09-24-1916	at St. Louis Browns	2-0	W	33-112-1
147-II	09-24-1916	at St. Louis Browns	2-3	L	33-113-1
148	09-27-1916	vs Washington Senators	3-13	L	33-114-1
149	09-28-1916	vs Washington Senators	1-4	L	33-115-1
150-I	09-30-1916	vs Washington Senators	6-8	L	33-116-1
151-II	09-30-1916	vs Washington Senators	10-9	W	34-116-1
152	10-02-1916	at Boston Red Sox	2-4	L	34-117-1
153-I	10-03-1916	at Boston Red Sox	5-3	W	35-117-1
154-II	10-03-1916	at Boston Red Sox	7-5	W	36-117-1

1916 American League: Final Standings

Team	W	L	GBL
Boston	91	63	—
Chicago	89	65	2
Detroit	87	67	4
New York	80	74	11
St. Louis	79	75	12
Cleveland	77	77	14
Washington	76	77	14.5
Philadelphia	36	117	54.5

Chapter Notes

Preface

1. Frederick G. Lieb, *Connie Mack: Grand Old Man of Baseball*, 187.

Connie Mack (Part 1)

1. Paul Dickson, *Baseball's Greatest Quotations*, 262.
2. Ibid., 87.
3. Ibid., 260.
4. Lieb, 42.
5. Ibid., 50.

Connie Mack (Part 2)

1. Dan O'Brien, *Rube Waddell SABR Biography,* sabr.org/bioproject.
2. Dickson, 261.
3. Ken Burns, *Baseball* (PBS-TV documentary series), 1994.
4. Ernie Harwell, at Brainyquote.com (website).
5. Lieb, 122.

Connie Mack's First Dynasty

1. Dickson, 261.
2. Ibid., 40.
3. Lieb, 160.
4. Dickson, 260.
5. Lieb, 185.
6. George Robinson and Charles Salzberg, *On a Clear Day They Could See Seventh Place* (New York: Dell, 1991), 80.

Prelude to Disaster

1. Robinson and Salzberg, 80.
2. Donald Honig, *Baseball America* (New York: Macmillan, 1985), 97.
3. Ibid., 97.
4. Lieb, 188.

June

1. Daniel Okrent, *Baseball Anecdotes* (New York: Oxford University Press, 1989), 72.

July

1. Robinson and Salzberg, *On a Clear Day They Could See Seventh Place*, 76.

August

1. Robinson and Salzberg, *On a Clear Day They Could See Seventh Place*, 86.
2. Ibid., 84.

August 26

1. Lieb, 188.

August 28 to Season's End

1. Dickson, 262.

The Aftermath

1. Ted Davis, *Connie Mack: A Life in Baseball* (Lincoln, NE: Writers Club Press, 2000), 194.
2. William C. Kashatus, *The Philadelphia Athletics* (Mount Pleasant, SC: Arcadia, 2002), 90.
3. Davis, 215.
4. Dickson, 402.
5. *Philadelphia Inquirer*, September 17, 2012.
6. Ibid.
7. Ibid.

Bibliography

Books

Davis, Ted. *Connie Mack: A Life in Baseball*. Lincoln, NE: Writers Club Press, 2000.

Dickson, Paul. *Baseball's Greatest Quotations*. New York: HarperCollins, 1991.

Gay, Timothy M. *Tris Speaker: The Rough-and-Tumble Life of a Baseball Legend*. Lincoln: University of Nebraska, 2005.

Hollingsworth, Harry. The *Best & Worst Baseball Teams of All Time*. New York: S.P.I. Books, 1994.

Honig, Donald. *Baseball America*. New York: Macmillan, 1985.

Jones, David (editor). *Deadball Stars of the American League*. Dulles, VA: Potomac Books, 2006.

Kashatus, William C. *The Philadelphia Athletics*. Mount Pleasant, SC: Arcadia, 2002.

Lieb, Frederick G. *Connie Mack: Grand Old Man of Baseball*. Kent, OH: Kent State University, OH, 2012 (reprint of Lieb's 1945 Mack biography).

Malone, Paul. *Dry Wells: A Century of No-Hitters*. Self-published, Forest Lake, MN, 1999.

Okkonen, Marc. *The Federal League of 1914–15: Baseball's Third Major League*. Garret Park, MD: Society for American Baseball Research, 1989.

Okrent, Daniel and Steve Wulf. *Baseball Anecdotes*. New York: Oxford University Press, 1989.

Ritter, Lawrence S. *The Glory of Their Times*. New York: Vintage Books, 1985.

Robinson, George & Charles Salzberg. *On a Clear Day They Could See Seventh Place*. New York: Dell, 1991.

Shatzkin, Mike, ed. *The Ballplayers*. New York: William Morrow, 1990.

Online Reference Sources

Baseball-Almanac.com
BaseballReference.com
la84foundation.org
PaperofRecord.com
Retrosheet.org
SABR.org
TheDeadballEra.com

Index

Numbers in **_bold italics_** indicate pages with photographs.

A. J. Reach & Co. 12
Alexander, Grover Cleveland 31, 64
Allison, Milo 134
Archer, Jimmy 21
Ashbridge, Samuel 14
Astroth, Joe 161
Austin, Jimmy 100, 116
Awful Teams League 170–174
Ayers, Yancey (Doc) 129

Bagby, Jim 66, 72, 97, 106
Baker, John Franklin (Home Run) 20, 22–23, 25, 29–30, 32, 34–35, 42, 46, 53–54, 57, 82, 88, 91, 99, 133, 138, 147
Baker Bowl 18, 54
Ball, Phil 25
Baltimore Orioles 108, 161, 170
Baltimore Orioles (original) 14
Baltimore Terrapins/Feds 36, 54
Barber, Turner 57
Barry, Jack 20–21, 30, 36, 44, 46–47, 52
Baseball Hall of Fame 13, 67, 124, 159, 166, 171
Baseball Magazine 3, 4, 30, 32, 35–37, 39, 52, 55, 61, 65, 114–115, 120, 148
Battle of the Somme 84–85
Battle of Verdun 33, 84
Bay, Harry 75
Beebe, Fred 97, 106, 118, 134
Bemis, Chester 116
Bender, Albert (Chief) 17, 18, 20, 22–24, 26, 28, 41–43, 54, 64, 124, 138
Benz, Joe 101, 105, 126–127, 137
Binghamton (New York State League) 42
Bishop, Max 158
Bisonette, Del 14
Blankenburg, Rudolph 6
Blume, Andrew 141
Bodie, Frank (Ping) 116, 127, 131, 141, 153
Boehler, George 59
Boehling, Joe 52
Boland, Bernie 58, 61, 108
Bonds, Barry 14
Boston (American Association) 10
Boston Braves 4, 26–28, 31, 39–40, 43, 142, 154, 161–162, 167, 171–172
Boston Pilgrims/Red Sox 1, 13, 16–17, 19, 23–26, 29–30, 32, 34–35, 44–51, 54, 57–58, 62, 64, 68–69, 73, 78–81, 85–86, 88, 95, 101–102, 105, 108, 111, 113, 115, 117, 124–125, 127, 129–131, 133–134, 136–137, 139–146, 149, 152, 154–157, 165–168, 174–178
Bowdoin College 99
Braves Field 142, 154
Brennan, Mike 75
Bressler, Raymond (Rube) 7, 24, 28, 35, 41, 43, 45, 53, 56, 61, 65, 68, 91, 143
Brissie, Lou 160
Broad Street Station 21
Brooklyn Dodgers/Robins 43, 54, 61, 133, 145–146, 154–155, 165, 167
Brooklyn Feds 25
Brounder, Ed 116
Brown, Carroll William (Boardwalk) 23
Brown, Jim 130, 132, 139
Brown, Mordecai (Three Finger) 129
Brown University 71, 75
Brush, John T. 16
Buckenberger, Al 10
Buffalo (Federal League) 36
Buffalo (International League) 104–105, 116
Buffalo Bisons (Players' League) 9, 12
Burns, George 59, 89, 115
Bush, (Bullet) Joe 2, 23–24, 27–29, 35, 41, 43, 45–47, 49, 50, 52, 55–56, 60–62, 64–73, 75–77, 79, 81–82, 86, 90, 98–103, 106–107, 109–111, 113–115, 118–125, **_123_**, 126–127, 129, 131, 133, 136–137, 139, 141, 147, 149–150, 157, 165–168

Cady, Forrest 157
Caldwell, Ray 70
Callahan, Jimmy 116
Carlton, Steve 15
Carrigan, Bill 34, 52
Carroll, Ralph Arthur (Doc) 80, 94, 98, 100, 104–105
Cartwright, Alexander 8
Catholic University of America 54
Cerv, Bob 160–161
Chance, Frank 21
Chapman, Ray 121
Chase, Hal 36–38
Chicago Cubs 18, 20–21, 129, 135, 142, 155, 158, 162, 167
Chicago Whales 25
Chicago White Sox 1, 14, 17–18, 25, 30, 34, 39,

181

182 Index

49, 61–62, 64–65, 93–94, 99, 101–102, 105–107, 109, 113, 126–127, 136–137, 139–144, 155–157, 168, 175–178
Chill, Ollie 59, 121, 127
Cicotte, Eddie 62, 94, 102, 105, 126
Cincinnati Reds 19, 34, 37, 58, 105, 128–129, 138, 165, 168
Cleveland Broncos/Naps/Indians 11, 15, 21, 34, 35, 45, 48, 50, 51, 57, 60, 62, 64–66, 68, 70–72, 78, 80, 89, 96–100, 106–107, 113, 115, 117–125, 131, 134–135, 140–141, 143–144, 149, 154, 167–168, 175–178
Cleveland Spiders 103
Coakley, Andy 17, 41
Cobb, Ty 9, 13, 18, 20–21, 24, 58, 73, 81, 88–89, 109–110, 114, 118, 136, 154, 158
Cochrane, Mickey 158
Coleman, Bob 122
Collins, Eddie 20, 25, 28, 35, 42, 46, 62, 65, 91, 137, 153
Columbia Park 12, 15, 17, 19, 25
Comiskey, Charles 25, 142
Comiskey Park 71, 101–102, 105, 136, 139, 151
Connecticut State League 8
Connolly, Tommy 96, 121–122
Coombs, Jack 20, 22, 28, 41, 43, 54, 64, 138, 155
Coumbe, Frederick (Fritz) 64–66, 98, 122
Coveleski, Harry 59, 89, 108, 113, 136
Coveleski, Stanley 71, 107, 120–122
Crane, Sam 31, 35–36, 46, 49, 58, 150, 152, 165–166
Crawford, Sam 18
Cross, Monte 75, 87, 138
Crowell, Minot Joy (Cap) 35, 49, 51–53, 59, 61–62, 68, 71, 75, 152
Cullop, Nick 69, 111
Cunningham, George 74, 89, 115

Danforth, Dave 105, 137
Dauss, George (Hooks) 73, 114
Davenport, Dave 61, 70, 93, 100, 111, 115
Davis, Harry 5, 20–21, 23, 38, 40, 75, 87, 91, 101, 104, 138
Davis, Harry, Jr. 5–6
DeBerry, Hank 135
DeMaestri, Joe 161
Detroit Tigers 4, 18, 21, 24, 30, 34, 48, 56, 58–61, 66, 68, 73–74, 88–89, 107–111, 113–115, 129–131, 135–137, 139, 141–142, 146, 168, 170, 175–178
Divis, Edwin George (Moxie) 106–107
Donovan, (Wild) Bill 34, 82, 88, 90, 92, 95, 127, 132–133, 138
Doyle, Larry 22
Driscoll, Michael 89
Dubuc, Jean 59, 73, 109
Duggan, Jimmy 82, 90, 92
Dumont, George 66, 77
Dunn, Jack 58
Dunn Park 106
Dykes, Jimmy 160

East Brookfield, MA 7, 8, 13, 162
Edwards, Henry P. 96–97, 118
Ehmke, Howard 125, 135–136, 162
Evans, Billy 25, 97, 110
Evers, Johnny 27

Faber, Urban (Red) 62, 101, 103, 126, 139
Falkenberg, Cy 42
Federal League 24–27, 29–30, 35–37, 54, 106, 137
Feller, Bob 168
Felsch, Happy (Oscar) 62, 101–102
Fenway Park 27, 30, 45–48, 50, 78, 80, 115, 142–143, 147, 154
Fisher, Ray 68, 82
Flaherty, Pat 104
Fohl, Lee 34, 64, 66, 96, 99–100
Ford, Edward (Whitey) 155
Foster, Eddie 129, 142
Foster, George (Rube) 47, 49, 51, 80, 124, 130
Fournier, Jack 102
Foxx, Jimmie 158–159
Fricano, Marion 160
Fromme, Art 117

Gallia, Bert 76, 128, 143
Gandil, Cahrles (Chick) 97–98, 121–122, 124
Garagiola, Joe 171
Gardner, Larry 46, 52, 130, 157
Gehrig, Lou 158
Giles, Warren 162
Gilhooley, Frank 69, 81, 88
Gill, George 171
Gilmore, James A. 25
Goddard Seminary 39
Gordon, Larry 162–163
Gould, Al 118, 135
Grahek, Mike 5
Graney, Jack 97, 121–124, 135
Griffith, Clark 34, 56–57
Griffith Stadium 52, 67, 127–129
Grimm, Charlie 102, 116
Groom, Bob 70–71, 101, 113, 140
Grove, Robert Moses (Lefty) 158–159
Grover, Roy 134–135, 145, 173

Haas, Bruno 30
Haley, Ray 101, 104–105, 108, 113, 116, 127, 131, 134–135, 152
Hallahan (Mack), Katherine 21
Hamilton, Earl 74, 90, 93, 101
Hamilton, Josh 14
Harper, Harry 53, 56, 128
Harridge, Will 162
Harris, Stanley (Bucky) 10
Hart, William 15
Harvard University 166
Harwell, Ernie 18
Healy, Thomas 65, 143, 145
Henry, John 143
Herzog, Charles Lincoln (Buck) 34

Index

Hesselbacher, George 82, 86, 90, 92–93, 97
High, Hugh 69, 81
Hilltop Park 88
Hoblitzell, Dick 47, 78–79
Hobson, Clell Lavern (Butch) 140–141
Hogan (Mack), Margaret 9
Hogan, Willie 9
Honig, Donald 13, 37
Hooper, Harry 46, 79, 143
Houck, Byron 23
Hughes, Charles Evans 85
Husting, Bert 15

Isaminger, Jimmy 157

Jackson, (Shoeless) Joe 62, 65, 94, 99, 101–102, 127, 149
James, Bill (pitcher) 26, 89, 114
James, Bill (statistician) 3, 21
Janvrin, Hal 79, 130
Jennings, Hughie 18, 34, 37, 60, 108, 115
Johnson, Arnold 161
Johnson, Bancroft (Ban) 11–16, 82, 88, 90, 96–97, 100, 155, 169
Johnson, Bill 139
Johnson, George 156
Johnson, Russell Conwell (Jing) 54, 80, 88, 105, 107, 113, 117–118, 126, 129–132, 136–137, 140, 145
Johnson, Walter 23, 25, 56–57, 64, 67, 80, 124–125, 127–128, 136, 146–147
Jones, Fielder 35, 90, 95–96, 99, 115–116, 134
Joost, Eddie 159, 161

Kansas City Packers 36
Kaufmann, Arthur C. 163
Kavanagh, Jack 165
Keating, Ray 56, 81
Kerr, William W. 10
Kiner, Ralph 171, 173
King, Lee 79, 82, 86–87, 89, 96
King, Silver 79, 87
Klem, Bill 22
Klepfer, Ed 107, 117
Kling, Johnny 21
Knowlson, Tom 29
Kofoed, J.C. 30, 35, 114
Koob, Ernie 70, 90, 101, 140
Kopf, Larry 29
Koufax, Sandy 16
Kucab, Johnny 160

Lajoie, Napoleon 2, 14–15, 29–30, 43–47, 55–58, 60, 62, 65, 75–77, 81, 85–87, 89, 94, 98, 103, 105–106, 110, 114, 117, 122, 125, 128, 134, 139, 150–151, 166, 173
Lambert, Dan 162
Lambeth, Otis 134–135
Lannin, Joe 105
Lanning, Lester Alfred (Red) 76, 81, 89, 94, 98, 100, 102, 105, 107

Lapp, Jack 30, 36, 38, 138
Lardner, Ring 31
LaRussa, Tony 10
Lavan, John (Doc) 116, 140
Lawry, Otis 75, 82, 87, 92, 94, 96, 113, 128, 130
Lemongello, Mark 172
Leonard, Hubert Benjamin (Dutch) 52, 79, 86, 124, 130
Leonard, Joe 128
Lewis, Duffy 52
Lieb, Fred 3, 11, 39, 124
Limmer, Lou 161
Lindstrom, Axel 145
Louisville Colonels 166
Love, Edward (Slim) 132
Lowdermilk, Grover 98

Macht, Norman L. 7, 12–13
Mack, Connie 2–6, 11–35, *34*, 38–51; 53–62, 64–82, 85–104, 106–111, 113–117, 119–125, 127–129, 131–137, 139–142, 144–150, 152–161, 163–173; code of conduct 155; death and funeral 161–162; as Milwaukee owner 11; 150th birthday celebrations 162–163; as Pittsburgh Pirates manager 10–11; as player 8–10; as youth 7–8
Mack, Earle 64, 159–160
Mack, Ruth 16
Magee, Lee 57, 88
Malone, Lewis 43–44, 75
Maranville, Walter (Rabbit) 171
Markle, Cliff 49
Marsans, Armando 70, 116, 140
Mathewson, Christy 13, 17, 22–24, 128–129
Mays, Carl 79, 86, 130
McAvoy, Jim 36
McBride, George 128
McCarthy, Joe 166
McElwee, Lee 86, 97, 99, 113, 137, 143
McGillicuddy, Mary 7–9, 16
McGillicuddy, Michael 7–8
McGinnity, Joe (Iron Man) 17
McGraw, John 10, 13, 14, 16–17, 40, 56, 142, 156
McInnis, John (Stuffy) 1, 21, 29–30, 45–48, 62, *63*, 80, 87, 91, 96–97, 99–100, 102, 110, 117, 121–122, 124, 126–128, 133, 135–136, 138, 140, 150, 157, 166
McKee, Ed 109
McMillan, Ralph E. 48, 78
McNally, Mike 143
Merkle, Fred 22
Meyer, Billy 1, 36, 39, 43, 47–48, 58, 69, 81, 86, 89, 91–92, 96, 98, 104, 116, 131, 150, 166–167, 171
Miller, Ward 98, 140
Milwaukee (Western League) 11
Mitchell, Willie 89, 110, 136
Mitterling, Ralph 89–90, 92, 94, 96, 98
Mogridge, George 85, 110
Moran, Pat 29, 116
Morgan, Cy 20, 41

Index

Morgan, Ray 142
Morrisette, Bill 35, 41, 56
Morton, Guy 66, 72, 107
Mt. St. Mary's College 75
Murnane, Tim 26, 30
Murphy, Danny 25
Murphy, Eddie 30, 46
Murphy, Mike 35–36, 42–43, 79, 90
Myers, Elmer 35, 39, 41, 42, 48, 50–51, 53, 57, 59–60, 62, 64–68, 70–72, 74–76, 81, 85, 89, 91–94, 97, 100–101, 103, 105, 107–108, 110, 113–114, 117, 126, 128, 130–132, 134–137, 139, 141–142, 145, 147, 150, 154, 167

Nabors, Jack 35, 42, 46–47, 49–51, 53, 56, 58–59, 67–68, 71–73, 76–79, 81–82, 86, 89, 93, 94, 98, 100–101, 103, 105, 107–108, 110–111, 113, 116–118, 127–130, 132, 135–137, 142–143, 145, 152–153, 167, 171
Nallin, Dick 56
Navin Field 108–109, 135
New York Giants 5, 10, 16–17, 22–24, 26, 52, 56, 117, 141, 156, 165, 168
New York Highlanders/Yankees 16, 20, 30, 34, 37, 49–51, 53–57, 68–70, 73, 77, 81–82, 85, 87–90, 92–96, 110–111, 124, 127, 131–134, 137–140, 142–143, 147, 151–153, 157–160, 165, 167–169, 171, 175–178
New York Mets 2, 4, 171–172
New York Times 154, 162
Nicholson, Bill 14

Oldring, Helen 27
Oldring, Reuben (Rube) 2, 22, 27, 31, 36, 43, 46, 52, 71, 77, 81, 87–88, 91, 93, 95, 96, 99, 133, 138, 151, 161, 173
O'Loughlin, Francis (Silk) 58
O'Neill, Steve 121–122, 124
Out of the Park Baseball 13 170–171
Owens, Clarence (Brick) 1, 77, 90, 92–93, 95–96, 152

Parnham, James (Rube) 137, 140, 144–145
Patten, Casey 171
Penner, Ken 135
Pennock, Herb 24, 29, 30, 30, 48, 50
Pennsylvania Supreme Court 14
Peoria (Three-I League) 36, 75
Phelon, W.A. 35
Philadelphia Athletics 1901 14; 1902 14–16; 1905 17–18; 1906 18; 1909 19; 1910 20–21; 1911 21–23; 1912 23; 1913 5–6, 23–24; 1914 24–28; 1915 16, 28–32; 1917 98, 131, 134, 141, 146, 153, 156, 165–169; 1918 133, 157, 167; 1919 157, 168, 170; 1920s 157–158; 1930s 158–159; 1940s 159; 1950s 159–161; effect of rainouts on 1916 team 72–73, 104–105, 151; move to Kansas City 161; tryouts 54, 73–74, 88, 104, 109, 153; *see also* spring training
Philadelphia Athletics Historical Society 4, 162–163

Philadelphia Evening Telegraph 3, 42, 168–169
Philadelphia Inquirer 44, 60, 163
Philadelphia Phillies 14, 18–19, 29, 31–32, 38, 42–43, 53–54, 67, 75, 108, 124–125, 133, 144–146, 160–161, 163, 166, 168, 171–172
Philadelphia Police Band 6
Philadelphia Public Ledger 19
Philadelphia Times 21
Picinich, Val 94, 98, 100–101, 104, 113, 121, 125, 130, 131
Pick, Charlie 1, 35, 36, 44, 46–47, 53, 55–56, 58, 61–62, 66, 72–73, 78, 85–86, 89, 93, 96, 110, 118, 121–122, 124, 128, 130, 132, 133, 135, 140–141, 150, 153, 167, 172
Pipp, Wally 81, 111, 133, 147
pitchers batting 61
Pittsburgh Pirates 10–11, 13, 16, 124, 165–168, 171–173
Plank, Eddie 5, 15, 17, 20, 22–24, 26, 28, 41–43, 60–61, 64, 65, 92, 111, 138–139
Players' League 9–10
Poindexter, George 116
Polo Grounds 22–24, 34, 49, 68, 70, 94, 110
Powers, John T. 24–25
Pratt, Del 70, 113, 116, 140

Quinn, Jack 158

Raleigh (North Carolina State League) 64
Ray, Carl 35–36, 42, 48, 50, 58
Ray, Johnny 65
Reyburn, John E. 19
Reyburn Park 163
Rice, Sam 67, 76, 143
Richardson, Jack 35–36, 41, 48
Robbins, George S. 106, 142
Robinson, George 4, 84, 171
Rommel, Ed 158
Rosen, Dick 163
Rosin, Harry 163
Roth, Robert (Braggo) 66, 117–118, 121–122, 124, 135
Rowe, Harland 78, 80–82, 87, 93, 142
Rowland, Clarence 34, 62
Rudolph, Dick 26
Russell, Allen 55, 81, 85, 132
Russell, Ewell (Reb) 101, 105, 137
Ruth, Babe 13, 47, 50, 80, 129, 143, 145, 154–155, 157–158, 171

St. Louis Browns 4, 15, 35, 48, 51, 56, 60–62, 64–72, 74, 80, 88–90, 92–93, 95–96, 98–105, 107, 109, 111, 113, 115–116, 124, 130, 131, 134, 136, 139–141, 147, 159, 161, 165, 168–169, 171–172, 175–178
St. Louis Cardinals 15, 130, 158
St. Louis Terriers 24, 35
St. Paul (American Association) 75
Salsinger, H.G. 107, 110, 136
Salzberg, Charles 84, 171
Schalk, Ray 102

Schang, Wally 1, 24, 27, 29, 36, 42–43, 46–47, 55, 57–58, 62, 73–74, 76, 79, 86, 93–94, 98–99, 104, 111, *112*, 115–116, 121–122, 126–127, 130–132, 134, 136, 138, 140, 147, 149–151, 157, 166–168, 173
Schroeder, Joe 38
Scott, Everett 46
Scott, Jim 93, 95, 105
Seibold, Harry (Socks) 137, 140–141, 143
Severeid, Hank 100
Shamokin Shammies (New York–Penn League) 168
Shaw, Jim 129, 142, 144
Shawkey, Bob 24, 29–30, 49, 68, 82, 111, 117, 133, 153
Sheehan, Tom 29, 41, 49, 51, 56, 59, 61–62, 70–72, 74, 78–82, 86, 88, 90, 93–94, 97–98, 101–103, 106–108, 115, 118, 127, 129, 130, 132, 135, 137, 153, 168
Shibe, Ben 12, 25, 28, 156–157, 159
Shibe, John 158
Shibe, Tom 158
Shibe Park 5, 6, 19–20, 22–23, 25–26, 29–31, 34, 38, 40–41, 50–51, 53–54, 56–58, 60, 62, 66, 68, 83–76, 81–82, 85, 87–88, 90–100, 104, 109, 113, 117, 120, 122, 124–126, 129, 130–132, 134, 142–144, 146, 149, 151, 153, 156, 158–161, 163, 166
Shocker, Urban 56, 110, 133
Shore, Ernie 48, 78, 86, 129, 145
Shorten, Chick 46
Shotton, Burt 61, 75, 101, 116, 140
Simmons, Al 158–159
Simons, Herbert 27
Sinclair, Harry F. 25
Sisler, George 75, 92, 96, 100, 116, 136, 140
Smith, Clarence (Pop-boy) 135
Smith, Elmer 129, 142
Smith, Red 160
Snodgrass, Fred 22
Spahn, Warren 15
Speaker, Tris 25, 35, 45–46, 50, 65–66, 114, 117–118, 120–122, 124, 134, 154, 158
The Sporting News 3, 5, 15–17, 22–24, 27–34, 37–44, 48–51, 53–54, 57–60, 62, 64–65, 67–68, 71–76, 78, 80–82, 87–88, 90–93, 95–96, 99–100, 104–111, 115–118, 120, 127, 130–131, 133–134, 136–139, 141–142, 145–146, 154–157, 168–169
Sportsman's Park 100, 136, 140, 169
spring training 33–45
Stallings, George 27
Stellbauer, Bill 35, 36, 48–49, 59, 75
Stengel, Casey 171
Strunk, Amos 43, 46, 49–50, 55, 57, 59, 62, 65–66, 76, 82, 98, 101, 106, 108, 10–111, 113–116, 122, 126, 129–131, 135–138, 141, 143, *144*, 147, 149, 157, 168, 172
Sunday baseball 51–53, 57, 60, 70–71, 74, 80, 94, 102, 107, 129, 132, 136, 140–141, 144, 163

Tesreau, Jeff 23
Thomas, Chester (Pinch) 47
Thomas, Hannah 27
Thomas, Ira 28, 38, 40, 44, 75, 88, 91, 104, 115–116
Thompson, James (Shag) 1, 35–36, 43, 49, 61, 151–152, 169
Thrasher, Frank (Buck) 127, 131, 141–143
Toronto Blue Jays 170, 172
Turner, Terry 57, 121–122, 124

United States 1916 presidential election 85
University of Alabama 141
University of Maine 54, 75, 81, 87
University of North Carolina 65
University of Pittsburgh 65
University of South Carolina 89, 91
Ursinus College 54, 88

Van Zelst, Eddie 29
Varitek, Jason 125
Veach, Bobby 114, 136
Vernon Coast League 117
Vila, Joe 50

Waddell, George Edward (Rube) 15–17, 24, 41
Walberg, Rube 158
Walker, Tilly 46, 79, 157
Walsh, Jimmy 1, 36, 43, 46–47, 66, 89–90, 92, 95–96, 101–102, 109, 114, 121–122, 127, 134, 152, 168
Wambsganss, Bill 98, 121–122
Ward, George S. 25
Washington National League team 8–10
The Washington Post 122, 124
Washington Senators 4, 11, 14, 23, 25, 31–32, 34, 41, 48, 52–54, 56–58, 60, 64–68, 76–78, 81, 88, 101, 109, 118, 125, 127–129, 131, 136, 139, 141–144, 146–147, 158–160, 165, 170–172, 175–178
Weart, William G. 3, 32, 38, 42–44, 53–54, 57, 59, 64, 65, 67, 71, 72, 74, 80, 82, 87, 90, 93, 95, 99, 104, 108, 111, 115, 124, 127, 130–131, 133, 138–139, 141, 146, 155–156, 168–169
Weaver, Buck 126–127
Weaver, Harry 42, 50, 56, 58, 65
Weeghman, Charlie 142
Weilman, Carl 71, 93, 100, 113, 115–116
Western League 11, 14
Whittaker, Walt 89
Williams, Claude (Lefty) 102, 126, 139
Williams, Joe 27
Williams, Marshall (Marsh) 89–92, 102, 105–106, 110–111, 115, 118, 153
Williams College 116
Wilson, Woodrow 85
Witt, Lawton (Whitey) 1, 35–36, 39, 44, 48–49, 52–53, 55–62, 67, 68–71, 73–74, 77–81, 85–87, 91–93, 96–97, 101, 103, 105–108, 110, 113–116, 118, 121–122, 126, 128–131, 133, 135–136, 139–140, 143–145, 147, 150, 152, 169, 172

Wolfgang, Mellie 102
World Series 6, 16–18, 23, 31–32, 41, 45–46, 56, 78–79, 88, 96, 100, 120, 134, 136, 138–139, 142, 144–145, 154–159, 161–163, 165, 167–169; 1905 17–18; 1910 3, 6, 20–21; 1911 3, 6, 20–23; 1913 3, 5, 23–24, 77; 1914 26–28, 61

Wyckoff, Weldon 24, 28, 35, 41, 43, 45, 67–69, 71, 80, 91

Young, George N. 134

Zernial, Gus 160

www.ingramcontent.com/pod-product-compliance
Lightning Source LLC
Chambersburg PA
CBHW030110170426
43198CB00009B/569